HITLER'S SECRET BOOK

HITLER'S
SECRET
BOOK

Introduction by
Telford Taylor

TRANSLATED BY SALVATOR ATTANASIO

GROVE PRESS, INC.   NEW YORK

First Hardcover Edition 1961
First Evergreen Edition 1983
First Printing 1983
ISBN: 0-394-62003-8
Library of Congress Catalog Card Number: 83-081374

Manufactured in the United States of America

GROVE PRESS, INC., 196 West Houston Street, New York, N.Y. 10014

5 4 3 2 1

TABLE OF CONTENTS

---

* In the original document, the first section is so
entitled (*Vorwort*). However, the ensuing chap-
ters are untitled and unnumbered, and are
separated merely by dashes. For the reader's
convenience, suitable chapter headings have been
added, together with the summaries, in the table
of contents.—*T.T.*

of the Earth. . . . Birth control eugenically unsound. . . . Spartan exposure logical. . . . Emigration sacrifices best elements. . . . Increase in productivity of no help competitively. . . . Export trade vanishing as other nations modernize. . . . Necessity of strife.

Weapons on hand no gauge of national strength. . . . National will the decisive factor. . . . Old German army as source of people's will and discipline. . . . National Socialist mission to revitalize national will. . . . Blood and folk values superior to international-mindedness. . . . Leadership superior to mass democracy.

Must learn from the past. . . . Must forge the instruments for change to a fruitful German foreign policy. . . . Correct ideas valueless unless translated into action. . . . The Pan-German League. . . . Necessity of taking risks. . . . Dangerous policies must be carried out ruthlessly. . . . Breaking the circle of enemies of Germany.

NSDAP is socialist and nationalist. . . . Bourgeois nationalists aim to restore Germany's pre-war frontiers. . . . NSDAP foreign policy aims at territorial expansion, and bringing Germans under German sovereignty. . . . Folkdom as basis of policy.

... Need for nationalist spirit. ... Army and people must be close. ... Border-restoration policy dead-ends into coalition of victor nations. ... Unsatisfactory goal. ... Beer-hall patriots' empty talk of "national honor". ... November criminals.

Germany today powerless to defend honor or borders. ... Increased production no solution. ... England won't tolerate merchant trade competition. ... Emigration no solution. ... American immigration quotas. ... Pan-Europeanism no solution, leads to loss of folk-values. ... American values based on dominant kindred groups.

Neutrality as policy means some other nation wins. ... Desirability of action. ... Worthlessness of League of Nations. ... American greatness the result of intervention in World War. ... Italy justified in deserting Triple Alliance.

Franco-Russian and Anglo-French alliances hem Germany in. ... Militarily indefensible German borders. ... Vulnerability of German cities to bombing attacks. ... Russian alliance would be catastrophic. ... France always the enemy. ... Soviet Russian goal is communist poisoning of Germany. ... Jews have destroyed Russian nationalism. ...

Russo-German alliance would mean invasion of Germany from West, with no help from Russia. . . . Russian alliance would block German expansion by conquest of Russian territory. . . . Slavs have no "state-forming" ability. . . . Jews dominate Russia.

South Tyrol. . . . Jews use Tyrol to set Italy and Germany at odds. . . . Germans in Alsace, Poland, etc., just as important as those in South Tyrol. . . . Advice to Mussolini. . . . The true villains who bear guilt for the South Tyrol. . . . William J. Flynn's article on stupidity of von Bernstorff.

Translator's Note

In the original document, Hitler, on occasion, indulges in his notorious lapses from correct German grammar. Since such lapses would be of interest only to the specialist (who can consult the original), they have not been noted in the translation. The original document also contained misspellings, and a number of obvious auditory mistakes. These have been corrected in accordance with the logical meaning inherent in the original sentence structure.

S. A.

INTRODUCTION

Telford Taylor

"Politics is history in the making," declared Adolf Hitler in 1928, as he began dictating the first chapter of this work to Max Amann. If the thought was hardly original, no one had a better right to give it voice, little as this was realized at the time. A few years later, Hitler's politics had become the stuff of an historical era, in the backwash of which mankind still flounders.

This long-buried screed is Hitler's second book or, if the two volumes of *Mein Kampf* each be counted, his third. Essentially it is an elaboration of the ideas on German foreign policy set forth in the second volume of *Mein Kampf,* and it is in the political events of the late twenties that the reasons for both the writing of the book and its suppression by the author are to be found.

As is well known, Hitler wrote most of the first volume of *Mein Kampf* in the prison at Landsberg-am-Lech, where he was confined after the unsuccessful Munich Beer Hall Putsch in November, 1923. Hitler soon started dictating to his acolytes, Emil Maurice and Rudolf Hess, who were imprisoned with him. He was paroled in December, 1924 and immediately set about reconstituting the Nazi Party. However, his fiery speech in Munich on February 27, 1925 caused the authorities to ban him from the public platform. This prohibition somewhat curtailed his political activities, but gave him more leisure for reflection and dictation to Hess. The first volume of *Mein Kampf* was published in the fall of 1925, and the second in December, 1926.

Commercially speaking, the work was by no means an immediate success. Max Amann, head of the Eher Verlag (the Nazi firm that published *Mein Kampf*) claimed a sale of 23,000 copies during the first year, but it is now known that the actual sales were less than 10,000 in 1925, less than 7,000 in 1926, barely 5,600 in 1927, and only 3,015 in 1928. Turgid in style and exasperatingly repetitious, the books contained little about the Beer Hall Putsch or other colorful adventures which Amann had hoped would attract readers.

Why, then, did Hitler again essay the author's role, less than two years after the completion of *Mein Kampf*? The answer is to be found in the slow growth of the Nazi movement in the late twenties, and in the nature of the criticism which its teachings provoked in what Hitler called "bourgeois national" (*bürgerlich nationalen*) circles.

Much had happened in Germany between the beginnings of *Mein Kampf* in 1924 and the spring of 1928. Friedrich Ebert, the first President of the Weimar Republic, had died early in 1925, and his successor was the venerable and venerated military hero and symbol of the *ancien régime,* Paul von Hindenburg. Gustav Stresemann's policies of reconciliation had borne fruit in the Locarno Pact, the end of the Inter-Allied Control Commission, the progressive Allied evacuation of the Rhineland, and Germany's admission to the League of Nations. The disastrous currency inflation of 1923 had run its course, and Germany had emerged into the brief glow of prosperity and good feeling that was to end in 1929. During these few years life was tolerable for most and good for many Germans, and therefore bad for the political fortunes of Adolf Hitler and the Nazi Party.

But if this was a lean period for Hitler, he was by no means wasting his time. On the contrary, he was busily and successfully putting down intra-Party rivalries, consolidating his control, and reorganizing the Party's structure. He had abandoned the idea of seizing power by an outright putsch, and had committed the Party to a strategy of propaganda and pressure intended to win success at the polls. Despite the lack of popular discontent on which to feed, the Nazi Party membership rose from 17,000 in 1926 to 40,000 in 1927. In the elections of May, 1928 the Party polled some 850,000 votes out of over 30 million cast, and took 12 of the 491 seats in the Reichstag.

It was a beginning, but not much more, and in 1928 Hitler was deeply concerned about the Party's obviously narrow popular appeal. Anti-Semitic and nationalistic as the Party was, Hitler knew (as he says in the Foreword to this book) that he could make little impression "on those who, in consequence of their general philosophical and political attitude, already regarded me as their most vehement opponent"—meaning, no doubt, the Communists, Social Democrats, and moderates of the Catholic Center.

But Hitler believed—and rightly, as events were soon to prove —that avenues could be found for effective appeal to conservative, monied, nationalistic circles. Since his party was "Socialist" and continued, at least nominally, to espouse economic policies favorable to "workers," that appeal, if addressed to conservative ears, had to be in the general area of foreign policy. Hence the drift and burden of this book.

If politically calculated, this approach was indubitably sincere. Whatever his other faults, Hitler was never one to underestimate himself, and it was in the field of high statecraft that he most fancied his own talents and concentrated his thoughts and energies. Precisely for this reason, it was "bourgeois national" attacks on his foreign policy program that most enraged Hitler. Here were men, so he thought, who shared many of his own patriotic and expansionist aims. How infernally stupid of them not to follow his lead! The more he dictated the angrier he became, and thus the book rapidly turned into a fierce denunciation of those very circles to which it was intended to appeal.

In 1928, the question of the South Tyrol* was an especially sharp thorn in the Nazi flesh. During the early twenties, the attitude of the Italian government toward the German-speaking people of the Alto Adige had been fairly liberal. But with the advent of Mussolini and fascism, a repressive program of Italianization was adopted, and in reaction a wave of Austrian "irredentism" swept not only that country and the South Tyrol, but Germany as well. Anti-Italian feeling was especially strong in Bavaria, where a movement arose for boycotting Italian goods. In February, 1926, Mussolini made a vigorous speech denouncing his German critics and threatening reprisals.

Two years later the issue flared up again, when the Italian language was introduced for religious instruction in the South Tyrol. A highly critical speech by the Austrian Chancellor (Ignaz Seipel) caused Mussolini to withdraw the Italian ambassador from Vienna. In March, 1928, these events precipitated public debate and extensive press comment in Germany.

All this was most difficult for Hitler. In *Mein Kampf* he had sung Mussolini's praises and advocated a policy looking to a close German alliance with Italy as well as England. He had likewise been at pains to explain that the South Tyrol issue was nothing but a "Jewish snare" concocted for the specific purpose of smearing Mussolini and blocking a German-Italian *rapprochement*.** Nevertheless the issue would not die, and in 1927 Hitler was sharply attacked in an open letter of the "German-Folkish Labor Society for the South Tyrol."

---

* The portion of the Tyrol south of the Alpine passes, embracing the predominantly German-speaking area around Bolzano known as the "Alto Adige" and, to the south, the Italian-speaking "Trentino." Both parts were under Austrian rule from the Congress of Vienna in 1815 to 1919, when the entire South Tyrol was awarded to Italy by the Treaty of St. Germain. The German-speaking population of the Alto Adige numbered about 215,000.

** *Mein Kampf* (trans. Ralph Manheim) pp. 465, 626-629, and 681 (Houghton Mifflin, 1943).

Needless to say, it was especially galling to Hitler to be attacked from the "folkish" and nationalist quarter as "soft" on an issue of German irredentism. The issue was always resurrecting itself at awkward moments; the Mussolini-Seipel controversy developed shortly before the German elections of May 20, 1928. Hitler spoke in Munich on May 19, and reiterated the charge that Jews and Marxists were exploiting the South Tyrol issue. On the next day (election day) the Social Democrats of Munich distributed posters charging that Hitler and ex-General Franz Ritter von Epp (a Nazi candidate for the Reichstag) had accepted financial aid from Mussolini in return for their helpful attitude on the South Tyrol question.

In the light of all this, Hitler's continued preoccupation with the issue is understandable. We know from internal evidence that the book was written in the late spring and early summer of 1928. The South Tyrol is mentioned in the third sentence of the Foreword; it is frequently referred to throughout the book, and is the subject of extensive discussion in the penultimate chapter, which reaches its denunciatory climax in the elaborate listing of those who, in Hitler's mind, bore the real guilt for the "betrayal" of the South Tyrol.*

We may safely say, then, that the South Tyrol issue was the most immediate cause of the writing of this book. But of course

---

* True to his stated principles, after he came to power Hitler brought about the *Anschluss* with Austria and, as part of the price, renounced all German claims to the South Tyrol by assuring Mussolini that the Brenner Pass would continue to mark the German-Italian boundary. Thereafter the two dictators jointly endeavored to settle the problem by encouraging the emigration of Germans from the Alto Adige to the Reich. Little came of this, and less of a war-born proposal to settle the South Tyroleans in the Crimea, referred to in *Hitler's Secret Conversations* (Farrar, Straus and Young, 1953), entry for July 2, 1942. The new Italian constitution of 1947 granted autonomous rights to the region, but this Austro-Italian controversy, which so exercised Hitler, is still very much alive today.

it was not the only one. With prosperity in Germany, domestic economic and social issues had somewhat faded into the background. In 1927 and 1928 such issues as German reparations, the Kellogg-Briand "peace" pact, the rights of German minorities in foreign countries, and German relations with the Soviet Union were the front-page issues. Stresemann's policies and relations with Aristide Briand suggested a trend toward German "internationalism" and burying the hatchet with France; the Treaty of Berlin (signed by Stresemann and Krestinski in April, 1924) confirmed the Rapallo policy of friendship with the Soviet Union.

Hitler was violently opposed to both of these trends. To him, France was an implacable enemy, Russia the promised land for German *Lebensraum*, and internationalism *à la* Geneva a snare and delusion. In alliance with England and Italy, Germany might regain her strength and embark on a program of territorial conquest *vi et armis*. This book was written to expound these ideas, and win converts in "nationalist" circles.

Why, then, was it never published? Here we are in the realm of inference. Internal evidence indicates that Hitler dictated at least some of the work in May, 1928,* and part of it is identical with a portion of a speech which Hitler delivered in Berlin on July 13, 1928. The typescript appears to be a first draft, dictated directly to the typist, and the typed corrections appear to have been made at the time of dictation. The draft of *Mein Kampf* was reviewed and revised prior to publication. From the lack of any signs of editing here, one may infer that this work was laid aside soon after its completion.

Other information about the attendant circumstances has

---

* See the reference (p. 189) to the destruction of the Bismarck tower in Bromberg, an episode which occurred early in May, 1928, and the long quotation (pp. 201-205) from the article by William J. Flynn, published in *Liberty* magazine on June 2nd, and reported in the *Münchener Neuesten Nachrichten* on June 26, 1928.

been furnished by one Josef Berg, formerly an employee of the Nazi publishing house Eher Verlag. According to Berg, Hitler dictated the contents directly to Max Amann, and two copies were made, only one of which has since come to light. Hitler gave strict orders that the work be kept secret, and in 1935 Berg put the typescript into an air-raid shelter for safekeeping. In 1945 the document was taken from Berg by an American officer, and it remained hidden in the mass of captured German documents from then until its location and identification in 1958.*

That Hitler did indeed order that his work be thus suppressed, as Berg says, seems highly probable, for only a single later reference to it by the author has been recorded. During one of his many monologues delivered at his headquarters on the Eastern front, Hitler on February 7, 1942 remarked that: "In 1925 I wrote in *Mein Kampf* (and also in an unpublished work) that world Jewry saw in Japan an enemy beyond its reach."**

It is possible that the reason Hitler so promptly abandoned his brain child was commercial. As we have seen, *Mein Kampf* was not selling well; indeed, 1928 was by far its poorest year in the market. Max Amann had a good head for business, and may well have taken a dim view of launching this long exposition, unrelieved by narrative passages, especially when *Mein Kampf* was doing so badly.

---

* The information concerning the typescript and the circumstances contemporaneous with its dictation is derived from the German publication of this work, *Hitlers Zweites Buch,* issued by the German *Institut für Zeitgeschichte* (Deutsche Verlags-Anstalt, Stuttgart, 1961) with an Introduction by Hans Rothfels and commentary by Gerhard L. Weinberg. The Institute obtained the information from Berg, and Mr. Weinberg located the document itself in the United States Records Center at Alexandria, Va.

** *Hitler's Secret Conversations, supra,* pp. 255-256. In fact there is such a passage in *Mein Kampf* (*supra,* p. 639), but not in the present work.

Such factors may well explain why the book was not published, but hardly account for its secret burial. Probable reason for its suppression may be found in the subsequent course of political events. The document soon outlived its initially intended uses.

The South Tyrol controversy subsided during the summer of 1928, and Hitler may well have thought that it would be worse than useless to belabor an issue on which he and his Party were on the defensive. New issues soon arose—such as the Young Plan for future German reparations payments—which called for revision of the text, if it were not to seem outdated.

Perhaps most important, Hitler began to draw support from those very "bourgeois national" circles that were so stridently condemned in the book. Apparently Hitler had better things to do with his time than revise the script, and within a few years he achieved power and had no further need of books for either financial or political purposes. So the typescript vanished into the secret files, from which it has now been exhumed by the industry and curiosity of scholars.

It remains to evaluate the work as an historical document. There are no new major themes herein, and that is hardly surprising, in view of its obvious purpose to restate and elaborate the foreign policy teachings of *Mein Kampf*. Confronted with the practical exigencies of statecraft, Hitler could chop and change and reverse his field, as he did in his 1939 pact with Stalin, and as he did, in a lesser way, by suppressing this very book. But the object in dictating it was reaffirmation, and so it is altogether natural that every important point he makes here is also to be found in *Mein Kampf*.

Nevertheless, this work is no mere repetition of the earlier writings, and it is in the particulars, illustrations, and overtones that its chief historical value lies. Especially interesting are the discussions of Russia, the United States, and the German Army.

The treatment of Russia is especially significant for what Hitler did *not* say on the subject. Military and diplomatic collaboration with the Soviet Union had been a basic part of General von Seeckt's policy since 1920, and in 1922 it found open manifestation in the Treaty of Rapallo. Under cover of strict secrecy, Seeckt then proceeded to exploit the friendly relationship for various military enterprises which, under the Treaty of Versailles, could not be carried out in Germany. Schools for the training of airplane pilots and tank crews were opened in Russia, and a stream of German officers was dispatched there to learn to use these and other Versailles-banned weapons.

In December, 1926, just as the second volume of *Mein Kampf* appeared, the Social Democratic politician Philip Scheidemann made a speech in the Reichstag exposing many of these secret activities and violently attacking the *Reichswehr*. The nationalist deputies denounced Scheidemann as a traitor and left the chamber in a body. Throughout 1927 the clandestine rearmament activities of the *Reichswehr* were in issue, and in January, 1928 they led to the retirement of Otto Gessler, the Minister of Defense.

These events must have been of consuming interest to Adolf Hitler; nevertheless, there is not a word about them in this book, and the reason is not far to seek. As a nationalist and an arch-critic of the Versailles Treaty he could hardly ally himself with Scheidemann or join in the liberals' denunciation of secret military exploitation of the Russian relationship. Nevertheless, the Russian orientation cut squarely athwart Hitler's violent castigation of the "Jewish Bolsheviks," and his selection of Russia as the field for future German aggrandizement.

Such factors no doubt account for the unwonted gentleness of Hitler's approach to the Russian question, as when he says (p. 128) that "there are still among us in Germany, even today, well-meaning national-minded men who in all earnestness believe that we must enter into an association with Russia." They also account for the extraordinary, tortured character of the arguments which Hitler put forward.

These arguments culminate in the fantastic passage (p. 132) in which Hitler puts forward the theory that "present-day Russia is anything but an anti-capitalist state," but rather "a country that has destroyed its own national economy . . . in order to give international finance capital the possibility of an absolute control." Hitler's thought seems to be that the Jews who, in his view, were governing Russia had deliberately created an economic vacuum there, into which Jewish-dominated "international finance capital" could step and, through loans, economic concessions, and international supervision, bring the Russian economy under international control. The ruling circles in Russia, Hitler concluded, could have only one aim as regards Germany: to "carry over the Bolshevist poisoning" and bring about "the complete rule of Jewry in Germany exactly as in Russia."

Scrutinizing the possibility that the Jews might be "crowded out" of the Russian regime and replaced by a "Russian national element," Hitler still found nothing to commend a German-Russian alliance. Russia, he thought, could be of no military assistance in the event that France should attack Germany—a judgment which hardly fits with his earlier-expressed analysis of France's power as based partly on her alliances with Poland and Czechoslovakia that "hemmed in" Germany.

More fundamental, however, was his objection that "Slavdom is lacking in state-forming forces." Past Russian greatness was the work of German Balts, he declared, and a truly Slavic national regime in Russia would soon "succumb to disintegration as a State." If all this makes strange reading in the hindsight of 1961, such arguments were not without appeal to the bourgeois Germans of 1927, many of whom had been taught that Slavs were inferior peoples, and had heard great scholars like Treitschke declare that "each dragoon who knocks a Croat on the head does more for the German cause than the finest political brain that ever wielded a trenchant pen."

The observations on the German Army are less contrived and

more revealing of Hitler's social nature. It has often been said that he hated and distrusted the aristocratic, ascetic temper of the German officer corps, but this is not really true. In *Mein Kampf* he sang the Imperial Army's praises as a "unique institution" which was "the mightiest school of the German nation" to which the German people owed "everything."*

The same note is struck in the present work (p. 26), where the "Old" Army is hailed as "the most magnificent [*grandioseste*] organization in the world," and the "breeding ground" of all the German virtues. This is accompanied now, however, by severe strictures on the "corrosion" which had set in, typified by the intermarriage of "individual officers, even of noble descent" with "of all things, department-store Jewesses." At a later point (p. 80) the *Reichswehr* is described as a "mercenary army . . . sinking to the level of policemen armed with special technical weapons."

This last comment reflects the resentment Hitler felt on account of the *Reichswehr*'s part in suppressing his own Putsch in 1923, and foreshadows his insistence, when he came to power, on keeping the *Wehrmacht* apart from police activities, which were thus turned over to the SS and Gestapo forces of Heinrich Himmler. More fundamentally, however, these passages reveal Hitler not as one who scorned, but rather envied, noble birth and aristocratic breeding, and who later castigated the officer corps not because it was too much, but rather too little like what he imagined it to have been in the time of Moltke and Schlieffen.

The United States emerges from these pages in a far more favorable light than anywhere else in Hitler's recorded pronouncements. In *Mein Kampf*, to be sure, he had described "the gigantic American colossus of states with the enormous wealth of its virgin soil."** In this later work, however, in the course of his

---

* *Mein Kampf, supra,* pp. 279-281.
** *Mein Kampf, supra,* p. 638.

argument against "Pan-Europeanism," he pays tribute to America in racial terms, as a country that "felt itself to be a Nordic-German state and in no way an international mishmash of peoples" (p. 108). The rising power of America is, herein, the factor on which Hitler most relies as a stimulant to a British alliance with Germany. Quite different were his comments after Pearl Harbor, when he described America as "a decayed country" without "much future," "half Judaised and the other half negrified."*

It is appropriate that the most striking parts of this work should be concerned with these three subjects, for the *Wehrmacht,* Russia, and the United States were the subjects of Hitler's most egregious mistakes, fatal to the fortunes of the Third Reich.

The German officer corps was probably the only group that could have broken Hitler after he came to power. It did not do so, and eventually Hitler broke the force and spirit of the corps. He corrupted and frightened its leaders to the point where their capacity for strategic guidance was badly undermined, and then set the *Wehrmacht* tasks (warfare in Britain and Africa) and involved it in campaigns (the Battle of Britain and the desert warfare) for which it lacked the sea and air power necessary for success.

Hitler attacked Russia not so much to win his openly coveted *Lebensraum,* but rather because it was the only target within reach of his land-bound Army, and he hoped that Russia's defeat would discourage the British and bring them to terms. He misjudged his opponent utterly, mistaking strength for weakness and still laboring under the delusion, reflected in these pages, that Slavs cannot build states. In the event, the Soviet state proved durable even when its armies were encircled and decimated, or pushed far back into the interior. Enlightened occupation policies might then have been the Germans' most effective weapon against

---

* *Hitler's Secret Conversations, supra,* p. 155, January 7, 1942.

the Soviet apparatus, but these too were prevented by the mythology of Nazism. In the end Hitler found the greater part of his one reliable weapon—the Army—buried deep in Russia while his other enemies gathered strength to assail him from the west.

Throughout these writings of the twenties, Hitler berates the leaders of post-Bismarck Imperial Germany for tying themselves to a worse than useless alliance with Austria-Hungary and for needlessly antagonizing the British. Yet he had an extraordinary penchant for repeating as a statesman the blunders that he so caustically described as a historian. How many times does Hitler say herein that Italy could not afford hostilities with Britain? Yet 1940 found Hitler confronting England with that very ally, Italy, which was to sap German resources while contributing nothing to the decisive campaigns. How often did Hitler inveigh against the stupidity of those who had led Germany into a two-front war, so prolonged that the American "colossus" was drawn in among Germany's enemies? Yet that is how the Third Reich eventually met its flaming, rubble-strewn end.

And so, if Hitler's book of 1928 is read against the background of the intervening years, it should interest not scholars only, but the general reader. Hitler was not a wise man, and in the long run lacked the energy, stability, and power of concentration to bring his aims to fulfillment. But if his vision was distorted, it was piercing; behind the speeches and headlines he saw many causes and relationships that were hidden to others. Perhaps more than any other man of this century he was able to transmute his own thoughts into events, and a corresponding concern and fascination thus attaches to this record of his thoughts in the year before his rise toward power began.

FOREWORD

In August, 1925, on the occasion of the writing of the second volume (*Mein Kampf*), I formulated the fundamental ideas of a National Socialist foreign policy, in the brief time afforded by the circumstances. Within the framework of that book I dealt especially with the question of the South Tyrol,* which gave rise to attacks against the movement as violent as they were groundless. In 1926 I found myself forced to have this part of the second volume published as a special edition. I did not believe that by so doing I would convert those opponents who, in the hue and cry over the South Tyrol, saw primarily a welcome means for the struggle against the hated National Socialist movement. Such people cannot be taught better because the question of truth or error, right or wrong, plays absolutely no part for them. As soon as an issue seems suitable for exploitation, partly for political party purposes, partly even for their highly personal interests, the truthfulness or rightness of the matter at hand is altogether irrelevant. This is all the more the case if they can thereby inflict damage on the cause of the general awakening of our people. For the men responsible for the destruction of Germany, dating from the time of the collapse, are her present rulers, and their attitude of that time has not changed in any respect up to now. Just as at that time they cold-heartedly sacrificed Germany for the sake of doctrinaire party views or for their own selfish advantage, today they likewise vent their hatred against anyone who contradicts their interests, even though he may have, a thousandfold, all the grounds for a German resurgence on his side. Even more. As soon as they believe the revival of our people, represented by a certain

---

* The "question of the South Tyrol" and its importance in stimulating Hitler to write this book are described in the Introduction, *supra* pp. xvi–xvii.—*T.T.*

name, can be seen, they usually take a position against everything that could emanate from such a name. The most useful proposals, indeed the most patently correct suggestions, are boycotted simply because their spokesman, as a name, seems to be linked to general ideas which they presume they must combat on the basis of their political party and personal views. To want to convert such people is hopeless [impossible].*

Hence in 1926 when my brochure on the South Tyrol was printed, I naturally gave not a second's thought to the idea that I could make an impression on those who, in consequence of their general philosophical and political attitude, already regarded me as their most vehement opponent. At that time I did entertain the hope that at least some of them, who were not at the outset malicious opponents of our National Socialist foreign policy, would first examine our view in this field and judge it afterward. Without a doubt this has also happened in many cases. Today I can point out with satisfaction that a great number of men, even among those in public political life, have revised their former attitude with respect to German foreign policy. Even when they believed they could not side with our standpoint in particulars, they nevertheless recognized the honorable intentions that guide us here. During the last two years, of course, it has become clearer to me that my writing of that time was in fact structured on general National Socialist insights as a premise. It also became clearer that many do not follow us, less out of ill-will than because of a certain inability. At that time, within the narrowly drawn limits, it was not possible to give a real fundamental proof of the soundness of our National Socialist conception of foreign policy. Today I feel compelled to make up for this. For not only have the attacks of the enemy been intensified in the last few years but through them the great camp of the indifferent has also been mobilized to a certain degree. The agitation that has been systematically conducted against Italy for the past five years threatens slowly to bear fruit: resulting in the possible death and destruction of the last hopes of a German resurgence.

Thus, as has often happened in other matters, the National So-

---

* Bracketed words are crossed out in original text.—*Trans.*

cialist movement in its foreign policy position stands completely alone and isolated within the community of the German people and its political life. The attacks of the general enemies of our people and fatherland are joined inside the country by the proverbial stupidity and ineptitude of the bourgeois national parties, the indolence of the broad masses, and by cowardice, as a particularly powerful ally: the cowardice that we can observe today among those who by their very nature are incapable of putting up any resistance to the Marxist plague, and who, for this reason, consider themselves downright lucky to bring their voices to the attention of public opinion in a matter which is less dangerous than the struggle against Marxism and which nevertheless looks and sounds like something similar to it. For when they raise their clamor over the South Tyrol today, they seem to serve the interests of the national struggle, just as, conversely, they come as close as they can to standing aside from a real struggle against the worst internal enemies of the German nation. These patriotic, national, and also in part folkish champions, however, find it considerably easier to launch their war cry against Italy in Vienna or Munich under benevolent support and in union with Marxist betrayers of their people and country, rather than fight an earnest war against these very elements. Just as so much nowadays has become appearance, the whole national pretense by these people has for a long time been only an outward show which, to be sure, gratifies them, and which a great part of our people does not see through.

Against this powerful coalition, which from the most varied points of view is seeking to make the question of the South Tyrol the pivot of German foreign policy, the National Socialist movement fights by unswervingly advocating an alliance with Italy against the ruling Francophile tendency. Thereby the movement, in contradistinction to the whole of public opinion in Germany, emphatically points out that the South Tyrol neither can nor should be an obstacle to this policy. This view is the cause of our present isolation in the sphere of foreign policy and of the attacks against us. Later, to be sure, it will ultimately be the cause of the resurgence of the German nation.

I write this book in order to substantiate this firmly held conception in detail and to make it understandable. The less importance I attach to being understood by the enemies of the German people, the more I feel the duty of exerting myself to present and to point out [make comprehensible] the fundamental National Socialist idea of a real German foreign policy to the national-minded elements of our people as such, who are only badly informed or badly led. I know that after a sincere examination [verification] of the conception presented here, many of them will give up their previous positions and find their way into the ranks of the National Socialist freedom movement of the German nation. They will thus strengthen that force which one day will bring about the final settlement with those who cannot be taught because their thought and action are determined not by the happiness of their people, but by the interests of their party or of their own person.

I

Politics is history in the making. History itself is the presentation of the course of a people's struggle for existence. I deliberately use the phrase "struggle for existence" here because in truth that struggle for daily bread, equally in peace and war, is an eternal battle against thousands upon thousands of resistances just as life itself is an eternal struggle against death. For men know as little why they live as does any other creature of the world. Only life is filled with the longing to preserve itself. The most primitive creature [could not without it] knows only the instinct of the self-preservation of its own "I," in creatures standing higher in the scale it is transferred to wife and child, and in those standing still higher to the entire species. While, apparently, man often surrenders his own instinct of self-preservation for the sake of the species, in truth he nevertheless serves it to the highest degree. For not seldom the preservation of the life of a whole people, and with this of the individual, lies only in this renunciation by the individual. Hence the sudden courage of a mother in the defense of her young and the heroism of a man in the defense of his people. The two powerful life-instincts, hunger and love, correspond to the greatness of the instinct for self-preservation. While the appeasement [fulfillment] of eternal hunger guarantees self-preservation, the satisfaction of love assures the continuance of the race. In truth these two drives are the rulers of life. And even though the fleshless aesthete may lodge a thousand protests against such an assertion, the fact of his own existence is already a refutation of his protest. Nothing that is made of flesh and blood can escape the laws which determined its coming into being. As soon as the human mind believes itself to be superior to them, it destroys that real substance which is the bearer of the mind.

5

What, however, applies to individual man also applies to nations. A nation is only a multitude of more or less similar individual beings. Its strength lies in the value of the individual beings forming it as such, and in the character and the extent of the sameness of these values. The same laws which determine the life of the individual, and to which he is subject, are therefore also valid for the people. Self-preservation and continuance are the great urges underlying all action, as long as such a body can still claim to be healthy. Therefore, even the consequences of these general laws of life will be similar among peoples, as they are among individuals.

If for every creature on this earth the instinct of self-preservation, in its twin goals of self-maintenance and continuance, exhibits the most elementary power, nevertheless the possibility of satisfaction is limited, so the logical consequence of this is a struggle in all its forms for the possibility of maintaining this life, that is the satisfaction of the instinct for self-preservation.

Countless are the species of all the earth's organisms, unlimited at any moment in individuals is their instinct for self-preservation as well as the longing for continuance, yet the space in which the whole life process takes place is limited. The struggle for existence and continuance in life waged by billions upon billions of organisms takes place on the surface of an exactly measured sphere. The compulsion to engage in the struggle for existence lies in the limitation of the living space; but in the life-struggle for this living space lies also the basis for evolution.

In the times before man, world history was primarily a presentation of geological events: the struggle of natural forces with one another, the creation of an inhabitable surface on this planet, the separation of water from land, the formation of mountains, of plains, and of the seas. This is the world history of this time. Later, with the emergence of organic life, man's interest concentrated on the process of becoming and the passing away of its thousandfold forms. And only very late did man finally become visible to himself, and thus by the concept of world history he began to understand first and foremost only the history of his own becoming, that is the presentation of his own evolution. This evolution is characterized by an eternal struggle of men against beasts and against men them-

6

selves. From the invisible confusion of the organisms there finally emerged formations, clans, tribes, peoples, states. The description of their origins and their passing away is but the representation of an eternal struggle for existence.

If, however, politics is history in the making and history itself the presentation of the struggle of men and nations for self-preservation and continuance, then politics is in truth the execution of a nation's struggle for existence. But [therefore] politics is not only the struggle of a nation for its existence as such; for us men it is rather the art of carrying out this struggle.

Since history as the representation of the hitherto existing struggles for existence of nations is at the same time the petrified representation of politics prevailing at a given moment, it is the most suitable teacher for our own political activity.

If the highest task of politics is the preservation and the continuance of the life of a people, then this life is the eternal stake with which it fights [consequently the life of a people always stands as the stake], for which and over which this struggle is decided. Hence its task is the preservation of a [that] substance made of flesh and blood. Its success is the making possible of this preservation. Its failure is the destruction, that is the loss of this substance. Consequently, politics is always the leader of the struggle for existence, the guide of the same, its organizer, and its efficacy will, regardless of how man formally designates it, [such a thing] carry with it the decision as to the life or death of a people.

It is necessary to keep this clearly in view because with this the two concepts—a policy of peace or war—immediately sink into nothingness. Since the stake over which politics wrestles is always life itself, the result of failure or success will likewise be the same, regardless of the means with which politics attempts to carry out the struggle for the preservation of the life of a people. A peace policy that fails leads just as directly to the destruction of a people, that is to the extinction of its substance of flesh and blood, as a war policy that miscarries. In the one case just as in the other, the plundering of the prerequisites of life is the cause of the dying out of a people. For nations have not become extinct on battlefields, lost battles rather have deprived them of the means for the preservation of life, or better expressed, have led to such a deprivation, or were not able to prevent it.

Indeed the losses which arise directly from a war are in no way proportionate to the losses deriving from a people's bad and unhealthy life as such. Silent hunger and evil vices in ten years kill more people than war could finish off in a thousand years. The cruelest war, however, is precisely the one which appears to be most peaceful to present-day humanity, namely the peaceful economic war. In its ultimate consequences this very war leads to sacrifices in contrast to which even those of the World War shrink to nothing. For this war affects not only the living but grips above all those who are about to be born. Whereas war at most kills off a fragment of the present, economic warfare murders the future. A single year of birth control in Europe kills more people than all those who fell in battle, from the time of the French Revolution up to our day, in all the wars of Europe, including the World War. But this is the consequence of a peaceful economic policy which has overpopulated Europe without preserving the possibility of a further healthy development for a number of nations.

In general, the following should also be stated:

As soon as a people forgets that the task of politics is to preserve its life with all means and according to all possibilities, and instead aims to subject politics to a definite mode of action, it destroys the inner meaning of the art of leading a people in its fateful struggle for freedom and bread.

A policy which is fundamentally bellicose can keep a people removed from numerous vices and pathological symptoms, but it can not prevent a change of the inner values in the course of many centuries. If it becomes a permanent phenomenon war contains an inner danger in itself, which stands out all the more clearly the more dissimilar are the fundamental racial values which constitute a nation. This already applied to all the known states of antiquity and applies especially today to all European states. The nature of war entails that, through a thousandfold individual processes, it leads to a racial selection within a people, which signifies a preferential destruction of its best elements. The call to courage and bravery finds its response in countless individual reactions, in that

8

the best and most valuable racial elements again and again voluntarily come forward for special tasks, or they are systematically cultivated through the organizational method of special formations. Military leadership of all times has always been dominated by the idea of forming special legions, chosen élite troops for guard regiments and assault battalions. Persian palace guards, Alexandrian élite troops, Roman legions of Praetorians, lost troops of *Landsknechte*, the guard regiments of Napoleon and Frederick the Great, the assault battalions, submarine crews and flying corps of the World War owed their origin to the same idea and necessity of seeking out of a great multitude of men those with the highest aptitude for the performance of correspondingly high tasks and bringing them together into special formations. For originally every guard was not a drill corps but a combat unit. The glory attached to membership in such a community led to the creation of a special *esprit de corps* which subsequently, however, could freeze and ultimately end up in sheer formalities. Hence not seldom such formations will have to bear the greatest blood sacrifices; that is to say, the fittest are sought out from a great multitude of men and led to war in concentrated masses. Thus the percentage of the best dead of a nation is disproportionately increased, while conversely the percentage of the worst elements is able to preserve itself to the highest degree. Over against the extremely idealistic men who are ready to sacrifice their own lives for the folk-community, stands the number of those most wretched egoists who view the preservation of their own mere personal life likewise as the highest task of this life. The hero dies, the criminal is preserved [remains alive]. This appears self-evident to an heroic age and especially to an idealistic youth. And this is good, because it is the proof of the still present value of a people. The true statesman must view such a fact with concern and take it into account. For what can easily be tolerated in one war, in a hundred wars leads to the slow bleeding away of the best, most valuable elements of a nation. Thereby victories will indeed have been won, but in the end there will no longer be a people worthy of this victory. And the pitifulness of the posterity, which to many seems incomprehensible, not seldom is the result of the successes of former times.

Therefore, wise political leaders of a people will never see in war the aim of the life of a people, but only a means for the preservation of this life. It must educate the human material entrusted to it to the highest manhood, but rule it with the highest conscientiousness. If necessary, when a people's life is at stake, they should not shrink from daring to shed blood to the utmost but they must always bear in mind that peace must one day again replace this blood. Wars which are fought for aims that, because of their whole nature, do not guarantee a compensation for the blood that has been shed, are sacrileges committed against a nation, a sin against a people's future.

Eternal wars, however, can become a terrible danger among a people which possesses such unequal elements in its racial composition that only part of them may be viewed as state-preserving as such, and therefore especially creative culturally. The culture of European peoples rests on the foundations which its infusion of Nordic blood has created in the course of centuries. Once the last remains of this Nordic blood are eliminated, the face of European culture will be changed, the value of the states decreasing, however, in accordance with the sinking value of the peoples.

A policy which is fundamentally peaceful, on the other hand, would at first make possible the preservation of its best blood carriers, but on the whole it would educate the people to a weakness which one day must lead to failure, once the basis of existence of such a people appears to be threatened. Then instead of fighting for daily bread the nation rather will cut down on this bread and, what is even more probable, limit the number of people either through peaceful emigration or through birth control in order in this way to escape an enormous distress. Thus the fundamentally peaceful policy becomes a scourge for a people. For what on the one hand is effected by permanent war, is effected on the other by emigration. Through it a people is slowly robbed of its best blood in hundreds of thousands of individual life catastrophes. It is sad to know that our whole national-political wisdom, insofar as it does not see any advantage at all in emigration, at most deplores the weakening of the number of its own people or at best speaks of a cultural fertilizer which is thereby given to other states. What is not perceived is the worst. Since the emigration does not proceed according to territory, nor according to age categories, but instead remains subject to the free rule of fate, it always drains away from a folk the most courageous and the boldest people, the most determined and most prepared for resistance. The peasant youth who emigrated to America 150 years ago was as much the most determined and most adventurous man in his village as the worker who today goes to Argentina. The coward and weakling would rather die at home than pluck up the courage to earn his bread in an unknown, foreign land. Regardless whether it is distress, misery, political pressure or religious compulsion that weighs on people, it will always be those who are the healthiest and the most capable of resistance who will be able to put up the most resistance. The weakling will always be the first to subject himself. His preservation is generally as little a gain for the victor as the stay-at-homes are for the mother country. Not seldom therefore the law of action is passed on from the mother country to the colonies, because there a concentration of the highest human values has taken place in a wholly natural way. However, the positive gain for the new country is thus a loss for the mother country. As soon as a people once loses its best, strongest and most natural forces through emigration in the course of centuries, it will hardly be able any more to muster the inner strength to put up the necessary resistance to fate in critical times. It will then sooner grasp at birth control. Even here the loss in numbers is not decisive, but the terrible fact that through birth control the highest potential values of a people are destroyed at the very outset. For the greatness and future of a people is determined through the sum of its capacities for the highest achievements in all fields. But these are personality values which do not appear linked to primogeniture. If we were to strike off from our German cultural life, from our science, indeed from our whole existence as such, all that which was created by men who were not first-born sons, then Germany would hardly be a Balkan state. The German people would no longer have any claim to being valued as a cultural people. Moreover, it must be considered that even in the case of those men who as first born nevertheless accomplished great things for their people, it must first be examined whether one of their ancestors at least had not been a first born. For when in

11

his whole ancestral series the chain of the first born appears as broken just once [one man], then he also belongs to those who would not have existed had our forefathers always paid homage to this principle. In the life of nations, however, there are no vices of the past that are [would be] right in the present.

The fundamentally peaceful policy, with the subsequent bleeding to death of a nation through emigration and birth control, is likewise all the more catastrophic the more it involves a people which is made up of racially unequal elements. For in this case as well the best racial elements are taken away from the people through emigration, whereas through birth control in the homeland it is likewise those who in consequence of their racial value have worked themselves up to the higher levels of life and society who are at first affected. Gradually then their replenishment would follow out of the bled, inferior broad masses and finally, after centuries, lead to a lowering of the whole value of the people altogether. Such a nation will have long ceased to possess real life vitality.

Thus a policy which is fundamentally peaceful will be precisely as harmful and devastating in its effects as a policy which knows war as its only weapon.

Politics must fight about the life of a people and for this life; moreover, it must always choose the weapons of its struggles so that life in the highest sense of the word is served. For one does not make politics in order to be able to die, rather one may only at times call upon men to die so that a nation can live. The aim is the preservation of life and not heroic death, or even [also] cowardly resignation.

II

A people's struggle for existence is first and foremost determined by the following fact:

Regardless of how high the cultural importance of a people may be, the struggle for daily bread stands at the forefront of all vital necessities. To be sure, brilliant leaders can hold great goals before a people's eyes, so that it can be further diverted from material things in order to serve higher spiritual ideals. In general the merely material interest will rise in exact proportion as ideal spiritual outlooks are in the process of disappearing. The more primitive the spiritual life of man, the more animal-like he becomes until finally he regards food intake as the one and only aim of life. Hence a people can quite well endure a certain limitation of material goals, as long as it is given compensation in the form of active ideals. But if these ideals are not to result in the ruin of a people, they should never exist unilaterally at the expense of material nourishment, so that the health of the nation seems to be threatened by them. For a starved people will indeed either collapse in consequence of its physical undernourishment or perforce bring about a change in its situation. Sooner or later, however, physical collapse brings spiritual collapse in its train. Then all ideals also come to an end. Thus ideals are good and healthy as long as they keep on strengthening a people's inner and general forces, so that in the last analysis they can again be of benefit in waging the struggle for existence. Ideals which do not serve this purpose are evil, though they may appear a thousand times outwardly beautiful, because they remove a people more and more from the reality of life.

But the bread which a people requires is conditioned by the

living space at its disposal. A healthy people, at least, will always seek to find the satisfaction of its needs on its own soil. Any other condition is pathological and dangerous, even if it makes possible the sustenance of a people for centuries. World trade, world economy, tourist traffic, etc., etc., are all transient means for securing a nation's sustenance. They are dependent upon factors which are partly beyond calculation and which, on the other hand, lie beyond a nation's power. At all times the surest foundation for the existence of a people has been its own soil.

But now we must consider the following:

The number of a people is a variable factor. It will always rise in a healthy people. Indeed, such an increase alone makes it possible to guarantee a people's future in accordance with human calculations. As a result, however, the demand for commodities also grows constantly. In most cases the so-called domestic increase in production can satisfy only the rising demands of mankind, but in no way the increasing population. This applies especially to European nations. In the last few centuries, especially in most recent times, the European peoples have increased their needs to such an extent that the rise in European soil productivity, which is possible from year to year under favorable conditions, can hardly keep pace with the growth of general life needs as such. The increase of population can be balanced only through an increase, that is an enlargement, of living space. Now the number of a people is variable, the soil as such, however, remains constant. This means that the increase of a people is a process, so self-evident because it is so natural that it is not regarded as something extraordinary. On the other hand, an increase in territory is conditioned by the general distribution of possessions in the world; an act of special revolution, an extraordinary process, so that the ease with which a population increases stands in sharp contrast to the extraordinary difficulty of territorial changes.

Yet the regulation of the relation between population and territory is of tremendous importance for a nation's existence. Indeed, we can justly say that the whole life struggle of a people in truth consists in safeguarding the territory it requires as a general prerequisite for the sustenance of the increasing population. Since the

14

population grows incessantly, and the soil as such remains stationary, tensions perforce must gradually arise which at first find expression in distress, and which for a certain time can be balanced through greater industry, more ingenious production methods or special austerity. But there comes a day when these tensions can no longer be eliminated by such means. Then the task of the leaders of a nation's struggle for existence consists in eliminating the unbearable conditions in a fundamental way, that is in restoring a tolerable relation between population and territory.

In the life of nations there are several ways for correcting the disproportion between population and territory. The most natural way is to adapt the soil, from time to time, to the increased population. This requires a determination to fight and the risk of bloodshed. But this very bloodshed is also the only one that can be justified to a people. Since through it the necessary space is won for the further increase of a people, it automatically finds manifold compensation for the humanity staked on the battlefield. Thus the bread of freedom grows from the hardships of war. The sword was the path-breaker for the plough. And if we want to talk about human rights at all, then in this single case war has served the highest right of all: it gave a people the earth which it wanted to cultivate industriously and honestly for itself so that its children might some day be provided with their daily bread. For this earth is not allotted to anyone, nor is it presented to anyone as a gift. It is awarded by Providence to people who in their hearts have [possess] the courage to take possession of [conquer] it, the strength to preserve it, and the industry to put it to the plough.

Hence every healthy, vigorous people sees nothing sinful in territorial acquisition, but something quite in keeping with nature. The modern pacifist who denies this holy right must first be reproached for the fact that he himself at least is being nourished on the injustices of former times. Furthermore, there is no spot on this earth that has been determined as the abode of a people for all time, since the rule of nature has for tens of thousands of years forced mankind eternally to migrate. Finally the present distribution of possessions on the earth has not been designed by a higher power but by man himself. But I can never regard a solution effected by man as an eternal value which Providence now takes under its protection and sanctifies into a law of the future. Thus, just as the earth's surface seems to be subject to eternal geological transformations, making organic life perish in an unbroken change of forms in order to discover the new, this limitation of human dwelling places is also exposed to an endless change. However, many nations, at certain times, may have an interest in presenting the existing distribution of the world's territories as binding forever, for the reason that it corresponds to their interests, just as other nations can see only something generally man-made in such a situation which at the moment is unfavorable to them and which therefore must be changed with all means of human power. Anyone who would banish this struggle from the earth forever would perhaps abolish the struggle between men, but he would also eliminate the highest driving power for their development; exactly as if in civil life he would want to eternalize the wealth of certain men, the greatness of certain business enterprises, and for this purpose eliminate the play of free forces, competition. The results would be catastrophic for a nation.

The present distribution of world space in a one-sided way turns out to be so much in favor of individual nations that the latter perforce have an understandable interest in not allowing any further change in the present distribution of territories. But the overabundance of territory enjoyed by these nations contrasts with the poverty of the others, which despite the utmost industry are not in a position to produce their daily bread so as to keep alive. What higher rights would one want to oppose against them if they also raise the claim to a land area which safeguards their sustenance?

No. The primary right of this world is the right to life, so far as one possesses the strength for this. Hence on the basis of this right a vigorous nation will always find ways of adapting its territory to its population size.

Once a nation, as the result either of weakness or bad leadership, can no longer eliminate the disproportion between its increased population and the fixed amount of territory by increasing the productivity of its soil, it will necessarily look for other ways. It will then adapt the population size to the soil.

16

Nature as such herself performs the first adaptation of the population size to the insufficiently nourishing soil. Here distress and misery are her devices. A people can be so decimated through them that any further population increase practically comes to a halt. The consequences of this natural adaptation of the population to the soil are not always the same. First of all a very violent struggle for existence sets in, which only individuals who are the strongest and have the greatest capacity for resistance can survive. A high infant mortality rate on the one hand and a high proportion of aged people on the other are the chief signs of a time which shows little regard for individual life. Since under such conditions all weaklings are swept away through acute distress and illness and only the healthiest remain alive, a kind of natural selection takes place. Thus the number of a people can easily be subject to a limitation, but the inner value can remain, indeed it can experience an inner heightening. But such a process cannot last for too long, otherwise the distress can also turn into its opposite. In nations composed of racial elements that are not wholly of equal value, permanent malnutrition can ultimately lead to a dull surrender to the distress, which gradually reduces energy, and instead of a struggle which fosters a natural selection a gradual degeneration sets in. This is surely the case once man, in order to control the chronic distress, no longer attaches any value to an increase of his number and resorts on his own to birth control. For then he himself immediately embarks upon a road opposite to that taken by nature. Whereas nature, out of the multitude of beings who are born, spares the few who are most fitted in terms of health and resistance to wage life's struggle, man limits the number of births and then tries to keep alive those who have been born with no regard to their real value or to their inner worth. Here his humanity is only the handmaiden of his weakness, and at the same time it is actually the cruelest destroyer of his existence. If man wants to limit the number of births on his own, without producing the terrible consequences which arise from birth control, he must give the number of births free rein but cut down on the number of those remaining alive. At one time the Spartans were capable of such a wise measure, but not our present, mendaciously senti-

17

mental, bourgeois-patriotic nonsense. The rule of six thousand Spartans over three hundred and fifty thousand Helots was only thinkable in consequence of the high racial value of the Spartans. But this was the result of a systematic race preservation; thus Sparta must be regarded as the first folkish state. The exposure of sick, weak, deformed children, in short their destruction, was more decent and in truth a thousand times more humane than the wretched insanity of our day which preserves the most pathological subject, and indeed at any price, and yet takes the life of a hundred thousand healthy children in consequence of birth control or through abortions, in order subsequently to breed a race of degenerates burdened with illnesses.

Hence it can be said in general that the limitation of the population through distress and human agencies may very well lead to an approximate adaptation to the inadequate living space, but the value of the existing human material is constantly lowered and indeed ultimately decays.

The second attempt to adapt the population size to the soil lies in emigration, which so long as it does not take place tribally, likewise leads to a devaluation of the remaining human material.

Human birth control wipes out the bearer of the highest values, emigration destroys the value of the average.

There are still two other ways by which a nation can try to balance the disproportion between population and territory. The first is called increasing the domestic productivity of the soil, which as such has nothing to do with so-called internal colonization; the second the increase of commodity production and the conversion of the domestic economy into an export economy.

The idea of increasing the yield of the soil within borders that have been fixed once and forever is an old one. The history of human cultivation of the soil is one of permanent progress, permanent improvement and therefore of increasing yields. While the first part of this progress lay in the field of methods of soil cultivation as well as in the construction of settlements, the second part lies in increasing the value of the soil artificially through the introduction of nutritious matter that is lacking or insufficient. This line leads from the hoe of former times up to the modern steam plough, from stable manure up to present artificial fertilizers. Without doubt the productivity of the soil has thereby been infinitely increased. But it is just as certain that there is a limit somewhere. Especially if we consider that the living standard of cultured man is a general one, which is not determined by the amount of a nation's commodities available to the individual; rather it is just as much subject to the judgment of surrounding countries and, conversely, is established [co-determined] through the conditions within them. The present-day European dreams of a living standard which he derives as much from the potentialities of Europe as from the actual conditions prevailing in America. International relations between nations have become so easy and close through modern technology and the communication it makes possible, that the European, often without being conscious of it, applies American conditions as a standard for his own life. But he thereby forgets that the relation of the population to the soil surface of the American continent is infinitely more favorable than the analogous conditions of European nations to their living spaces. Regardless of how Italy, or let's say Germany, carry out the internal colonization of their soil, regardless of how they increase the productivity of their soil further through scientific and methodical activity, there always remains the disproportion of the number of their population to the soil as measured against the relation of the population of the American Union to the soil of the Union. And if a further increase of the population were possible for Italy or Germany through the utmost industry, then this would be possible in the American Union up to a multiple of theirs. And when ultimately any further increase in these two European countries is no longer possible, the American Union can continue to grow for centuries until it will have reached the relation that we already have today.

The effects that it is hoped to achieve through internal colonization, in particular, rest on a fallacy. The opinion that we can bring about a considerable increase in the productivity of the soil is false. Regardless of how, for example, the land is distributed in Germany, whether in large or in small peasant holdings, or in plots for small settlers, this does not alter the fact that there are, on the average, 136 people to one square kilometer. This is an unhealthy relation. It is impossible to feed our people on this basis and under this premise. Indeed it would only create confusion to set the slogan of internal colonization before the masses, who will then latch their hopes onto it and thereby think to have found a means of doing away with their present distress. This would not at all be the case. For the distress is not the result of a wrong kind of land distribution, say, but the consequence of the inadequate amount of space, on the whole, at the disposal of our nation today.

By increasing the productivity of the soil, however, some alleviation of a people's lot could be achieved. But in the long run this would never exempt it from the duty to adapt the nation's living space, become insufficient, to the increased population. Through internal colonization, in the most favorable circumstances, only amelioration in the sense of social reform and justice could take place. It is entirely without importance as regards the total sustenance of a people. It will often be harmful for a nation's foreign policy position because it awakens hopes which can remove a people from realistic thinking. The ordinary, respectable citizen will then really believe that he can find his daily bread at home through industry and hard work, rather than realize that the strength of a people must be concentrated in order to win new living space.

Economics, which especially today is regarded by many as the savior from distress and care, hunger and misery, under certain pre-conditions can give a people possibilities for existence which lie outside its relation to its own soil. But this is linked to a number of prerequisites of which I must make brief mention here.

The sense of such an economic system lies in the fact that a nation produces more of certain vital commodities than it requires for its own use. It sells this surplus outside its own national community and with the proceeds therefrom it procures those foodstuffs and also the raw materials which it lacks. Thus this kind of economics involves not only a question of production, but in at least as great a degree a question of selling. There is much talk, especially at the present time, about increasing production, but it is completely forgotten that such an increase is of value only as long as a buyer is at hand. Within the circle of a nation's economic life every increase in production will be profitable to the degree that it increases the number of goods which are thus made available to the individual. Theoretically, every increase in the industrial production of a nation must lead to a reduction in the price of commodities and in turn to an increased consumption of them, and consequently put the individual folk-comrade in a position to own more vital commodities. In practice, however, this in no way changes the fact of the inadequate sustenance of a nation as a result of insufficient soil. For to be sure we can increase certain industrial outputs, indeed many times over, but not the production of foodstuffs. Once a nation suffers from this need, an adjustment can take place only if a part of its industrial over-production can be exported in order to compensate from the outside for the foodstuffs that are not available in the homeland. But an increase in production having this aim achieves the desired success only when it finds a buyer, and indeed a buyer outside the country. Thus we stand before the question of the sales potential, that is the market, a question of towering importance.

The present world commodity market is not unlimited. The number of industrially active nations has steadily increased. Almost all European nations suffer from an inadequate and unsatisfactory relation between soil and population. Hence they are dependent on world export. In recent years the American Union has turned to export, as has also Japan in the East. Thus a struggle automatically begins for the limited markets, which becomes tougher the more numerous the industrial nations become and, conversely, the more the markets shrink. For while on the one hand the number of nations struggling for world markets increases, the commodity market itself slowly diminishes, partly in consequence of a process of self-industrialization on their own power, partly through a system of branch enterprises which are more and more coming into being in such countries out of sheer capitalist interest. For we should bear the following in mind: the German people, for example, has a lively interest in building ships for China in German dockyards because thereby a certain number of men of our nationality get a chance to feed themselves which they would not have on our own soil, which is no longer sufficient. But the German people has no interest, say, in a German financial group or even

21

a German factory opening a so-called branch dockyard in Shanghai which builds ships for China with Chinese workers and foreign steel, even if the corporation earns a definite profit in the form of interest or dividend. On the contrary the result of this will be only that a German financial group earns so and so many million, but as a result of the orders lost a multiple of this amount is withdrawn from the German national economy.

The more pure capitalist interests begin to determine the present economy, the more the general viewpoints of the financial world and the stock exchange achieve a decisive influence here, the more will this system of branch establishments reach out and thus artificially [suddenly] carry out the industrialization of former commodity markets and especially curtail the export possibilities of the European mother countries. Today many can still afford to smile over this future development, but as it makes further strides, within thirty years people in Europe will groan under its consequences.

The more market difficulties increase, the more bitterly will the struggle for the remaining ones be waged. Although the primary weapons of this struggle lie in pricing and in the quality of the goods with which nations competitively try to undersell each other, in the end the ultimate weapons even here lie in the sword. The so-called peaceful economic conquest of the world could take place only if the earth consisted of purely agrarian nations and but one industrially active and commercial nation. Since all great nations today are industrial nations, the so-called peaceful economic conquest of the world is nothing but the struggle with means which will remain peaceful for as long as the stronger nations believe they can triumph with them, that is, in reality for as long as they are able to kill the others with peaceful economics. For this is the real result of the victory of a nation with peaceful economic means over another nation. Thereby one nation receives possibilities of survival and the other nation is deprived of them. Even here what is at stake is always the substance of flesh and blood, which we designate as a people.

If a really vigorous people believes that it cannot conquer another with peaceful economic means, or if an economically weak people does not wish to let itself be killed by an economically stronger one, as the possibilities for its sustenance are slowly cut off, then in both cases [it will seize the sword] the vapors of economic phraseology will be suddenly torn asunder and war, that is the continuation of politics with other means, steps into its place.

The danger to a people of economic activity in an exclusive sense lies in the fact that it succumbs only too easily to the belief that it can ultimately shape its destiny through economics. Thus the latter from a purely secondary place moves forward to first place, and finally is even regarded as state-forming, and robs the people of those very virtues and characteristics which in the last analysis make it possible for nations and states to preserve life on this earth.

A special danger of the so-called peaceful economic policy, however, lies above all in the fact that it makes possible an increase in the population, which finally no longer stands in any relation to the productive capacity of its own soil to support life. This overfilling of an inadequate living space with people not seldom also leads to the concentration of people in work centers which look less like cultural centers, and rather more like abscesses in the national body in which all evil, vices and diseases seem to unite. Above all they are breeding grounds of blood mixing and bastardization, and of race lowering, thus resulting in those purulent infection centers in which the international Jewish racial-maggots thrive and finally effect further destruction.

Precisely thereby is the way open to decay in which the inner strength of such a people swiftly disappears, all racial, moral and folk values are earmarked for destruction, ideals are undermined, and in the end the prerequisite which a people urgently needs in order to take upon itself the ultimate consequences of the struggle for world markets is eliminated. Weakened by a vicious pacifism, peoples will no longer be ready to fight for markets for their goods with the shedding of their blood. Hence as soon as a stronger nation sets the real strength of political power in the place of peaceful economic means, such nations will collapse. Then their own delinquencies will take revenge. They are overpopulated, and now in consequence of the loss of all the real basic requirements they no longer have any possibility of being able to feed their overgrown mass of people adequately. They have no strength to break the chains of the enemy, and no inner value with which to bear their fate with dignity. Once they believed they could live, thanks to their peaceful economic activity, and renounce the use of violence. Fate will teach them that in the last analysis a people is preserved only when population and living space stand in a definite natural and healthy relation to each other. Further, this relation must be examined from time to time, and indeed must be re-established in favor of the population to the very same degree that it shifts unfavorably with respect to the soil.

For this, however, a nation needs weapons. The acquisition of soil is always linked with the employment of force.

If the task of politics is the execution of a people's struggle for existence, and if the struggle for existence of a people in the last analysis consists of safeguarding the necessary amount of space for nourishing a specific population, and if this whole process is a question of the employment of a people's strength, the following concluding definitions result therefrom:

Politics is the art of carrying out a people's struggle for its earthly existence.

Foreign policy [Domestic policy] is the art of safeguarding the momentary, necessary living space, in quantity and quality, for a people.

Domestic policy is the art of preserving the necessary employment of force [power content] for this in the form of its race value and numbers.

III

Here at this point I want [would like] to discuss that bourgeois concept which views power chiefly as a nation's supply of weapons, and to a lesser degree perhaps also the army as an organization. If the concept of these people were pertinent, that is if the power of a nation really lay in its possession of arms and in its army as such, then a nation which has lost its army and weapons through any reasons whatsoever must be done for permanently. These bourgeois politicians themselves hardly believe that. By their very doubt of this they admit that weapons and army organization are things which can be replaced; and that consequently they are not of a primary character, that there is something which stands above them and which at least is also the source of their power. And so it is. Weapons and army forms are destructible and are replaceable. As great as their importance perhaps is for the moment, just so is it limited when viewed over longer periods of time. What is ultimately decisive in the life of a people is the will to self-preservation and the living forces that are at its disposal for this purpose. Weapons can rust, forms can be outdated; the will itself can always renew both and move a people into the form required by the need of the moment. The fact that we Germans had to give up our arms is of very slight importance, insofar as I look at the material side of it. And yet this is the only thing our bourgeois politicians see. What is depressing about the surrender of our arms, at most, lies in the attendant circumstances in which it took place, in the attitude which it made possible, as well as in the wretched manner of doing it which we experienced. It is outweighed by the destruction of the organization of our army. But even there the major misfortune is not the elimination of the organization as the bearer of the weapons we possess, but rather the abolition of an institution for the training of our people to manliness, which was possessed by no other state in the world and which, indeed, no people needed more than our Germans. The contribution of our old army to the general disciplining of our people for the highest achievements in all fields is incommensurable. Precisely our people, which in its racial fragmentation so very much lacks qualities which, for example, characterize the English—a determined sticking together in time of danger—has received at least a part of this, which in other nations is a natural, instinctive endowment, by way of its training through the army. The people who chatter so happily about socialism do not at all realize that the highest socialist organization of all has been the German Army. This is also the reason for the fierce hatred of the typical capitalistically inclined Jews against an organization in which money is not identical with position, dignity, to say nothing of honor, but rather with achievement; and in which the honor of belonging among people of a certain accomplishment is more greatly appreciated than the possession of property and riches. This is a conception which to Jews seems as alien as it is dangerous and which, if only it became the general patrimony of a people, would signify an immunizing defense against every further Jewish danger. If, for example, an officer's rank in the army could be bought, this would be comprehensible to Jews. They cannot understand an organization—indeed they find it weird—which surrounds with honor a man who either possesses no property at all, or whose income is only a fragment of that of another man who precisely in this organization is neither honored nor esteemed. But therein lay the chief strength of this incomparable old institution which unfortunately in the last thirty years of peace, however, also showed signs of slowly becoming corroded. As soon as it became fashionable for individual officers, especially of noble descent, to pair off with, of all things, department-store Jewesses, a danger arose for the old army which, if the same development continued, might have some day grown into a great evil. At any rate in the times of Kaiser Wilhelm I there was no understanding [shown] for such events. Nevertheless, all in all, the Germany Army at the turn of the century was the most magnificent organization in the world and its effect on our German people one that was more than beneficial. The breeding ground of German discipline, German efficiency, forthright disposition, frank courage, bold aggressiveness, tenacious persistence and granite honorableness. The conception of honor of a whole profession slowly but imperceptibly became the general patrimony of a whole people.

That this organization was destroyed through the peace treaty of Versailles was all the worse for our people as our internal enemies thereby finally received a free path for effecting their worst intentions. But our incompetent bourgeoisie, for lack of any genius and ability to improvise, could not even find the most primitive substitute.

Thus, to be sure, our German people has lost possession of arms and their bearer. But this has been the case countless times in the history of nations, without the latter having perished because of it. On the contrary: nothing is easier to replace than a loss of weapons and every organizational form can again be created or renewed. What is irreplaceable is the spoiled blood of a people, the destroyed inner value.

For in opposition to the present bourgeois conception that the Treaty of Versailles has deprived our people of arms I can reply only that the real lack of weapons lies in our pacifistic-democratic poisoning, as well as in internationalism, which destroys and poisons our people's highest sources of power. For the source of a people's whole power does not lie in its possession of weapons or in the organization of its army, but in its inner value which is represented through its racial significance, that is the racial value of a people as such, through the existence of the highest individual personality values, as well as through its healthy attitude toward the idea of self-preservation.

In coming before the public as National Socialists with this conception of the real strength of a people, we know that today the whole of public opinion is against us. But this is indeed the deepest meaning of our new doctrine, which as a world view separates us from others.

Since our point of departure is that one people is not equal to another, the value of a people is also not equal to the value of another people. If, however, the value of a people is not equal to another, then every people, apart from the numerical value deriving from its count, still has a specific value which is peculiar to it and which cannot be fully like that of any other people. The expressions of this specific, special value of a people can be of the most varied kind and be in the most varied fields; but collected together they result in a standard for the general valuation of a people. The ultimate expression of this general valuation is the historical, cultural image of a people, which reflects the sum of all the radiations of its blood value or of the race values united in it.

This special value of a people, however, is in no way merely aesthetic-cultural, but a general life value as such. For it forms the life of a people in general, molds and shapes it and, therefore, also provides all those forces which a people can muster in order to overcome the resistances of life. For every cultural deed, viewed in human terms, is in truth a defeat for the hitherto existing barbarism, every cultural creation [thereby] a help to man's ascent above his formerly drawn limitations and thereby a strengthening of the position of these people. Thus a power for the assertion of life truly also lies in the so-called cultural values of a people. Consequently the greater the inner powers of a people in this direction, the stronger also the countless possibilities for the assertion of life in all fields of the struggle for existence. Consequently the higher the race value of a people, the greater its general life value [through] which it can stake in favor of its life, in the struggle and strife with other peoples.

The importance of the blood value of a people, however, only becomes totally effective when this value is recognized by a people, properly valued and appreciated. Peoples who do not understand this value or who no longer have a feeling for it for lack of a natural instinct, thereby also immediately begin to lose it. Blood mixing and lowering of the race are then the consequences which, to be sure, at the beginning are not seldom introduced through a so-called predilection for things foreign, which in reality is an underestimation of one's own cultural values as against alien peoples. Once a people no longer appreciates the cultural expression of its own spiritual life conditioned through its blood, or even begins to feel ashamed of it, in order to turn its attention to alien expressions of life, it renounces the strength which lies in the harmony of its blood and the cultural life which has sprung from it. It becomes torn apart, unsure in its judgment of the world picture and its expressions, loses the perception and the feeling for its own purposes, and in place of this it sinks into a confusion of international ideas, conceptions, and the cultural hodge-podge springing from them. Then the Jew can make his entry in any form, and this master of international poisoning and race corruption will not rest until he has thoroughly uprooted and thereby corrupted such a people. The end is then the loss of a definite unitary race value and as a result, the final decline.

Hence every existing race value of a people is also ineffective, if not indeed endangered, as long as a people does not consciously remind itself of its own and nurse it with great care, building and basing all its hopes primarily on it.

For this reason international-mindedness is to be regarded as the mortal enemy of these values. In its place the profession of faith in the value of one's own people must pervade and determine the whole life and action of a people.

The more the truly eternal factor for the greatness and the importance of a people is sought in the folk value, the less will this value as such achieve a total effectiveness if the energies and talents of a people, at first slumbering, do not find the man who will awaken it.

For so little as mankind, which is made up of different race values, possesses a uniform average value, just as little is the personality value within a people the same among all members. Every deed of a people, in whatever field it might be, is the result of the creative activity of a personality. No distress can be redressed solely by the wishes of those affected by it, as long as this general wish does not find its solution in a man chosen from a people for this task. Majorities have never wrought creative achievements. Never have they given discoveries to mankind. The individual person has always been the originator of human progress. Indeed a people of a definite inner race value, so far as this value is generally visible in its cultural or other achievements, must at the outset possess the personality values, for without their emergence and creative ac-

29

tivity the cultural image of that people would never have come into being and therefore the possibility of any inference as to the inner value of such a people would be lacking. When I mention the inner value of a people, I appraise it out of the sum of achievements lying before my eyes and thereby at the same time I confirm the existence of the specific personality values which acted as the representatives of the race value of a people and created the cultural image. As much as race value and personality value seem to be linked together, because a racially valueless people cannot produce important creative personalities from this source—as, conversely, it seems impossible to infer, for example, the existence of race value from the lack of creative personalities and their achievements—just as much can a people, nevertheless, by the nature of the formal construction of its organism, of the folk community or of the state, promote the expression of its personality values, or at least facilitate it, or indeed even prevent it.

Once a people installs the majority as the rulers of its life, that is to say, once it introduces present-day democracy in the Western conception, it will not only damage the importance of the concept of personality, but block the effectiveness of the personality value. Through a formal construction of its life it prevents the rise and the work of individual creative persons.

For this is the double curse of the democratic-parliamentary system prevailing today: not only is it itself incapable of bringing about really creative achievements, but it also prevents the emergence and thereby the work of those men who somehow threateningly rise above the level of the average. In all times the man whose greatness lies above the average measure of the general stupidity, inadequacy, cowardice, and arrogance too, has always appeared most threatening to the majority. Add to this that through democracy inferior persons must, almost as a law, become leaders, so that this system applied logically to any institution devaluates the whole mass of leaders, insofar as one can call them that at all. This resides in the irresponsibility lying in the nature of democracy. Majorities are phenomena that are too elusive to be grasped so that they can somehow be charged with responsibility. The leaders set up by them are in truth only executors of the will of the majorities. Hence their task is less that of producing creative plans or ideas, in order to carry them out with the support of an available administrative apparatus, than it is to collect the momentary majorities required for the execution of definite projects. Thus the majorities are adjusted less to the projects than the projects are to the majorities. No matter what the result of such an action may be, there is no one who can be held concretely accountable. This is all the more so as each decision that is actually adopted is the result of numerous compromises, which each will also exhibit in its character and content. Who then is to be made responsible for it?

Once a purely personally drawn responsibility is eliminated, the most compelling reason for the rise of a vigorous leadership falls away. Compare the army organization [institution], oriented to the highest degree toward authority and responsibility of the individual person, with our democratic civil institutions, especially in relation to the results of the leadership training on both sides, and you will be horrified. In one case an organization of men who are as courageous and joyous in responsibility as they are competent in their tasks, and in the other, incompetents too cowardly to assume responsibility. For four and a half years the German army organization withstood the greatest coalition of enemies of all times. The civil, democratically decomposed domestic leadership literally collapsed at the first thrust of a few hundred ragamuffins and deserters.

The pitiful lack of really great leading minds among the German people finds its most simple explanation in the desolate disintegration which we see before us through the democratic-parliamentary system which is slowly corroding our whole public life.

Nations must decide. Either they want majorities or brains. The two are never compatible. Up to now, however, brains have always created greatness on this earth, and what they created was again destroyed mostly through majorities.

Thus on the basis of its general race value a people can certainly entertain a justified hope that it can bring real minds into existence. But then it must seek forms in the mode of construction of its national body which do not artificially, indeed systematically, restrict such brains in their activity, and erect a wall of stupidity against them, in short, which prevent them from achieving efficacy.

Otherwise one of the most powerful sources of a people's strength is blocked.

The third factor of the strength of a people is its healthy natural instinct for self-preservation. [As a third factor of the inner strength of a people, we have education for self-assertion.] From it result numerous heroic virtues, which by themselves make a people take up the struggle for life. No state leadership will be able to have great successes, if the people whose interests it must represent is too cowardly and wretched to stake itself for these interests. No state leadership, of course, can expect that a people possess heroism, which it itself does not educate to heroism. Just as internationalism harms and thereby weakens the existing race value, and as democracy destroys the personality value, so pacifism paralyzes the natural strength of the self-preservation of peoples.

These three factors—the race value as such, the existing personality values, as well as the healthy instinct of self-preservation—are the sources of strength, from which a wise and bold domestic policy time and again can draw the weapons which are necessary for the self-assertion of a people. Then the army establishments and the technical questions regarding weapons always find the solutions suitable to support a people in the hard struggle for freedom and daily bread.

If the domestic leadership of a people loses sight of this standpoint or believes that it must arm for the struggle in terms of weapon technique only, it can achieve as much momentary success as it pleases, but the future does not belong to such a people. Hence the limited preparation for a war was never the task of truly great legislators and statesmen of this earth, but rather the unlimited inner, and thorough training of a people, so that its future could be secured almost as by law, according to all human reason. Then even wars lose the isolated character of more or less immense surprises, but instead are integrated into a natural, indeed self-evident, system of fundamental, well-grounded, permanent development of a people.

That present state leaders pay little attention to this viewpoint is partly due to the nature of democracy, to which they owe their very existence, but secondly to the fact that the state has become a

32

purely formal mechanism which appears to them as an aim in itself, which must not in the least coincide with the interests of a specific people. People and state have become two different concepts. It will be the task of the National Socialist movement to bring about a fundamental change here.

IV

Consequently if the task of domestic policy—besides the obvious one of satisfying the so-called questions of the day—must be the steeling and strengthening of a nation by means of a systematic cultivation and promotion of its inner values, the task of foreign policy is to correspond to and collaborate with this policy in order to create and to secure the vital prerequisites abroad. A healthy foreign policy, therefore, will always keep the winning of the basis of a people's sustenance immovably in sight as its ultimate goal. Domestic policy must secure the inner strength of a people so that it can assert itself in the sphere of foreign policy. Foreign policy must secure the life of a people for its domestic political development. Hence domestic policy and foreign policy are not only most closely linked, but must also mutually complement one another. The fact that in the great conjunctures of human history domestic policy as well as foreign policy has paid homage to other principles is not at all a proof of soundness, but rather proves the error of such action. Innumerable nations and states have perished as a warning example to us, because they did not follow the above-mentioned elementary principles. How little man thinks of the possibility of death during his life is a noteworthy fact. And how little he arranges the details of his life in accordance with the experiences that innumerable men before him had to have and which, as such, are all known to him. There are always exceptions who bear this in mind and who, by virtue of their personality, try to force on their fellow men the laws of life that lay at the base of the experiences of past epochs. Hence it is noteworthy that innumerable hygienic measures which perforce redound to the advantage of a people, and which individually are uncomfortable, must be formally forced upon the main body of a people through the autocratic standing of individual persons, in order however to disappear again when the authority of the personality is extinguished through the mass insanity of democracy. The average man has the greatest fear of death and in reality thinks of it most rarely. The important man concerns himself with it most emphatically and nevertheless fears it the least. The one lives blindly from day to day, sins heedlessly, in order suddenly to collapse before the inevitable. The other observes its coming most carefully and, to be sure, looks it in the eye with calm and composure.

Such is exactly the case in the lives of nations. It is often terrible to see how little men want to learn from history, how with such imbecilic indifference they gloss over their experiences, how thoughtlessly they sin without considering that it is precisely through their sins that so and so many nations and states have perished, indeed vanished from the earth. And indeed how little they concern themselves with the fact that even for the short time-span for which we possess an insight into history, states and nations have arisen which were sometimes almost gigantic in size but which two thousand years later vanished without a trace, that world powers once ruled cultural spheres of which only sagas give us any information, that giant cities have sunk into ruins, and that their rubble-heap has hardly survived to show present-day mankind at least the site on which they were located. The cares, hardships and sufferings of these millions and millions of individual men, who as a living substance were at one time the bearers and victims of these events, are almost beyond all imagination. Unknown men. Unknown soldiers of history. And truly, how indifferent is the present. How unfounded its eternal optimism and how ruinous its willful ignorance, its incapacity to see and its unwillingness to learn. And if it depended on the broad masses, the game of the child playing with the fire with which he is unfamiliar would repeat itself uninterruptedly and also to an infinitely greater extent. Hence it is the task of men who feel themselves called as educators of a people to learn on their own from history and to apply their knowledge practically [now], without regard to the view, understanding, ignorance or even the refusal of the mass. The greatness of a man is all the more important, the greater his courage, in opposition to a generally prevailing but ruinous view, to lead by his better insight to general victory. His victory will appear all the greater, the more enormous the resistances which had to be overcome, and the more hopeless the struggle seemed at first.

The National Socialist movement would have no right to regard itself as a truly great phenomenon in the life of the German people, if it could not muster the courage to learn from the experiences of the past, and to force the laws of life it represents on the German people despite all resistance. As powerful as its inner reform work will be in this connection, equally it must [may] never forget that in the long run there will be no resurgence of our people if its activity in the sphere of foreign policy does not succeed in securing the general pre-condition for the sustenance of our people. Hence it has become the fighter for freedom and bread in the highest sense of the word. Freedom and bread is the simplest and yet, in reality, the greatest foreign-policy slogan that can exist for any people: the freedom of being able to order and regulate the life of a people, according to its own interests, and the bread that this people requires for its existence.

If today, therefore, I come forward as a critic of our people's leadership in the sphere of foreign policy both past and present, I am aware that the errors which I see today have also been seen by others. What distinguishes me from the latter perhaps is only the fact that in most cases [in one case] it has only involved critical perceptions having no practical consequences, whereas, on the basis of my insight into the errors and faults of former and present German domestic and foreign policy, I strive to deduce proposals for a change and improvement and to forge the instrument with which these changes and improvements can some day be realized.

For example, the foreign policy of the Wilhelminian period was in many cases viewed by not a few people as catastrophic and characterized accordingly. Innumerable warnings came, especially from the circles of the Pan-German League* of that time, which were jus-

---

* The Pan-German League (*Alldeutscher Verband*) was formally established in 1894 to promote the geographical and economic expansion of Germany, in line with ideas that had been current since the founding of the German Empire in 1871. Hitler refers here to books by Pan-German writers such as Heinrich Class, President of the League and author of several strongly nationalist books published in the decade preceding the first World War.—*T.T.*

tified in the highest sense of the word. I can put myself in the tragic
situation that befell all these men who raised their voices in warning
and who saw how and in what a people perishes, and yet were not
able to help. In the last decades of the unfortunate foreign policy
of the prewar period in Germany, parliament, that is democracy,
was not powerful enough to choose the heads for the political leadership of the Reich by itself. This was still an imperial right, whose
formal existence no one yet dared to shake. But the influence of
democracy had grown so strong, however, that a certain direction
already seemed to be prescribed to the imperial decisions. Hence
this had disastrous consequences, for now a national-minded man
who raised his voice in warning, on the one hand, could no longer
count on being invested with a very responsible post against the pro-
nounced tendency of democracy, whereas, conversely, on the basis
of general patriotic ideas he could not fight against His Majesty the
Kaiser with the final weapon of opposition. The idea of a March
on Rome in prewar Germany would have been absurd. Thus the
national opposition found itself in the worst of situations. Democracy had not yet triumphed, but it already stood in a furious struggle
against the monarchic conceptions of government. The monarchical
state itself responded to the struggle of democracy not with the
determination to destroy the latter, but rather with endless concessions. Anyone who at that time took a stand against one of the two
institutions ran the danger of being attacked by both. Anyone who
opposed an imperial decision on national grounds was proscribed by
patriotic circles as much as he was abused by the adherents of
democracy. Anyone who took a position against democracy was
fought by democracy and left in the lurch by the patriots. Indeed,
he ran the danger of being most ignominiously betrayed [sacrificed]
by German officialdom in the wretched hope that through such
a sacrifice it could gain Jehovah's approval and temporarily stop
the yelping of the pack of Jewish press hounds. Under the conditions
of that time there was no prospect at hand of making one's way
to a responsible position in the leadership of the German government against the will of the democrats or against the will of His
Majesty the Kaiser, and thereby being able to change the course of
foreign policy. Further this led to the fact that German foreign

37

policy could be contested exclusively on paper, which consequently launched a criticism that necessarily took on the characteristic features of journalism, the longer it continued. The consequence of this, however, was that increasingly less value was placed on positive proposals, in view of the lack of any possibility of their realization, whereas the purely critical consideration of foreign policy occasioned the innumerable objections that one could adduce in all their fullness, all the more so because it was hoped that thereby one could overthrow the bad regime responsible. To be sure this was not achieved by the critics of that time. It was not the regime of that time which was overthrown, but the German empire and consequently the German people. What they had foretold for decades had now come to pass. We cannot think of these men without a deep compassion, men condemned by fate to foresee a collapse for twenty years, and who now, having not been heeded and hence in no position to be of help, had to live to see their people's most tragic catastrophe.

Aged in years, care-worn and embittered, and yet full of the idea that, now after the overthrow of the Imperial Government, they had to help, they again tried to make their influence felt for the resurgence of our people. For ever so many reasons this was futile to be sure.

When the revolution shattered the Imperial scepter and raised democracy to the throne, the critics of that time were as far from the possession of a weapon with which to overthrow democracy as formerly they had been from being able to influence the imperial government. In their decades of activity they had been geared so much to a purely literary treatment of these problems that they not only lacked the real means of power to express their opinion on a situation which was only a reaction to the shouting in the streets; they had also lost the capacity to try to organize a manifestation of power which had to be more than a wave of written protests if it were to be really effective. They had all seen the germ and the cause of the decline of the German Empire in the old parties. With a sense of their own inner cleanliness they had to scorn the suggestion that they too now wanted to play the game of the political parties. And yet, they could carry out their view in practice only if a large number gave them the opportunity of representing it. And even though they wanted a thousand times to smash the political parties, they still indeed first had to form a party which viewed its task as that of smashing the other parties. That such did not come to pass was due to the following reasons: the more the political opposition of these men was forced to express itself purely journalistically, the more it adopted a criticism which, though it exposed all the weaknesses of the system of that time and shed light on the defects of the individual foreign policy measures, failed to produce positive proposals because these men lacked any possibility of personal responsibility, especially since in political life there is naturally no action which does not have its dark as well as its bright sides. There is no political combination in foreign policy that we can ever regard as completely satisfactory. For as matters stood then, the critic, forced to view his main task as the elimination of a regime recognized as altogether incompetent, had no occasion, outside of the useful critical consideration of this regime's actions, to come forward with positive proposals, which in consequence of the objections attached to them could just as easily have been subjected to a critical elucidation. The critic will never want to weaken the impact of his criticism by bringing forward proposals which themselves could be subjected to criticism. Gradually, however, the purely critical thinking of those who then represented the national opposition became such a second nature that even today they consider domestic and foreign policy critically, and deal with it only critically. Most of them have remained critics, who therefore cannot even today make their way to a clear, unambiguous, positive decision neither in domestic nor in foreign policy, partly because of their insecurity and irresoluteness, partly because of their fear of thereby furnishing the enemy with ready ammunition for criticism of themselves. Thus they would like to bring about improvements in a thousand things and yet cannot decide upon taking a single step because even this very step is not completely satisfactory, and possesses doubtful points; in short it has its darker sides which they perceive and which make them fearful. Now, leading a nation from a deep and difficult illness is not a question of finding a prescription that itself is completely free of poison; not seldom it involves destroying a poison through an antidote. In order to eliminate conditions recognized as deadly we must have the courage to make and carry out decisions which contain dangers in themselves. As a critic I have the right to examine all the possibilities of a foreign policy and to take them apart in detail according to the doubtful aspects or possibilities they bear in themselves. As the political leader, however, who wants to make history, I must decide upon one way, even if sober consideration a thousand times tells me that it entails certain dangers and that it also will not lead to a completely satisfying end. Hence I cannot renounce the possibility of success because it is not a hundred percent certain. I must neglect no step for the reason that perhaps it will not be a full one, if the spot in which I momentarily find myself might bring my unconditional death the next instant. Neither, therefore, may I renounce a political action for the reason that besides benefiting my people it will also benefit another people. Indeed, I may never do this when the benefit to the other people will be greater than that to my own, and when in the case of a failure to take action the misfortune of my people remains with absolute certainty.

Indeed right now I encounter the most stubborn resistance in the purely critical way of viewing things that many people have. They recognize this and this and this as good and as correct, but despite this they cannot join us because this and this and this is dubious. They know that Germany and our people will perish, but they cannot join the rescue action because here too they detect this or that which is at least a blemish that mars its beauty. In short, they see the decline and cannot muster up the strength of determination to battle against it, because in the resistance and in this deed itself they already again begin to smell out some possible objection or other.

This deplorable mentality owes its existence to [springs from] a still further evil. Today there are not a few men, especially the so-called educated ones, who, when they finally make up their minds to fall in line with a certain action or even to promote it, first carefully weigh the percentage of the probability of its success, in order then to calculate the extent of their active involvement likewise on the basis of this percentage. Thus this means: because, for example, any decision on foreign policy or domestic policy is not completely satisfying and hence does not seem certain to succeed, one should also not espouse it unreservedly with the full dedication of all his powers. These unhappy souls have no understanding at all of the fact that, on the contrary, a decision which I deem to be necessary, whose success however does not seem completely assured, or whose success will offer only a partial satisfaction, must be fought for with an increased energy so that what it lacks in the possibility of success in percentage points, must be made up for in the energy of its execution. Thus only one question is to be examined: whether a situation demands a definite decision or not. If such a decision is established and recognized as incontestably necessary, then its execution must be carried out with the most brutal ruthlessness and the highest employment of strength even if the ultimate result will be a thousand times unsatisfactory or in need of improvement or possibly will meet with only a small percentage of probability of success.

If a man appears to have cancer and is unconditionally doomed to die, it would be senseless to refuse an operation, because the percentage of the possibility of success is slight and because the patient, even should it be successful, will not be a hundred percent healthy. It would be still more senseless were the surgeon to perform the operation itself only with limited or partial energy in consequence of these limited possibilities. But it is this senselessness that these men expect uninterruptedly in domestic and foreign policy matters. Because the success of a political operation is not fully assured or will not be completely satisfactory in result, not only do they renounce its execution but expect, should it take place nevertheless, that at least it will ensue only with restrained power, without a complete dedication, and always in silent hope that perhaps they can keep a little loophole open through which to make their retreat. This is the soldier who is attacked by a tank on an open battlefield and who in view [in consequence] of the uncertainty of the success of his resistance conducts it at the outset with only half his strength. His little loophole is flight and certain death his end.

No, the German people is today attacked by a pack of booty-hungry enemies from within and without. The continuation of this

41

state of affairs is our death. We must seize every possibility of breaking it, even if its result may a thousand times likewise have its weaknesses or objectionable sides as such. [He who has fallen into the hands of the devil has little choice as regards his allies.] And every such possibility must therefore be fought out with the utmost energy.

The success [victory] of the battle of Leuthen was uncertain, but it was necessary to fight it. Frederick the Great did not win because he went toward the enemy with only half his strength, but because he compensated for the uncertainty of success by the abundance of his genius, the boldness and determination of his troop dispositions and the derring-do of his regiments in battle.

I'm afraid, indeed, that I will never be understood by my bourgeois critics, at least as long as success does not prove to them the soundness of our action. Here the man of the people has a better counselor [instinct]. He sets the assurance of his instinct [feeling] and the faith of his heart in place of the sophistry of our intellectuals.

If I deal with foreign policy in this work, however, I do so not as a critic but as the leader of the National Socialist movement which I know will some day make history. If I am therefore nevertheless forced to consider the past and the present critically, it is only for the purpose of establishing the only positive way and to make it appear understandable. Just as the National Socialist movement not only criticizes domestic policy, but possesses its own philosophically grounded program, likewise in the sphere of foreign policy it must not only recognize what others have done wrongly, but deduce its own action on the basis of this knowledge.

Thus I know well that even our highest success will not create a hundred percent happiness, for in view of human imperfection and the general circumstances conditioned by it, ultimate perfection always lies only in programmatic theory. I also know, further, that no success can be achieved without sacrifice, just as no battle can be fought without losses. But the awareness of the incompleteness of a success will never be able to keep me from preferring such an incomplete success to the perceived complete downfall. I will then strain every nerve to try to offset what is lacking in the probability of success or the extent of success through greater determination, and to communicate this spirit to the movement led by me. Today we are fighting against an enemy front which we must and will break through. We calculate our own sacrifices, weigh the extent of the possible success and will stride forward to the attack, regardless of whether it will come to a halt ten or a thousand kilometers behind the present lines. For wherever our success ends, it will always be only the point of departure for a new struggle.

V

I am a German nationalist. This means that I proclaim my nationality. My whole thought and action belongs to it. I am a socialist. I see no class and no social estate before me, but that community of people who are linked by blood, united by a language, and subject to a same general fate. I love this people and hate only its majority of the moment, because I view the latter to be just as little representative of the greatness of my people as it is of its happiness.

The National Socialist movement which I lead today views its goal as the liberation of our people within and without. It aims to give our people domestically those forms of life which seem to be suitable to its nature and to be a benefit to it as the expression of this nature. It aims thereby to preserve the character of this people and to further cultivate it through the systematic fostering of its best men and best virtues. It fights for the external freedom of this people, because only under freedom can this life find that form which is serviceable to its people. It fights for the daily bread of this people because it champions [in hunger] this people's right to life. It fights for the required space, because it represents this people's right to life.

By the concept "domestic policy" the National Socialist movement therefore understands the promotion, strengthening and consolidation of the existence of our people through the introduction of forms and laws of life which correspond to the nature of our people, and which can bring its fundamental powers to full effectiveness.

By foreign policy it understands the safeguarding of this development through the preservation of freedom and the creation of the most necessary prerequisites for life.

Thus in terms of foreign policy the National Socialist movement is distinguished from previous bourgeois parties by, for example, the following: The foreign policy of the national bourgeois world has in truth always been only a border policy; as against that, the policy of the National Socialist movement will always be a territorial one. In its boldest plans, for example, the German bourgeoisie will aspire to the unification of the German nation, but in reality it will finish with a botched-up regulation of the borders.

The National Socialist movement, on the contrary, will always let its foreign policy be determined by the necessity to secure the space necessary to the life of our people. It knows no Germanizing or Teutonizing, as in the case of the national bourgeoisie, but only the spread of its own people. It will never see in the subjugated, so-called Germanized, Czechs or Poles a national, let alone folkish, strengthening, but only the racial weakening of our people. For its national conception is not determined by earlier patriotic ideas of government, but rather by folkish, racial insights. Thus the point of departure of its thinking is wholly different from that of the bourgeois world. Hence much of what seems to the national bourgeoisie like the political success of the past and present, is for us either a failure or the cause of a later misfortune. And much that we regard as self-evident seems incomprehensible or even monstrous to the German bourgeoisie. Nevertheless a part of German youth, especially from bourgeois circles, will be able to understand me. Neither I nor the National Socialist movement figure to find any support whatsoever in the circles of the political-national bourgeoisie, active at present, but we certainly know that at least a part of the youth will find its way into our ranks.

[For them . . .]

VI

The question of a nation's foreign policy is determined by factors which lie partly within a nation, and partly given [determined] by the environment. In general the internal factors are the basis for the necessity of a definite foreign policy as well as for the amount of strength required for its execution. Peoples living on an impossible soil surface fundamentally will tend to enlarge their territory, consequently their living space, at least as long as they are under healthy leadership. This process, originally grounded only in the concern over sustenance, appeared so beneficent in its felicitous solution that it gradually attained the fame of success. This means that the enlargement of space, at first grounded in pure expediencies, became in the course of mankind's development a heroic deed, which then also took place even when the original pre-conditions or inducements were lacking. Later, the attempt to adapt the living space to increased population turned into unmotivated wars of conquest, which in their very lack of motivation contained the germ of the subsequent reaction. Pacifism is the answer to it. Pacifism has existed in the world ever since there have been wars whose meaning no longer lay in the conquest of territory for a people's sustenance. Since then it has been war's eternal companion. It will again disappear as soon as war ceases to be an instrument of booty- or power-hungry individuals or nations, and as soon as it again becomes the ultimate weapon with which a people fights for its daily bread.

Even in the future the enlargement of a people's living space for the winning of bread will require staking the whole strength of the people. If the task of domestic policy is to prepare this commitment of the people's strength, the task of a foreign policy is to wield this strength in such a manner that the highest possible success seems assured. This, of course, is not conditioned only by the strength of the people, ready for action at any given time, but also by the power of the resistances. The disproportion in strength between peoples struggling with one another for land leads repeatedly to the attempt, by way of alliances, either to emerge as conquerors themselves or to put up resistance to the over-powerful conqueror.

This is the beginning of the policy of alliances.

After the victorious war of 1870-1871 the German people achieved a position of infinite esteem in Europe. Thanks to the success of Bismarckian statesmanship and Prusso-German military accomplishments a great number of German states, which heretofore had been only loosely linked and which, indeed, had not seldom in history faced each other as enemies, were brought together in one Reich. A province of the old German Reich, lost 170 years before, permanently annexed at that time by France after a brief predatory war, came back to the mother country. Numerically thereby the greatest part of the German nation, at least in Europe, was amalgamated in a unitary state structure. It was cause for concern that ultimately this state structure included . . . . million Poles and . . . . Alsatians and Lorrainers become Frenchmen.* This did not correspond either with the idea of a national or of a folkish state. The national state of bourgeois conception must at least secure the unity of the state language, indeed down to the last school and the last street sign. Further it must include the German idea in the education and life of these people and make them the bearers of this idea.

There have been weak attempts at this; perhaps it was never seriously wanted and in practice the opposite has been achieved.

The folkish state, conversely, must under no conditions annex Poles with the intention of wanting to make Germans out of them some day. On the contrary it must muster the determination either to seal off these alien racial elements, so that the blood of its own people will not be corrupted again, or it must without further ado

---

* The figures here, as elsewhere in the book, were omitted by Hitler at the time of dictation, and never filled in.—*Trans.*

remove them and hand over the vacated territory to its own national comrades.

That the bourgeois-national state was not capable of such a deed is obvious. Neither had anyone ever thought about it, nor would anyone ever have done such a thing. But even if there had been a will to do this, there would not have been sufficient strength to carry it out, less because of the repercussions in the rest of the world than because of the complete lack of understanding that such an action would have found in the ranks of the so-called national bourgeoisie. The bourgeois world had once presumed it could overthrow the feudal world, whereas in reality it continued the latter's mistakes through bourgeois pepper-sacks,* lawyers and journalists. It has never possessed an idea of its own, but indeed a measureless conceit and money.

But a world cannot be conquered with this alone, nor another one built. Hence the period of bourgeois rule in world history will be as brief as it is indecently contemptible.

Thus, right from its foundation, the German Reich had also assimilated toxins into the new state structure whose deleterious effect could all the less be evaded as bourgeois equality, to top things off, gave Jews the possibility of using them as their surest shock troops.

Aside from that the Reich nevertheless encompassed only a part of the German nation, even though the largest. It would have been self-evident that even if the new state had not possessed any great foreign policy aim of a folkish character, at least as a so-called bourgeois-national state it should have kept in view further unification and consolidation of the German nation, as its minimum foreign policy aim. This was something that the bourgeois-national Italian state never forgot.

Thus the German people had gotten a national state which in reality did not completely encompass the nation.

Thus the new borders of the Reich, viewed in a national-political

---

* *Pfeffer-Säcke,* a colloquial term for grocers, shopkeepers, etc. A variant given here was "professors."—*Trans.*

48

sense, were incomplete. They ran straight across German language areas, and even through parts which, at least formerly, had belonged to the German Union, even if in an informal way.

But these new borders of the Reich were even more unsatisfactory from a military viewpoint. Everywhere were unprotected, open areas which especially in the West were, in addition, of decisive importance for the German economy, extending far beyond the border areas. These borders were all the more unsuitable in a military-political sense since grouped around Germany were several great states [on the border] with foreign policy aims as aggressive as their military means were plentiful. Russia in the East, France in the West. Two military states, one of which cast covetous glances at East and West Prussia, while the other tirelessly pursued its centuries-old foreign policy goal for the erection of a frontier on the Rhine. In addition there was England, the mightiest maritime power of the world. The more extensive and unprotected the German land borders were in the East and West, the more restricted, by contrast, was the possible operational basis of a naval war. Nothing had made the fight against German submarine warfare easier than the spatially conditioned restriction of its port areas. It was easier to close off and patrol the triangle-shaped body of water* than would have been the case with a coast, say, 600 or 800 kilometers long. Taken all in all the new borders of the Reich as such were not at all satisfactory from a military point of view. Nowhere was there a natural obstacle or a natural defense. As against this, however, everywhere were highly developed power states with hostile thoughts in the back of their minds. The Bismarckian premonition that the new Reich founded by him would once again have to be protected with the

---

* The "triangle-shaped body of water" is the North Sea, and Hitler's complaint was that Germany's short coast line could be easily sealed off by closing the passage between Scotland, the Orkneys, and Norway. This was a favorite theme in German naval circles, and in 1929 Vize-admiral Wolfgang Wegener published a book (*Die Strategie des Welt-krieges*) pointing to the value of naval bases in Norway, by means of which Germany might more easily break out of a British blockade and more effectively wage submarine warfare. These ideas in part motivated the German conquest of Norway in 1940.—*T.T.*

sword was most deeply justified. Bismarck expressed what was fulfilled forty-five years later.

As little satisfactory as the new Reich borders could be in a national and military-political sense, they were nevertheless even still more unsatisfactory from the standpoint of the possibility of sustenance of the German people.

Germany in fact was always an overpopulated area. On the one hand this lay in the hemmed-in position of the German nation in Central Europe, on the other in the cultural and actual importance of this people and its purely human fertility. Since its historical entry into world history the German people has always found itself in need of space. Indeed, its first political emergence was forced primarily by that need. Since the beginning of the migration of peoples, our people has never been able to settle this need for space, except through conquest by the sword or through a reduction of its own population. This reduction of the population was sometimes effected through hunger, sometimes through emigration, and at times through endless, unfortunate wars. In recent times it has been effected by voluntary birth control.

The wars of the years '64, '66 and '70-'71 had their meaning in the national-political unification of a part of the German people and thus in the final end of German state-political fragmentation. The black, white, red flag of the new Reich therefore did not have the slightest ideological meaning, but rather a German-national one in the sense that it overcame the former state-political fragmentation. Thus the black, white, red flag became a symbol of the German Federal State which had overcome the fragmentation. The fact that, notwithstanding and despite its youth, it enjoyed a positively idolatrous veneration lay in the manner of its baptism, for indeed the very birth of the Reich towered infinitely above otherwise similar events. Three victorious wars, the last of which became a literal miracle of German statesmanship, Germany military leadership and German heroism, are the deeds from which the new Reich was born. And when it finally announced its existence to the surrounding world in the imperial proclamation, through its greatest imperial herald, the thunder and rumbling of the batteries at the front surrounding Paris re-echoes [rumbles] in the blare and the flourish of the trumpets.

Never before had an empire been proclaimed in such a fashion.

But the black, white, red flag appeared to the German people as the symbol of this unique event exactly as the black, red and yellow flag is and will remain a symbol of the November Revolution.

As much as the individual German states increasingly fused with one another under this banner and as much as the new Reich secured their state-political prestige and recognition abroad, the founding of the empire still did not change anything with regard to the major need, our people's lack of territory. The great military-political deeds of our people had not been able to give the German people a border within which it would have been able to secure its sustenance by itself. On the contrary: in proportion as the esteem of German nationality rose through the new Reich, it became all the more difficult for the individual German to turn his back on such a state as an emigrant, whereas, conversely, a certain national pride and a joy in life, which we find almost incomprehensible today, taught that large families were a blessing rather than a burden.

After 1870-1871 there was a visibly rapid increase in the German population. In part its sustenance was covered through the utmost industry and great scientific efficiency with which the German now cultivated his fields within the secured frontiers of his people. But a great part, if not the greatest, of the increase in German soil productivity was swallowed up by an at least equally great increase of the general living requirements which the citizen of the new state now likewise claimed. "The nation of sauerkraut-eaters and potato-annihilators," as the French derisively characterized it, now slowly began to adjust its living standard to that of other peoples in the world. Thus only a part of the yield of the increase of German agriculture was available for the net population increase.

As a matter of fact the new Reich never knew how to banish this need. Even in the new Reich at first an attempt was made to keep the relation between population and land within tolerable limits through a permanent emigration. For the most shattering proof of the soundness of our assertion of the towering importance of the relation between population and land lies in the fact that in consequence of this disproportion, specifically in Germany during the '70's, '80's and '90's, the distress led to an epidemic of emigration which even at the beginning of the '90's had swollen to a figure of nearly one and a quarter million people a year.

Thus the problem of the sustenance of the German people had not been solved for the existing human mass, not even by the foundation of the new Reich. A further increase of the German nation, however, could not take place without such a solution. Regardless of how such a solution might turn out, it had to be found in any case. Hence the most important problem of German foreign policy after 1870-1871 had to be the question of solving the problem of sustenance.

VII

Among Bismarck's innumerable utterances there is hardly another which the bourgeois political world could have been more fond of quoting than the one that politics is the art of the possible. The smaller the political minds which had to administer the legacy of the great man, the greater the force of attraction this utterance possessed. For with this proposition, to be sure, they could embroider, indeed justify even the most wretched political bunglers, by simply appealing to the great man and trying to prove that, for the moment, it was impossible to do other than what was being done, that politics was the art of the possible and that consequently they were acting with a Bismarckian spirit and in a Bismarckian sense. Thereby even a Herr Stresemann can receive some sort of an Olympian wreath to put around his head which, if not really Bismarckian, is at least bald.

Bismarck had an exactly demarcated and clearly outlined political goal before his eyes. It is an impudence to want to saddle him with the idea that he achieved his life work only through an accumulation of specific political possibilities and not through a mastery of specific momentary situations with an eye on a visualized political aim. This political aim of Bismarck was to solve the German question through blood and iron. Elimination of the Hapsburg-Hohenzollern dualism. Formation of a new German Reich under Prussian-Hohenzollern leadership. Highest possible external security of this Reich. Organization of its inner administration on the Prussian model.

In the pursuit of this aim Bismarck utilized every opportunity and worked through the diplomatic art as long as it promised success; he threw the sword into the scales if force alone was in a position to bring about a decision. A master of politics, for whom the operational sphere extended from the parquet floors of drawing rooms to the blood-soaked earth of battlefields.

Such was the master of the politics of possibilities.

His successors have neither a political aim nor even a political idea. In contrast to him they muddle through from today to tomorrow and from tomorrow to the day after, and then with conceited insolence quote that man—whom partly they themselves, partly their spiritual predecessors had occasioned the most difficult concerns and most bitter battles—in order to present their politically senseless and aimless, ruinous stammering as the art of the possible.

When, in his three wars, Bismarck set up the new Reich—all due, however, to his brilliant political activity—this was actually the highest achievement that could be realized at that time. But this was only the indispensable, necessary prerequisite for any future political representation of the vital interests of our people. For without the creation of the new Reich the German people would have never discovered the power-structure without which the fateful struggle could not be carried on in the future too. It was equally clear that at the outset the new Reich certainly had to be joined together on the battlefield, but that internally the component states first had to grow accustomed to each other. Years of adjustment had to pass before this consolidation of German states into a union could in the first instance result in a real federal state. This was when the Iron Chancellor discarded the cuirassier's boot in order then, with infinite cleverness, patience, and with a wise understanding and a wonderful sensitivity, to replace the pressure of Prussian hegemony by the power of trust. The achievement of making a coalition of states, formed on the battlefield, into a Reich interconnected in a touching love, belongs with the greatest ever brought about by the art of politics.

That Bismarck at first limited himself to this was just as much due to the wisdom of his insight, as it was the good fortune of the German nation. These years of the inner peaceful construction of the new Reich were necessary, if one was not to succumb to a mania for conquest whose results would have been all the more uncertain since the executive power within the empire itself was still lacking in that homogeneity which would have been a prerequisite for the fusing of further territories.

Bismarck achieved his life goal. He solved the German question, eliminated the Hapsburg-Hohenzollern dualism, raised Prussia to German hegemony, subsequently united the nation, consolidated the new Reich within the limits of the possible of that time, and worked out the military defense in such a way that this whole process of newly establishing the German Reich internally, which indeed necessarily took decades, could not be disrupted in essentials by anybody.

Thus the more Bismarck could, as the aged old Reich Chancellor, look back on a finished life work, the less did this work signify the end of the life of the German nation. Through Bismarck's founding of the new Reich the German nation, after centuries of governmental decay, had again found an organic form which not only united the German people, but also endowed this united people with an expression of vigor which was as real as it was ideal. If the flesh and blood of this people was the substance whose preservation in this world had to be sought, the instrument of power through which the nation could henceforth again attend to its right to life in the framework of the rest of the world had come into being with the new Reich.

The task of the post-Bismarck period was to resolve what further step had to be taken in the interest of preserving the substance of the German people.

Hence the further detailed political work depended on these decisions, which had to be of a fundamental character and which thereby signified the setting of a new goal. Hence this means: just as Bismarck, as an individual man, had resolved to set a goal for his political action, which only then allowed him to act from situation to situation according to all possibilities, in order to arrive at this goal, so did the post-Bismarck period also have to set itself a definite goal, as necessary as it was possible, whose achievement imperatively promoted the interests of the German people, and for the achievement of which one could then likewise utilize all possibilities, beginning with the arts of diplomacy up to the art of war.

The setting of this goal, however, was left undone.

It is not necessary, and indeed hardly possible, to specify all the causes of this neglect. The principal reason lies first of all in the lack of a really brilliant, towering political personality. But reasons which partly lie in the very nature of the founding of the new Reich weigh almost as heavily in the scales. Germany had become a democratic state, and even though the leaders of the Reich were subject to imperial decisions, nevertheless these decisions themselves could escape only with difficulty the impact of that general opinion which found its particular expression in the parliamentary institution, the makers of which were the political parties as well as the press, which in turn themselves received their ultimate instructions from a few recognizable wirepullers. Thereby the interests of the nation receded more and more into the background in comparison to the interests of definite and special grot ps. This was all the more the case, since only little clarity on the real interests of the nation prevailed among the broadest circles of public opinion, whereas, conversely, the interests of definite political parties or of the newspaper world were much more concrete since Germany was now indeed a national state. But the concept of a national attitude was in the end only a purely governmental-patriotic-dynastic one. It had almost nothing to do with folkish insights. Hence a general vagueness prevailed as to the future and as to the directional goal of a future foreign policy. Viewed from a national standpoint the next task of the state, after the completion of its inner state structure, should have been the resumption and the final achievement of national unity. No foreign policy aim could have been more obvious for the strictly formal national state of that time than the annexation of those German areas in Europe which, partly through their former history, had to be an obvious part not only of the German nation but of a German Reich. Nevertheless such an obvious goal had not been set because, apart from other resistances, the so-called national concept was much too vague, [too] little thought through and worked out, to be able to motivate such a step sufficiently by itself. To have kept in view and carried out, with all means, the incorporation of the German element of the old eastern frontier of the Reich as the next aim would have run counter to patriotic-legitimist ideas, as well as counter to feelings of poorly defined sympathies.

The "venerable" House of Hapsburg, to be sure, would thereby have lost its throne. All beer-table patriotism would also have been most grievously offended, but nevertheless this would have been the only reasonable next aim which the new Reich could set for itself—that is, from the point of view of a so-called national state. Not only because through it Germans living in the area of the Reich would have considerably increased numerically, which naturally would have also been expressed militarily, but at that time we could have rescued that, the loss of which we deplore today. Had Germany herself joined [then] in the partition of the impossible Hapsburg state, indeed had she presented this partition to herself as her own political aim for national-political reasons, Europe's whole development would have taken another path. Germany would not have made enemies out of a whole number of states which in themselves had nothing against Germany, and in the south the frontiers of the Reich would not run across the Brenner. At least the predominantly German part of the South Tyrol would be in Germany today.

But that this was prevented lay not only in the lack of a national concept at that time, but just as much in the definite interests of definite groups. Centrist circles under all circumstances desired a policy aimed at preserving the so-called "Catholic" Hapsburg state, in connection with which they talked mendaciously about "clan brothers," whereas they knew very well that in the Hapsburg monarchy these clan brothers were slowly but surely being driven to the wall and robbed of their membership in the clan. But for the Center, German viewpoints were not a standard, indeed not even in Germany proper. The gentlemen were fonder of any Pole, any Alsatian traitor and Francophile than they were of the German who did not want to join such a criminal organization. Under the pretext of representing Catholic interests this party even in peacetime had lent a helping hand to harm and ruin the major bulwark of a real Christian world view, Germany, in all possible ways. And this most mendacious party did not even shrink from going arm in arm, in the closest friendship, with avowed deniers of God, atheists, blasphemers of religion, as long as they believed they could thereby harm the German national state and the German people.

Thus in the establishment of the insane German foreign policy the Center, the Christian-Catholic pious Center, had Jewish-God-denying Marxists as loving allies at its side.

For just as the Center did everything it could to protect itself against any anti-Hapsburg policy, the Social Democrats, as the then representatives of the Marxist world view, did exactly the same, albeit for other reasons. To be sure, the ultimate intention in both parties was the same: to harm Germany as much as possible. The weaker the state, the more unlimited becomes domination of these parties, and therefore the greater advantage to their leaders.

If the old Reich wanted to resume the unification of the German element in Europe on the basis of national-political viewpoints, then the dissolution of the Hapsburg conglomeration of states, necessarily linked to it, entailed a new grouping of European powers. It was self-evident that such a dissolution of the Hapsburg state was inconceivable without entering into relations with other states which had to pursue similar interests. Thus a European coalition for the achievement of this goal, by pursuing all possibilities thereto, would automatically have come into being, which would have determined Europe's fate at least for the next decades.

To be sure the Triple Alliance had first to be liquidated in fact. I say in fact, because in practice the liquidation had already been accomplished long ago.

The alliance with Austria had a real meaning for Germany as long as through this alliance she could hope to get additional power in the hour of danger. It became senseless from the moment in which the additional power was smaller than Germany's military burden brought about by this alliance. Properly considered, this was the case from the very first day of the Triple Alliance, if for example Russia were to become Germany's enemy in consequence of this Alliance or on the basis of this Alliance. Bismarck had also pondered this most scrupulously and therefore saw himself induced to conclude the so-called Reinsurance treaty with Russia. Briefly the sense of the Reinsurance treaty was that if Germany should be pushed into a conflict with Russia through the Alliance, she would drop Austria. Thus Bismarck had already perceived the problematic importance of the Triple Alliance in his time, and in accordance with his art of the possible he had taken the necessary precautions to meet all circumstances.

In its time this Reinsurance treaty contributed to the banishment of the greatest German statesman of our age.

As a matter of fact the situation feared by Bismarck had already arisen in the beginning of the '90's after the occupation of Bosnia by Austria-Hungary and in consequence of the powerfully inflamed Pan-Slav movement arising therefrom. The alliance with Austria had brought enmity with Russia.

This enmity with Russia, however, was the reason why Marxists, even though they were not in accord with German foreign policy, nevertheless in reality used every means to make another one impossible.

Thus Austria's relation to Italy as such always remained the same. Formerly Italy had entered the Triple Alliance as a precaution against France, but not out of love for Austria. On the contrary, Bismarck even here had correctly perceived the "inner cordiality" of the Italian-Austrian relationship when he asserted that there were only two possibilities between Austria and Italy: either an alliance or war. In Italy—aside from a few Francophile fanatics—a real sympathy existed only for Germany. And this was also understandable. It speaks for the completely bottomless lack of political training and the political ignorance of the German people, especially of its so-called bourgeois-national intelligentsia, that they believed they could carry over the Triple Alliance, based on political law, to the sphere of friendly inclinations. This was not even the case between Germany and Austria, for even here the Triple Alliance, or more correctly, the alliance with Germany was humanly anchored only in the hearts of a relatively small part of the Germans in Austria. The Hapsburgs would have never made their way to the Triple Alliance if any other possibility of preserving their corpse of a state had existed. When in the July days of 1870 the German people were inflamed with indignation over France's unprecedented provocations and hastened to the old battlefields in defense of the German Rhine, in Vienna it was hoped that the hour to revenge Sadowa had come. Conferences followed one another in rapid succession, one crown council alternated with another, couriers flew hither and thither, and the first call-up of the reserves was issued when suddenly, to be sure, the first communiqués from the theaters of war also began to arrive. And when Weissenburg was followed by a Wörth, and Wörth by a Gravelotte, a Metz, a Mars la Tour, and finally a Sedan, then the Hapsburgs, under the pressure of the suddenly released clamor of the new German opinion, first began to discover their German heart. If at that time Germany had lost only the first battles the Hapsburgs, and with them Austria, would have done the very thing for which they later greatly reproached Italy. And that which, moreover, they not only intended to do in the World War for the second time, but actually perpetrated as the basest betrayal of the state which had unsheathed its sword for them. For the sake and on account of this state Germany had taken the worst bloody hardships upon herself and she was betrayed not only in a thousand individual cases by this state, but finally by the representative of the state himself, all things and truths about which our bourgeois national patriots prefer to keep silent, in order to be able to shriek against Italy today.

When later the House of Hapsburg crept into the Triple Alliance, it was really only because without the Triple Alliance this House would long ago have been swept to where it finds itself today. When I once more examine the sins of this House in the history of the German people, to me it seems distressing that this time the mills of God were propelled by forces which lay outside the German people.

But thus the Hapsburgs also had every reason to want the alliance, especially with Germany, because this alliance in reality indeed surrendered Germanism in Austria. The denationalization policy of the Hapsburgs in Austria, their Czechization and Slavization of German elements would have never become possible, if the Reich itself had not held its moral shield over it. Because what right did the German-Austrian have to protest, and on national grounds, against a state policy to which corresponded the quintessence of the German national idea, as it was embodied in the Reich for the German-Austrian?

And conversely could Germany now exert any pressure at all to prevent the slow de-Germanization in Austria, if after all the

Hapsburgs themselves were the allies of the Reich? We must know the weakness of the political leaders of the Reich in order to know that anything else would sooner have been possible rather than an attempt to exercise a real energetic influence on the ally which would have affected her domestic affairs. The wily Hapsburgs knew this well, just as in general Austrian diplomacy was toweringly superior to the German in artfulness and craftiness. And, conversely, these very Germans, as though stricken with blindness, seemed not to have the remotest idea of events and conditions inside the country of their ally. Only the war may have opened the eyes of most people.

Thus the very alliance-based friendship of the Hapsburgs for Germany was all the more fateful since through it the ultimate undermining of the prerequisite for this alliance was guaranteed. For now that the Hapsburgs were in a position to wipe out Germanism in Austria at their leisure and without having to worry about German interference, the worth of this whole alliance for Germany herself became increasingly problematic. What meaning should an alliance have for Germany which was not earnestly intended by the ruling house—for the House of Hapsburg had never thought to regard German interests as taken for granted in the matter of the alliance, so that the few real friends of this alliance perforce slowly fell prey to de-Germanization. For in the rest of Austria the alliance was viewed with indifference at best, but in most cases it was inwardly hated.

In the period of the last twenty years before the war the metropolitan press in Vienna was already much more oriented along pro-French rather than pro-German lines. The press of the Slavic provinces, however, was deliberately hostile to Germany. In proportion as Slavism was culturally fostered to the utmost by the Hapsburgs, and now acquired focal points of its own national culture in their capitals, it also gave rise to centers having a special political will of their own. It is an historical punishment for the House of Hapsburg not to have seen that one day this national hatred, which was first mobilized against the Germans, would devour the Austrian state itself. But for Germany the alliance with Austria became especially senseless the moment when, thanks to the influence of the German-Austrian Marxists, treasonable to the *Volk*, so-called universal suffrage finally broke the hegemony of Germanism in the Austrian state. For actually indeed the Germans numbered only a third of the population of Cisleithania, that is of the Austrian half of the Austro-Hungarian state. Once universal suffrage became the foundation of Austrian parliamentary representation, the situation of the Germans became hopeless, the more so since the clerical parties wanted a deliberate representation of the national viewpoints as little as did the Marxists, who deliberately betrayed them. The same Social Democrats who today hypocritically talk about Germanism in the South Tyrol betrayed and sold out Germanism in old Austria in the most shameless way at every opportunity that offered itself. They always stood on the side of the enemies of our people. The most impertinent Czech arrogance has always found its representatives in so-called German Social Democracy. Every oppressive act directed against Germany found their approbation. And every example of a German deterioration saw the German Social Democrats as collaborators. Under such circumstances what could Germany still expect from a state whose political leadership, insofar as it was specifically expressed in parliament, was four-fifths consciously and deliberately anti-German?

The advantages of the alliance with Austria lay really only on Austria's side, whereas Germany had to bear the disadvantages. And these were not few.

The nature of the Austrian state entailed that a whole number of surrounding states had Austria's dissolution in view as the goal of their national policy. For what post-Bismarckian Germany was never able to bring about had been done by even the smallest Balkan states; namely, setting a definite foreign policy goal which they tried to achieve with, and according to, all the possibilities at hand. All these to some extent freshly arisen national states, lying on Austria's borders, saw their highest future political task as the "liberation" of the racial comrades who ethnically belonged to them, but who lived under the scepter of Austria and the Hapsburgs. It was self-evident that this liberation could take place only through military action. Likewise that this must necessarily lead to Austria's dissolution. The Austrians' own power of resistance constituted an obstacle to this all the less so as they were dependent primarily on those who were to be liberated. In case of a coalition war of Russia, Rumania, and Serbia against Austria the North- and South-Slav elements would fall from the outset outside the frame of Austrian resistance, so that at best Germans and Magyars would remain as the bearers of the main struggle. Now, experience shows that the elimination of specific fighting forces on folkish grounds leads to disintegration and thus to a complete paralysis of Austria's front. By herself Austria would have been able to offer only little resistance to such a general offensive war. This was known in Russia as well as in Serbia, and very well known in Rumania. Thus what really supported Austria was only her mighty ally, on whom she was able to steady herself. But what was more natural than that by this time the idea should form in the brains of the leading anti-Austrian statesmen, as well as in public opinion, that the way to Vienna must lead through Berlin?

The more states there were which fancied to inherit Austria and could not do so in consequence of the military partnership, all the more were the states which Germany herself necessarily incurred as enemies.

At the turn of the century the weight of these enemies, set against Germany because of Austria, was already several times greater than the possible armed help that Austria could ever furnish Germany.

Thus the inner meaning of this alliance policy was converted exactly into its opposite.

The matter was complicated still further by the third member of the alliance, Italy. As has already been mentioned, Italy's relation to Austria was never a matter of cordiality, and hardly one of reason, but actually only the result and the consequence of an overwhelming necessity. The Italian people primarily, and the Italian intelligentsia, were always able to rally sympathy for Germany. At the turn of the century every ground already existed for an alliance of Italy with Germany alone. The opinion that Italy as such would be a faithless ally is so stupid and dumb that armchair politicians can serve it only to our unpolitical so-called national bourgeoisie. The most shattering counter-proof is provided by the history of our own people, namely, the time when Italy had once been allied with Germany against Austria, of course. To be sure, the Germany of that time was the Prussia led by Bismarck's genius and not that led by the political incapacity of the later bunglers of the mishandled Reich.

Certainly the Italy of that time had suffered defeats in battles on land and sea, but she honorably fulfilled the obligations of her alliance, as Austria did not do in the World War, into which she had pushed Germany. For at that time, when Italy was offered a separate peace which would have given her everything which she was able to achieve only later, she proudly and indignantly rejected it despite the military defeats she had suffered, whereas the Austrian government leaders not only coveted such a separate peace, but were ready to drop Germany completely. If this did not come to pass, the reason for it did not lie in the Austrian state's strength of character but rather in the nature of the demands which the enemy made upon her and which in practice signified her disintegration. The fact that Italy suffered military defeats in 1866 could not really be viewed as a sign of faithlessness to the alliance. For certainly she would have preferred gathering victories to defeats, but the Italy of that time could not indeed be compared to Germany then and even later, because she lacked that very superior power of military crystallization which Germany had in Prussia. A German Union without the base of the Prussian military power would have identically succumbed to the attack of so old and not yet nationally dismembered a military power such as Austria possessed, as was the case with regard to Italy. But the essential thing lay in the fact that the Italy of that time made possible the decision in Bohemia in favor of the later German Reich, by tying up a considerable and great part of the Austrian army. For whoever bears in mind the critical situation on the day of the battle of Königgrätz cannot assert that it would have been a matter of indifference to Germany's fate, whether Austria had been on the battlefield with an additional 140,000 men, as she could have done on the strength of Italian commitment.

That naturally the Italy of that time did not conclude this alliance in order to make possible the national unity of the German people, but rather that of the Italians, is understood. It really requires the proverbial political naiveté of a patriotic leaguer to be able to see cause for reproach or for slander in that. The idea of obtaining an alliance which from the outset possesses only prospects of success or gain is a childish stupidity. For the Italians had exactly the same right to make the same reproach to the Prussia of that time and to Bismarck himself, namely, that they had concluded the alliance not for love of Italy but also in pursuit of their own interests. Unfortunately, I am inclined to say, it is humiliating that this stupidity is committed only north of the Alps and not also to the south of them.

Such a stupidity becomes understandable only if we consider the Triple Alliance, or better still, the alliance between Germany and Austria, which really is a rare case wherein one state, Austria, obtains everything from an alliance and the other, Germany, nothing at all. An alliance in which one party stakes its interests and the other its "shining armor." The one has a cold purposefulness [purposeful reason] and the other a Nibelungen loyalty. At least this has happened only once in history to such an extent and in this way, and Germany has received the most terrible returns for this kind of political state leadership and alliance policy.

Thus if the alliance with Italy, insofar as it concerned Austria's relation with Italy, was of the most dubious value from the outset, this was not so much because with Italy, say, it could involve a fundamentally wrong partner but because for Italy this very alliance with Austria did not promise a single reciprocal value.

Italy was a national state. Her future necessarily had to lie on the shores of the Mediterranean. Thus every neighboring state is more or less an obstacle for the development of this national state. If in addition we take into account that Austria herself had over 800,000 Italians within her borders and further [conversely] that these same Hapsburgs—who on the one hand surrendered the Germans to Slavization, on the other hand understood very well how to play Slavs and Germans against Italians—had every interest in slowly denationalizing these 800,000 Italians, then the future task of Italian foreign policy was hardly in doubt. It had to be an anti-Austrian one, as pro-German as it could be. And this policy also found the liveliest support, indeed a glowing enthusiasm,

65

among the Italian people itself. For the wrongs that the Haps-burgers—and Austria was their political weapon for this—had committed against Italy in the course of the centuries, seen from an Italian viewpoint, cried out to heaven. For centuries Austria had been the obstacle to Italy's unification; again and again the Hapsburgs had supported corrupt Italian dynasties; indeed even at the turn of the century hardly a party congress of the clerical and Christian social movement closed with anything but a demand that Rome be restored to the Holy Father. No bones were made about the fact that this was regarded as a task of Austrian policy; but on the other hand they had the impertinence to expect that people in Italy perforce exhibit a ringing enthusiasm over the alliance with Austria. Thus Austrian policy toward Italy in the course of the centuries had by no means always used kid gloves. What France had been for centuries to Germany, Austria was for centuries to Italy. The north Italian lowlands were always the field of operations on which the Austrian state showed its policy of friendship toward Italy. Croatian regiments and *Panduren* were the culture bringers and bearers of Austrian civilization, and it is a pity that all this has, in part, also clung to the German name. If today we frequently hear an arrogant deprecation, indeed a contemptuous insulting of German culture on Italian lips, then for this the German people must thank that state which was camouflaged as German on the outside, but which exposed the character of its inner being to the Italian through a coarse soldiery who in their own Austrian state were viewed by the beneficiaries thereof as a true scourge of God. The battle fame of the Austrian army was in part built on successes which necessarily aroused the undying hatred of the Italians for all time.

It was a misfortune for Germany never to have understood this, a misfortune, on the contrary, to have covered it up indirectly, if not directly. For thus did Germany lose the state which, as matters then stood, could have become our most loyal ally, as it once had been a very dependable ally for Prussia.

Thus the attitude of the broadest public opinion in Austria on the occasion of the war in Tripoli was especially decisive for Italy's inner relation to Austria. That Vienna should look askance at the Italian attempt to set foot in Albania was still understandable in view of the state of affairs. Austria thought her own interests were being threatened there. But the general and decidedly artificial incitement against Italy when the latter set out to conquer Tripoli was incomprehensible. The Italian step, however, was self-evident. No man could blame the Italian government if it attempted to carry the Italian flag to areas which by their very location had to be the acknowledged colonial area for Italy. Not only because the young Italian colonists fell into the footsteps of the ancient Romans, but the Italian action should have been welcome precisely to Germany and Austria for still another reason. The more Italy was engaged in North Africa, the more the natural oppositions between Italy and France would perforce one day develop. A superior German state leadership, at least, should have sought with all means to create difficulties for the threatening spread of French hegemony over North Africa, and in general to the French opening up of the Dark Continent, even in consideration of the possible military strengthening of France also on European battlefields. For the French governments and especially their military leaders left no doubt at all that for them the African colonies actually had another importance other than just being showpieces [plantations] of French civilization. For a long time they had already seen in them a reservoir for soldiers for the next European contest of arms. That this could take place only with Germany was likewise clear. What would have been more natural, then, from a German point of view than to favor every interference of another power, especially if this other power was her own ally. Moreover, the French nation was sterile and had no need for enlarging its living space, whereas the Italian people, exactly like the German, had to find a way out somewhere. Let no one say that this would have involved a theft committed against Turkey. For then all colonies are indeed stolen areas. Only, without them the European cannot live. We had no interest, and should not have had any, in bringing about an estrangement with Italy out of a completely unreal sympathetic feeling for Turkey. If ever there was a foreign political action in which Austria and Germany could have fully stood behind Italy, this was precisely it. It was simply scandalous how the Austrian press of that time, indeed all public opinion, behaved toward an Italian action whose ultimate aim was nothing but the annexation of Bosnia-Herzegovina by Austria herself. A hate suddenly flared up at that time which showed the real inner disposition of this Austrian-Italian relation all the more clearly since there had been no actual grounds for it at all. I was in Vienna at that time and was inwardly disgusted by the stupid as well as shameless way in which the ally was stabbed in the back then. Thus, under such circumstances, to demand from this very ally a loyalty which in reality would have been Italy's suicide, is at least as incomprehensible as it is naive.

For in addition there is the following: Italy's natural military-geographical situation will always force this state to formulate a policy which does not bring it into conflict with a superior naval power, to which the Italian fleet and fleets allied with it would not be in a position, human foresight indicates, to put up any resistance. As long as England possesses uncontested supremacy on the seas and as long as this hegemony can still be strengthened by a Mediterranean French fleet, without Italy and her allies being able to make a promising resistance, Italy can never assume an anti-English attitude. We must not demand from the leaders of a state that, out of an idiotic sympathy for another state whose reciprocal love had been clearly shown precisely by the war in Tripoli, they end by surrendering their own people to certain destruction. Anyone who subjects the coastal conditions of the Italian state to the most cursory examination must immediately arrive at the conviction that a struggle against England on Italy's part under prevailing circumstances is not only hopeless but absurd. Thus Italy found herself in exactly the same situation as Germany had likewise found herself; namely, just as for Bismarck, once the risk of war with Russia, caused by Austria, appeared so monstrous to him that in such an eventuality he committed himself, through the famous Reinsurance treaty, to disregard the matter of the otherwise existing alliance, likewise for Italy the alliance with Austria was also untenable the moment she made an enemy of England as a result of it. Anyone who does not want to grasp or understand this is incapable of thinking politically and therefore, at best, capable of making policy in Germany. But the German people sees the result of the policy of this sort of people before it, and must bear the consequences.

All these are aspects that had to lower the value of the alliance with Austria to a minimum. For it was thereby certain that Germany, because of her alliance with Austria, would also presumably make enemies, besides Russia, of Rumania, Serbia and Italy. For, as has been said, there is no alliance that can be built on the basis of ideal sympathies or ideal loyalty or ideal gratitude. Alliances will be all the stronger, the more the individual contracting parties may hope to derive private advantages from them. It is fantastic to wish to form an alliance on any other basis.

I would never expect Italy to enter into an alliance with Germany out of sympathy for Germany, out of love for Germany, with the intention of thereby procuring an advantage for Germany. Just as little would I ever want to enter into a contractual relationship out of love for another state, out of sympathy for it, or out of a desire to serve it. If today I advocate an alliance between Italy and Germany I do so only because I believe that both states can thereby achieve useful advantages. Both states would prosper as a result.

The advantage of the Triple Alliance lay exclusively on Austria's side. Certainly, in consequence of the determining factors in the policy of the individual states, only Austria could be the beneficiary of this alliance. For by its whole nature the Triple Alliance had no aggressive tendency. It was a defensive alliance which at the utmost, according to its provisions, was only supposed to safeguard the preservation of the status quo. Germany and Italy, in consequence of the impossibility of feeding their populations, were compelled to pursue an aggressive policy. Only Austria had to be happy to preserve at least the corpse of a state which, in itself, was already impossible. Since Austria's own defensive power would never have sufficed for this, through the Triple Alliance, the offensive forces of Germany and Italy were harnessed in the service of maintaining the Austrian state. Germany remained in the harness and thereby perished, Italy leapt out of it and saved herself. Only a man for whom politics is not the duty of preserving the life of a people with all means and according to all possibilities could want to censure such an action.

69

Even if old Germany as a formal national state had set herself only the further unification of the German nation as a goal, the Triple Alliance should perforce have been dropped instantaneously, respectively the relation with Austria changed. She would thereby have been spared from incurring a number of enmities which in no way could be compensated by the employment of Austrian strength.

Thus even prewar Germany should no longer have let her foreign policy be determined by purely formal national viewpoints, if these did not lead to necessary folkish goals.

Already in the prewar period, the future of the German people was a question of solving the problem of their sustenance. The German people could no longer find their daily bread within their existing territory. All industry and competence, as well as all scientific methods of soil cultivation could at best alleviate the distress somewhat, but ultimately they could not prevent it. Even in the years of exceptionally good harvests they no longer could completely cover their own food requirements. During average or bad harvests they were already dependent on imports to a considerable degree. Even the raw material supply of many industries ran into serious difficulties and could be procured only abroad.

There were various ways to overcome this distress. Emigration and birth control had to be categorically rejected even from the standpoint of the national state of that time. In this case the knowledge of biological consequences was less decisive than the fear of numerical decimation. Thus for the Germany of that time only two possibilities existed for securing the nation's preservation for a future time without having to limit the population itself. Either an effort had to be made to solve the need for space, that is, to acquire new soil, or the Reich had to be converted into a great export firm. This meant that the production of certain commodities was to be increased beyond domestic needs, in order to be able to exchange them for foodstuffs and raw materials by way of export.

The knowledge of the necessity of an enlargement of German living area existed, albeit at least partly at that time. It was believed that the best way to act in this sense was to lead Germany into the ranks of the great colonial peoples. In reality, however, a flaw in the inner logic was already present in the form of the execution of this idea. For the sense of a sound territorial policy lies in the fact that a people's living space is enlarged by allotting new areas for settlement to the surplus of the population which, then, if it is not to take on the character of an emigration, must be in close political and governmental relation with the mother country. This no longer applied to the colonies which were still at all available at the end of the nineteenth century. Their distance in space as well, particularly as the climatic conditions of these areas by themselves prevented settlement such as the English had previously been able to carry out in their American colonies, the Dutch in South Africa and again the English in Australia. Added to this was the whole character of the inner establishment of German colonial policy. Thereby the problem of settlement receded entirely into the background in order to put in their place business interests which were identical with the general interests of the German people only in the smallest measure. Thus from the beginning the value of German colonies lay more in the possibility of obtaining certain markets, which by providing different colonial products and partly also raw materials would make the German economy independent of foreign countries.

This would have surely succeeded up to a certain degree in the future, but it would not in the least have resolved the problem of Germany's overpopulation, unless it was decided to guarantee the sustenance of the German people fundamentally through an increase of its export economy. Then naturally the German colonies, through the more favorable delivery of raw materials, could one day give the different industries a greater capacity to compete on the international markets. Thus German colonial policy in the deepest sense was indeed no territorial policy, but had become an instrument of German economic policy. Actually, even the numerically direct relief of German internal overpopulation through the settlement of the colonies was completely insignificant.

If in addition one wanted to go over to a real territorial policy, then the colonial policy pursued before the war was all the more senseless, as it could not lead to a relief of German overpopulation. Conversely, however, one day, all human foresight indicates, its very execution necessitated the same staking of blood as would have been required in the worst cases for a really useful territorial policy. For while this kind of German colonial policy in the most favorable situation could bring only a strengthening of the German economy, one day it had to become a cause for a physical conflict with England. For a German world economic policy could never avoid a decisive struggle with England. Export industry, world trade, colonies and merchant marine had then to be protected with the sword from that power which, for the same viewpoint of self-preservation as Germany's, had long ago seen itself forced to embark upon this path. Therefore, this peaceful economic struggle for the conquest of a place in the sun could take place for just as long as England could count on bringing about the collapse of German competition with purely economic means, because then we would never emerge from the shade. But if Germany succeeded in pushing England back in this peaceful economic way, it was self-evident that the phantom of this peaceful economic conquest of the world would be replaced by the resistance of bayonets.

Without doubt it was, however, a political idea to allow the German people the increase of its number through the increase of industrial production and sale on the international world market. This idea was not folkish, but it corresponded to the prevailing ideas of the bourgeois-national world of that time. This way could be traveled in any case, only it then placed a wholly definite and narrowly outlined duty on German foreign policy: the end of German world trade policy could only be war with England. But then the task of German foreign policy was to arm itself, through farseeing alliance measures, for a conflict with a state which on the basis of an experience of more than a hundred years itself would not neglect to bring about a general mobilization of allied states. If Germany wanted to defend her industrial and economic policy against England, then she first had to seek to cover her rear with Russia. Russia then was the only state which could be considered a valuable ally because she alone had no need to be essentially opposed to Germany, at least for the moment. To be sure the selling price for this Russian alliance, as matters stood, could lie only in giving up the alliance with Austria. For then the dual alliance with Austria was madness, indeed insanity. Only when

Germany's rear was completely covered by Russia could she pass over to a maritime policy which deliberately aimed at the day of reckoning. Only then could Germany also commit the enormous means necessary for the completion of a fleet which, not being up to date in all details, lagged five years behind especially in speed and thereby displacement.

But the entanglement in the Austrian alliance was so great that a solution could no longer be found and Russia, which had begun to orient herself anew after the Russo-Japanese war, had to be repelled for good. But thereby the whole German economic and colonial policy was a more than dangerous game. The fact was that Germany indeed also shunned the final settlement with England and accordingly for years her attitude was determined by the principle of not antagonizing the adversary. This determined all German decisions which would have been necessary for the defense of German economic and colonial policy, until on August 4, 1914 the English declaration of war brought an end to this unfortunate period of German blindness.

Had Germany of that time been ruled less by bourgeois-national than by folkish viewpoints, only the other path to a solution of German distress would have been considered, namely that of a large-scale territorial policy in Europe itself.

Hence the German colonial policy which necessarily had to bring us into conflict with England, whereby France could always be regarded as siding with the enemy, was especially unreasonable for Germany because our European base was weaker than any other colonial people of world political importance. For ultimately the fate of the colonies was obviously decided in Europe. In consequence every German foreign policy was directed primarily toward strengthening and safeguarding Germany's military position in Europe.

Thus we could expect only little decisive help from our colonies. Conversely every broadening of our European territorial base automatically would have led to a strengthening of our position. It is not the same, if a people has a closed area of settlement of 560,000 or, let us say, one million square kilometers. Wholly apart from the difficulty, in the case of war, of sustenance, which should remain as independent as possible from the effects of enemy action, military protection already resides in the size of the territory, and to that extent our operations, which force us to wage wars on our own soil, will be considerably easier to bear.

In general, then, a certain defense against rash attacks lies in the size of a state territory. Above all, however, only through a territorial policy in Europe can the human resources shifted there be preserved for our people, including their military utilization. An additional 500,000 square kilometers in Europe can provide new homesteads for millions of German peasants, and make available millions of soldiers to the power of the German people for the moment of decision.

The only area in Europe that could be considered for such a territorial policy therefore was Russia. The thinly settled western border regions which already once had received German colonists as bringers of culture, could likewise be considered for the new territorial policy of the German nation. Therefore the aim of German foreign policy unconditionally had to be to free its rear against England and conversely to isolate Russia as much as possible. Then with a dauntless logic we had to give up our economic and world trade policy, and if necessary completely give up the fleet, in order to concentrate the nation's whole strength again on the land army as once before. Then, more than ever, the alliance with Austria had to be dropped, for nothing more would stand in the way of an isolation of Russia than a state whose defense was guaranteed by Germany, whose partition was desired by a whole number of European powers, but which they would have been able to carry out only in an alliance with Russia. Since these states had recognized in Germany the greatest defense of Austria's preservation, all the more were they forced to be against Russia's isolation as the Czarist Empire more than ever could appear to them as the only possible power factor for the final destruction of Austria.

It was obvious, however, that all these states especially could not wish for a strengthening of Austria's only defense at the cost of the strongest enemy of the Hapsburg state.

For in this case too France would have always sided with Germany's enemy, the possibility of forming an anti-German coalition would always have been present, unless we decided to liquidate the alliance with Austria at the end of the century, and surrender the Austrian state to its fate, but thereby save the German areas for the Reich.

Something different happened. Germany wanted world peace. Therefore she avoided a territorial policy which as such could only have been fought out aggressively, and ultimately turned to a limitless economic and trade policy. We thought to conquer the world with peaceful economic means, and thereby we supported ourselves neither on one nor another power but instead clung all the more doggedly to the dying Hapsburg state the more a general political isolation resulted therefrom. Broad circles within Germany welcomed this, partly out of real political incompetence and also partly out of wrongly understood patriotic-legitimist ideas and finally also partly in the hope, still nourished, that the hated Hohenzollern empire could one day be thereby led to collapse.

When the World War burst forth blood-red on August 2, 1914, the prewar alliance policy had as a matter of fact already suffered its actual defeat. In order to help Austria, Germany had been pushed into a war which then was to revolve only around her own existence. Her enemies were the adversaries of her world trade as well as of her general greatness altogether, and those who were awaiting the fall of Austria. Her friends, the impossible Austrian-Hungarian state structure on the one side and the constantly weak and ailing Turkey on the other. Italy, however, took the step that Germany perforce should have taken and carried out herself, had her destiny been guided by the genius of a Bismarck instead of weak philosophers and bragging hurrah-patriots. The fact that later Italy finally undertook an offensive against a former ally, again merely matched Bismarck's prophetic foresight, namely, that only two conditions could exist at all between Italy and Austria: an alliance or war.

VIII

On November 11, 1918, the armistice was signed in the forest of Compiègne. For this, fate had chosen a man who was one of those bearing major guilt for the collapse of our people. Matthias Erzberger, deputy of the Center, and according to various assertions the bastard son of a servant-girl and a Jewish employer, was the German negotiator who affixed his name to a document which, compared and measured against the four and a half years of heroism of our people, seems incomprehensible if we do not assume the deliberate intention to bring about Germany's destruction.

Matthias Erzberger himself had been a petty-bourgeois annexationist, that is one of those men who especially at the beginning of the war had tried to remedy the lack of an official war aim in their own way and manner. For even though in August, 1914 the entire German people instinctively felt that this struggle involved their being or non-being, nevertheless once the flames of the first enthusiasm were extinguished, they were not in any way clear either about the threatening non-being or the necessity of remaining in being. The enormity of the idea of a defeat and its consequences was slowly blotted out through a propaganda which had complete free rein within Germany and which twisted or altogether denied the real aims of the Entente in a way that was as adroit as it was mendacious. In the second and especially in the third year of the war it had also succeeded to some extent in removing the fear of defeat from the German people, since thanks to this propaganda people no longer believed in the enemy's annihilatory will. This was all the more terrible as, conversely, nothing was allowed to be done which could inform the people of the minimum that had to be achieved in the interests of its future self-preservation, and as a reward for its unprecedented sacrifices. Hence the discussion over a possible war aim took place only in more or less irresponsible circles and acquired the expression of the mode of thought as well as the general political ideas of its respective representatives. While the sly Marxists, who had an exact knowledge of the paralyzing effect of a lack of a definite war aim, forbade themselves to have one altogether, and for that matter talked only about the reestablishment of peace without annexations and reparations, at least some of the bourgeois politicians sought to respond to the enormity of the bloodshed and the sacrilege of the attack with definite counterdemands. All these bourgeois proposals were purely border rectifications and had nothing at all to do with geopolitical ideas. At best they still thought of satisfying the expectations of German princes who were unemployed at the time by the formation of buffer states. Thus even the founding of the Polish state appeared as a wise decision in national-political terms to the bourgeois world, aside from a few exceptions. Individuals pushed economic viewpoints to the foreground according to which the border had to be formed; for example, the necessity of winning the ore basin of Longwy and Briey, other strategical opinions, for example, the necessity of possessing the Belgian fortresses on the Meuse River, etc.

It should be self-evident that this was no aim for a state engaged in a war against twenty-six states, in which the former had to take upon itself one of the most unprecedented bloodsheddings in history while at home an entire people was literally surrendered to hunger. The impossibility of justifying the necessity for enduring the war helped to bring about its unfortunate outcome.

Hence when the collapse took place in the homeland, a knowledge of war aims existed even less, as their former weak representatives had meanwhile moved further away from their former meager demands. And this was quite understandable. For to want to conduct a war of this unprecedented extent so that the borders instead of running through Herbesthal should run through Liége, or so that instead of a Czarist commissar or governor a German princeling could be installed as potentate over some Russian province or other, would have been really irresponsible and monstrous. It lay in the nature of German war aims, so far as they were at all subject to discussion, that they were later altogether denied. Truly for such baubles a people should not have been kept for even an hour longer in a war whose battlefields had slowly become an inferno.

The sole war aim that the monstrous bloodshed would have been worthy of could consist only in the assurance to German soldiers of so and so many hundred thousand square kilometers, to be allotted to front line fighters as property, or to be placed at the disposal of a general colonization by Germans. With that the war would have quickly lost the character of an imperial enterprise and instead would have become a cause of the German people. For after all the German grenadiers really had not shed their blood so that Poles might acquire a state or so that a German prince might be set on a plush-covered throne.

Thus in 1918 we stood at the end of a completely senseless and aimless squandering of the most precious German blood.

Once more had our people infinitely staked its heroism, courageous sacrifice, indeed defiance of death and joyousness in responsibility and [in order to] nevertheless been forced to leave the battlefields weakened and beaten. Victorious in a thousand battles and skirmishes and in the end nevertheless defeated by those who had been beaten. This was the handwriting on the wall for the German domestic and foreign policy of the prewar time and the four and a half years of the bloody struggle itself.

Now after the collapse there arose the alarmed question, whether our German people had learned anything from this catastrophe, whether those who had deliberately betrayed it up to this time would still determine its fate, whether those who had so pitifully failed until this time would henceforth also dominate the future with their phrases, or whether finally our people would be educated to a new way of thinking about domestic and foreign policy and shift its action accordingly.

For if a miracle does not take place for our people, its path will be one of ultimate doom and destruction.

What is Germany's present situation and what are the prospects for her future and what kind of a future will this be?

The collapse which the German people suffered in 1918 lies, as I want once more to establish here, not in the overthrow of its military organization, or in the loss of its weapons, but rather in its inner decay which was revealed at that time and which today increasingly appears. This inner decay lies just as much in respect to the worsening of its racial value as in the loss of all those virtues which condition the greatness of a people, guarantee its existence and promote its future.

Blood value, the idea of personality and the instinct for self-preservation slowly threatened to be lost to the German people. Internationalism triumphs in its stead and destroys our folk-value, democracy spreads by stifling the idea of personality and in the end an evil pacifistic liquid manure poisons the mentality favoring bold self-preservation. We see the effects of this vice of mankind appear in the whole life of our people. Not only does it make itself noticeable in the field of poltical concerns, no, but also in that of economy, and not least in that of our cultural life, so that if it is not brought to a halt once and for all our people will be excluded from the number of nations with a future.

The great domestic task of the future lies in the elimination of these general symptoms of the decay of our people. This is the mission of the National Socialist movement. A new nation must arise from this work which overcomes even the worst evils of the present, the cleavage between the classes, for which the bourgeoisie and Marxism are equally guilty.

The aim of this reform work of a domestic political kind must finally be the regaining of our people's strength for the prosecution of its struggle for existence and thereby the strength to represent its vital interests abroad.

Our foreign policy is also presented by this with a task that it must fulfill. For the more domestic policy must furnish the folkish instrument of strength to foreign policy, the more must also foreign policy, through the actions and measures it adopts, promote and support the formation of this instrument.

If the foreign policy task of the old bourgeois-national state had primarily been that of the further unification in Europe of those belonging to the German nation in order then to work up to a higher territorial policy viewed in folkish terms, then the foreign policy task of the postwar period must at the outset be one that promotes the forging of the internal instrument of power.

For the foreign policy aspirations of the prewar period had at their disposal a state that perhaps was not very highly exigent in a folkish sense, but which had a wonderful army establishment. Even if Germany of that time had long since ceased to place such an emphasis on the military, as for example old Prussia, and therefore was outmatched by other states, especially in the extent of the army organization, nevertheless the inner quality of the old army was incomparably superior to all other similar institutions. At that time this best instrument of the art of war stood at the disposal of a state leadership with a bold foreign policy. In consequence of this instrument as well as of the general high esteem which it enjoyed, the freedom of our people was not only a result [matter] of our factually proved strength, but rather of the general credit that we possessed [enjoyed] in consequence of this remarkable army instrument as well as partly in consequence of the rest of the exemplarily clean state apparatus.

The German people no longer possesses this most important instrument for the defense of a nation's interests, or at least it possesses it to a completely insufficient extent, and very far removed from the foundation which conditioned its former strength.

The German people has acquired a mercenary army. In Germany these mercenary troops run the danger of sinking to the level of policemen armed with special technical weapons. The comparison of the German mercenary army with the English turns out unfavorably to the Germans. The English mercenary army was always the bearer of England's military defense and aggressive ideas as well as of her military tradition. In her mercenary troops and the militia system peculiar to her England possessed the army organization which in view of her insular position sufficed, indeed seemed suitable for fighting to the finish for England's vital interests. The idea of manifesting English power of resistance in such a form in no way sprang from cowardice, in order thereby to be able to spare shedding the blood of the English people. On the contrary. England fought with mercenaries as long as they sufficed for the defense of England's interests. She called for volunteers immediately the struggle required a greater commitment. She introduced general military conscription immediately the needs of the country demanded it. For regardless of how the momentary organization of the English power of resistance looked, it was always committed in a dauntless struggle for England. And the formal army organization in England was always only an instrument for the defense of English interests, committed with a will, which did not even shrink, if necessary, from demanding the blood of the whole nation. Wherever England's interests were decisively at stake, she at any rate knew how to preserve a hegemony which, considered purely technically, goes as far as the demand for a two-power standard. If we compare the infinitely responsible [solicitous] care shown here with the frivolousness with which Germany, and national-bourgeois Germany at that, neglected her armaments in the prewar period, we must still today be gripped by a deep sadness. Just as England knew that her future, indeed her existence, depended on the strength of her fleet, so should this bourgeois-national Germany have known that the existence and future of the German Reich depended on the strength of our land power. In Europe Germany should have had to counter the two-power standard on land to the two-power standard on the seas. And just as England with an iron determination saw a reason for going to war at every violation of this standard, so did Germany have to prevent every attempt in Europe to outflank her army through France and Russia by a military decision, even one which had to be precipitated, and for which more than one favorable opportunity had presented itself. Even here this bourgeoisie misused one of Bismarck's utterances in a most senseless way. Bismarck's assertion that he did not intend to wage preventive war was joyfully seized upon by all weak, energyless and also irresponsible armchair politicians as a cover for the disastrous consequences of their "anything goes" policy. Only thereby they completely forgot that all three wars which Bismarck had conducted were wars which, at least according to the conceptions of these anti-preventive-war peace philosophers, could have been avoided. Consider, for example, what insults by Napoleon III in 1870 would have to be heaped on the German Republic of today for it to decide to request M. Benedetti to moderate his tone somewhat. Neither Napoleon nor the whole French people would ever have been able to incite the German Republic of today to a

Sedan: or does one believe that if Bismarck had not wanted a decision, the war of 1866 could not have been prevented? Now here it can be objected that this was a question of wars with clearly set aims and not of a kind whose only ground lies in the fear of an attack by the enemy. But in reality this is only wordsplitting. Because Bismarck was convinced that the struggle with Austria was inevitable he prepared himself for it and carried it through when the occasion suited Prussia. The reform of the French army by Marshal Niel made clearly perceptible the intention to give French policy and French chauvinism a forceful weapon for an attack against Germany. As a matter of fact it would doubtless have been possible for Bismarck to bring the conflict to some kind of a peaceful solution in 1870. But it was more expedient for him to fight it out to the finish at a time when the French army organization had not yet arrived at its full efficiency. Moreover all these interpretations of Bismarckian utterances suffer from one thing, namely, they confuse Bismarck the diplomat with a republican parliamentarian. How Bismarck himself judged such utterances is best shown in his reply to a questioner before the outbreak of the Prussian-Austrian war, who would have very much liked to know whether Bismarck really intended to attack Austria, whereupon the latter with an impervious expression replied, "No, I have no intention of attacking Austria, but neither would I have the intention of telling them, in case I wanted to attack her."

Moreover, the hardest war that had ever been fought by Prussia was a preventive war. When Frederick the Great had received final knowledge of the intention of his old enemies through a scribbler-soul, he did not wait until the others attacked, on the grounds of a fundamental rejection of a preventive war, but went immediately over to the attack himself.

For Germany any violation of the two-power standard of necessity should have been a cause for a preventive war. For what would it have been easier to answer before history: for a preventive war in 1904, which could have defeated France when Russia seemed to be entangled in East Asia, or for the World War which ensued from this neglect and which required many times the blood and plunged our people into the abyss of defeat?

England never had such scruples. Her two-power standard on the seas seemed to be the prerequisite for the preservation of English independence. As long as she had the strength she allowed no change to be made in this situation. When, however, this two-power standard was given up after the World War, it was then only under the pressure of circumstances which were stronger than any contrary British intention. With the American Union, a new power of such dimensions has come into being as threatens to upset the whole former power and orders of rank of the states.

At any rate up to now the English fleet was always the most striking proof, regardless of how the form of the organization of the land army looked, that decisively determined England's will to self-preservation. This was the reason why the English mercenary army never acquired the bad characteristics of other mercenary troops. It was a fighting military body of wonderful individual training with excellent weapons and a conception of service which viewed it as a sport. Thus what endowed this small body of troops with a special importance was the direct contact with the visible manifestations in life of the British world empire. As this mercenary army had fought for England's greatness in almost all parts of the world, it had thereby in like measure also come to know England's greatness. The men who now in South Africa, now in Egypt and at times in India represented England's interests as the possessors of her military prestige, through this also received an indelible impression of the immense greatness of the British Imperium.

Such an opportunity is completely lacking to the present-day German mercenary troops. Indeed, the more we feel ourselves induced to make concessions to this spirit in the small army itself, under the pressure of pacifistic-parliamentary majorities, which in reality represent traitors to their people and country, it gradually ceases to be an instrument of war. Instead it becomes a police corps for the maintenance of peace and order, which means, in reality, of peaceful subjugation. No army with a high intrinsic value can be trained, if the preparation for war is not the aim of its existence. There are no armies for the maintenance of peace, but rather only for the victorious fighting of wars to the end. The more, in short, one tries finally to unhinge the *Reichswehr* from the tradition of the old army, the more will it itself become traditionless.

For with troops the value of a tradition does not lie in a few successful quellings of internal strike-revolts, or in preventing the plundering of foodstuffs, but in the glory gained through victorious battles. In reality, however, the German *Reichswehr* departs from the tradition of this glory in proportion as from year to year it ceases to be a representative of the national idea. The more it finally kills the conscious, national, hence nationalistic spirit in its own ranks, and removes its representatives, in order to give their posts to democrats and altogether ordinary ambitious persons, all the more will it become alien to the people. Let the sly gentlemen not fancy that they can make contact with the people by concessions to the pacifistic-democratic part of our people. Any military organization as such is deeply hated by this part of the German people, as long as it is indeed military and not the burglar-protection agency of international-pacifistic stock-exchange interests. The only part to which an army can have an inner relationship in a militarily valuable sense, is that nationally conscious core of our people which not only thinks in a soldierly manner out of tradition, but rather, out of national love, is also the only part ready to wear the gray tunic in defense of honor and freedom. It is necessary, however, that a military body maintain intimate relations with those from whom it itself in the hour of need can supplement itself and not with those who betray it at every opportunity. Hence the present leaders of our so-called *Reichswehr* can act as democratically as they please, nevertheless they will thereby never attain to a closer bond with the German people, because the German people for which this is appropriate is not to be found in the democratic camp. Since, however, the former chief of the German *Reichswehr* especially, General von Seeckt,* not only did not put up any resistance to the removal of hardened, deliberately national-minded officers, but

---

* Generaloberst Hans von Seeckt, who had been Chief of the Army Command (*Chef der Heeresleitung*) since 1920, was dismissed early in October, 1926. In technical violation of the Treaty of Versailles, he had permitted the former Crown Prince's eldest son to appear in uniform at army exercises, and Seeckt was forced to resign in consequence of widespread public criticism from liberal elements in Germany.—*T.T.*

84

rather even [himself] advocated it, they themselves finally created the instrument which dropped him with a relatively light heart.

Since General von Seeckt's retirement, however, the democratic-pacifistic influence has been tirelessly active in order to make out of the *Reichswehr* that which the present rulers of the state have in their minds as the most beautiful ideal: a republican-democratic parliamentary guard.

Obviously a foreign policy cannot be conducted with such an instrument.

Hence today the first task of German domestic policy ought to be that of giving the German people a military organization suitable to its national strength. Since the forms of the present *Reichswehr* could never suffice for this goal and, conversely, are determined by foreign policy motives, it is the task of German foreign policy to bring about all the possibilties that could permit the reorganization of a German national army. For that must be the immovable aim of any political leadership in Germany, so that one day the mercenary army will again be replaced by a truly German national army.

For just as the purely technical-military qualities of the present are superior, so must the general qualities of the German *Reichswehr* deteriorate in their development in the future. The former without doubt is to be credited to General von Seeckt and to the *Reichswehr's* Officers' Corps altogether. Thus the German *Reichswehr* could really be the army framework for the future German national army. Just as in general the task of the *Reichswehr* itself must be, by the educational stress placed on the national fighting task, to train the mass of [later] officers and sergeants for the later national army.

No true national-thinking German can dispute that this aim must be held immovably in sight. Even less can he dispute that its execution is possible only if the nation's foreign policy leaders assure the general necessary prerequisites.

Thus the first task of German foreign policy is primarily the creation of conditions which make possible the resurrection of a German army. For only then will our people's vital needs be able to find their practical representation.

85

Fundamentally, however, it must be further observed that the political actions which are to guarantee the resurrection of a German army must lie in the framework of a necessary future development for Germany as such.

Hence there is no need to stress that a change of the present army organization, wholly apart from the present internal political situation as well as for reasons of foreign policy, cannot materialize as long as purely German interests and German viewpoints alone speak for such a change.

It lay in the nature of the World War and in the intention of Germany's main enemies, to carry out the liquidation of this greatest battle action of the earth in such a way that as many states as possible would be interested in its perpetuation. This was achieved through a system of distribution of territories in which even states with otherwise divergent desires and aims were held together in a solid antagonism by the fear that they could in that case suffer losses through a Germany once more become strong.

For if ten years after the World War it is still possible, against all the experience of world history, to maintain a kind of coalition of the victor states, the reason lies only in the fact, glorious for Germany, of the recollection of that struggle in which our fatherland had stood up to twenty-six states all together.

Thus it will also last as long as the fear of suffering losses through a resurrected German power Reich is greater than the difficulties between these states. And it is further obvious that it will last as long as no will exists anywhere to allow the German people a rearmament which can be viewed as a threat by these "victor states." On the basis of the knowledge that first a real representation of German vital interests in the future cannot take place through an inadequate German *Reichswehr* but rather only through a German national army, that, second, the formation of a German national army is impossible for as long as the present foreign policy strangulation of Germany does not slacken, third, that a change of foreign policy obstacles to the organization of a national army appears possible only if such a new formation is not in general felt as a threat, the following fact emerges with respect to a German foreign policy possible at this time:

Under no circumstances must present-day Germany see her foreign policy in terms of a formal border policy. Once the principle of the restoration of the borders of the year 1914 is laid down as the set goal of foreign policy, Germany will face a closed phalanx of her former enemies. Then any possibility is excluded of setting up another army which serves our interests more, as against the one whose definite form was determined by the peace treaty. Hence the foreign policy slogan of restoration of the borders has become a mere phrase, because it can never be realized for the lack of the necessary strength for this.

It is characteristic that precisely the so-called German bourgeoisie, again headed by the patriotic leagues, has made its way to this most stupid foreign policy aim. They know that Germany is powerless. They know further that, wholly apart from our internal decline, military means would be required for the restoration of our borders, and they know further that we do not possess these means as a result of the peace treaty, and also that we cannot acquire them in consequence of the solid front of our enemies [they further know that we . . . the 1914 borders . . .]. But nevertheless they proclaim a foreign policy slogan which precisely because of its essential character forever removes the possibility of achieving those means of power which would be necessary in order to carry out the slogan.

This is what is called bourgeois statesmanship and in its fruits that we see before us it exhibits the incomparable spirit that dominates it.

The Prussia of that time required only seven years, from 1806 to 1813, for her resurgence. In the same time [And in ten years] bourgeois statesmanship, in union with Marxism, has led Germany up to Locarno. Which is a great success in the eyes of the present bourgeois Bismarck, Herr Stresemann, because it offers the possible which even the above-mentioned Herr Stresemann could achieve. And politics is the art of the possible. If Bismarck had ever imagined that fate would have damned him to endorse with this utterance the statesmanlike qualities of Herr Stresemann, he would have surely omitted the utterance, or in a very small note he would have denied Herr Stresemann the right to refer to it.

Thus the slogan of the restoration of the German borders as an aim for the future is doubly stupid and dangerous, because in reality it in no way encompasses any useful aim worth striving for.

The German borders of the year 1914 were borders which presented something incomplete in exactly the same way as the borders of all nations are at all times incomplete. The territorial distribution of the world at any time is the momentary result of a struggle and a development which by no means is concluded, but one which clearly continues further. It is stupid to take the border of any sample year in a nation's history and offhand to represent it as a political aim. We can, of course, present the border of the year 1648 or that of 1312, etc., just as well as the border of the year 1914. This all the more so as indeed the border of the year 1914 was not satisfactory in a national, military or geopolitical sense. It was only the momentary situation in our people's struggle for existence which has been going on for centuries. And even if the World War had not occurred, this struggle would not have had its end in 1914.

If the German people had in fact achieved the restoration of the borders of the year 1914, the sacrifices of the World War would have been no less in vain. But also, there would not be the slightest gain for our people's future in such a restoration. This purely formal border policy of our national bourgeoisie is just as unsatisfactory in its possible end result as it is intolerably dangerous. Indeed it need not even be covered by the dictum of the art of the possible, for this is above all only a theoretical phrase, which nevertheless seems suitable to destroy every practical possibility.

As a matter of fact such a foreign policy aim also cannot stand up to a real critical examination. Hence attempts are made to motivate it less on logical grounds than on grounds of "national honor."

National honor requires that we restore the borders of the year 1914. This is the tenor of the discussions at the beer evenings which the representatives of national honor hold on all sides.

First of all national honor has nothing to do with the obligation to conduct a stupid and impossible foreign policy. For the result of a bad foreign policy can be the loss of a people's freedom, whose consequence is slavery, and which certainly cannot be viewed as a condition of national honor. To be sure a certain degree of national dignity and honor can still be preserved under oppression, but then this is not a question of shouting or national phrases, etc., but on the contrary, the expression which is to be found in the decorum with which a people bears its fate.

Let there be no talk in present-day Germany, above all, of national honor, let no one try to make himself conspicuous, as though one could [again] preserve the national honor outwardly by any kind of rhetorical barking. No, this cannot be done, and for the reason that it is no longer there. And by no means is it no longer there because we lost the war or because the French occupied Alsace-Lorraine, or the Poles stole Upper Silesia or the Italians took the South Tyrol. No, the national honor is no longer there because the German people, in the most difficult time of its struggle for existence, exposed to the light of day a lack of character, an unabashed servility, a doglike, crawling fawning that can only be called shameless. For the reason that we subjected ourselves miserably without being forced to do so, indeed because the leaders of this people, against eternal historical truth and our own knowledge, themselves assumed the war guilt, and indeed burdened our whole people with it, because there was no oppression by the enemy which would have not found thousands of creatures as willing helpers among our people. Because, conversely, there were those who shamelessly reviled the time of the great deeds of our people, spat upon the most glorious flag of all times, indeed defiled it with dirt, tore the cockades from home-coming soldiers before whom the world had trembled, pelted the flag with mud balls, ripped off ribbons and badges of honor and degraded a thousandfold even the memory of Germany's greatest period. No enemy had so reviled the German army as it was defiled by the representatives of the November crime. No enemy had disputed the greatness of the commanders of the German army as much as they were calumniated by the scoundrelly representatives of the new idea of government. And which was more certain dishonor for our people: the occupation of German areas by the enemy, or the cowardice with which our bourgeoisie surrendered the German Reich to an organization of pimps, pickpockets, deserters, black marketeers and hack journalists? Let not the gentlemen prattle now about German honor, as long as they bow under the rule of dishonor. They have no right to want to conduct a foreign policy in the name of national honor, if the domestic policy is one characterized by the most anti-nationalist shamelessness which has ever afflicted a great nation.

Whoever wants to act in the name of German honor today must first launch a merciless war against the infernal defilers of German honor. They are not the enemies of yore, but they are the representatives of the November crime. That collection of Marxist, democratic-pacifistic, destructive traitors of our country who pushed our people into its present state of powerlessness.

To revile former enemies in the name of national honor and recognize the shameless allies of this enemy as the rulers within their own country—that suits the national dignity of this present-day so-called national bourgeoisie.

I frankly confess that I could reconcile myself to any of the former enemy, but that my hatred against the betrayers of our own people in our ranks is and remains irreconcilable.

What the enemy inflicted on us is grievous and deeply humiliating to us, but the wrong committed by the men of the November crime is the most dishonorable, the basest crime of all times. I am helping to make amends for German honor by striving to bring about a situation in which these creatures will some day be called to account.

I must, however, reject the idea that any other grounds could be a standard for the ordering of foreign policy save that of the responsibility of securing the freedom and the future of the life of our people.

The whole senselessness of the patriotic-national bourgeois border policy shows itself on the basis of the following consideration:

If the avowal of German as the mother tongue is used as a basis the German nation numbers . . . . people.

Of this figure . . . . millions are in the mother country.
In which

90

IX

Consequently of all the Germans in the world there are only . . . . millions within the present Reich territory, who represent . . . . per cent of the total number of our people altogether. Of the Germans not united with the motherland, in consequence of the slow loss of dedicated racial comrades the . . . . must be regarded, ... ,* i.e. a total number of approximately . . . . million Germans find themselves in a situation which in all human probability will one day cause their de-Germanization. In no case, however, will they be able to take further part in the motherland's fateful struggle in any kind of decisive form, and just as little, too, in the cultural development of their people. Whatever the German element individually accomplishes in North America, it will not be reckoned to the benefit of the German people as such, but adds to the cultural aggregate of the American Union. Here the Germans are really only the cultural fertilizers for other peoples. Indeed, in reality the greatness of these nations is, in general, not seldom to be ascribed to the high percentage of German contributions and accomplishments. Once we keep the size of this constant loss of people in view, we will immediately be able to estimate the slight importance of the border policy sponsored by the bourgeois world.

Even if a German foreign policy were to restore the borders of the year 1914, the percentage of Germans living within the Reich territory, that is belonging to our nation, would rise despite this only from . . . . per cent to . . . . per cent. Thus the possibility of enlarging this percentage considerably could hardly be in question any more.

---

* At this place in the original about one-third of a page was left blank.— *Trans.*

If, notwithstanding, the German element abroad wants to remain true to the nation, this can at the outset be only a question of a language and cultural loyalty, in that the more it rises to a consciously manifested feeling of belongingness, the more does the motherland of the German nation honor the German name in the dignity of her representatives.

Thus the more Germany as a Reich transmits a mark of the greatness of the German people to the world, the more will the German element conclusively lost to the state receive a stimulus at least to take pride in belonging spiritually to this people. On the other hand, the more wretchedly the motherland herself attends to her interests, and accordingly transmits a bad impression abroad, the weaker will the inner inducement be felt to belong to such a people.

Since the German people does not consist of Jews, the German element, especially in Anglo-Saxon countries, nevertheless and unfortunately will increasingly be anglicized and presumably likewise be lost to our people, spiritually and ideologically as well. Just as its practical work accomplishments are already lost to them.

Insofar, however, as it is a matter of the fate of those Germans who were broken off from the German nation by the events of the World War and the peace treaty, it must be said that their fate and future is a question of regaining the motherland's political power.

Lost territories will not be retrieved by protest actions, but rather by a victorious sword. Thus whoever today desires the liberation of any territory whatsoever in the name of national honor must also be ready to stake all, with iron and blood for the liberation, otherwise such a chatterbox should keep his mouth shut. Along with this, to be sure, follows the duty also of carefully considering whether we possess the power to carry out such a struggle, and secondly whether the blood risked leads, or can lead, to the desired success, and thirdly whether the success achieved matches the blood that must be staked.

I most solemnly protest against the claim that a duty of national honor exists which compels us to have two million men bleed to death on the battlefield in order that, under the most favorable result, we may be able to enter a total of a quarter million men, women and children on our books. This is not national honor that is made manifest here, but rather a lack of principle, or madness. It is no national honor, however, for a people to be ruled by madmen.

Certainly a great people will protect even its last citizen with collective action. But it is an error to impute this to sentiment, to honor, rather than primarily to a sagacious insight and human experience. As long as a nation tolerates an injustice that is inflicted on some of its citizens, it will slowly but increasingly weaken its own position, since such a tolerance would serve the inner strengthening of an aggressive-minded enemy just as it grinds down trust in the strength of one's own state. We know all too well what the consequences are in history of a constant yielding in little things, not to know how to be able to judge the necessary consequences in big things. Hence a solicitous state leadership will all the more preferably attend to the interests of its citizens in the smallest things, as with that the risk of its own commitment is reduced in proportion as that of the adversary rises. If today in any state an injustice is committed against an English citizen and England undertakes her citizen's defense, the danger of England being involved in a war on account of this one Englishman is no greater for England than for the other state, which inflicts the injustice. Hence the firm action of a government respected as such in defense of even a single person is altogether not an unbearable risk, since indeed the other state will have just as little interest in starting a war on account of a trifling injustice that may have been inflicted on a single person. A general conception of honor has been formulated on the basis of this knowledge and the thousand-year-old application of this principle, namely, that a powerful state take every individual citizen under its protection and defend him with all its might.

Further, through the nature of European hegemony, a certain practice has been developed in the course of time to demonstrate this conception of honor in more or less cheap examples, so as to raise the prestige of individual European states, or at least to give it a certain stability. As soon as an alleged, or even faked, injustice was committed against a Frenchman or an Englishman in certain countries that were weak and less powerful militarily, this subject's defense with armed power was undertaken. That is to say a couple of warships put on a military demonstration, which in the worst cases was firing practice with live ammunition, or an expeditionary force of some kind was landed with which the power to be punished was to be chastised. Not seldom, at the same time, the wish that thus an excuse for intervention might be obtained, was father to the thought.

It would probably never occur to the English even to exchange a note with North America on account of a trifling incident for which they would take bloody revenge on Liberia.

Thus the more the defense of the individual citizen is undertaken on grounds of pure expediency and with every means in a strong state, the less can a Reich, made completely defenseless and powerless, be expected to undertake a foreign policy step on the grounds of so-called national honor, which perforce must lead, after all, to the destruction of its last prospects for the future. For if the German people justifies its present border policy, espoused in the so-called national circles, by the necessity of representing German honor, the result will not be the redemption of German honor but rather the eternalization of German dishonor. That is to say, it is not at all dishonorable to have lost territories, but it is dishonorable to conduct a policy which must needs lead to a complete enslavement of one's own people. And all this only so as to be able to give vent to just ugly talk and to avoid action. For this is just a question of empty talk. If we really wanted to establish a policy having national honor as its goal, then we must at least entrust this policy to persons worthy of esteem according to all common notions of honor. As long, however, as German domestic and foreign policy is conducted by forces which, with cynical smirks, proclaim in the Reichstag that for them there exists no fatherland called Germany, for just so long will it be the first task of these national bourgeois and patriotic phrase-mongering heroes merely to secure the simplest recognition of the idea of national honor in Germany through their domestic policy. But why do they not do it; indeed, on the contrary, why do they enter coalitions with avowed betrayers of the country at the expense of this so-called national honor? Because otherwise a difficult struggle would be necessary, whose outcome they view with small confidence, and which, indeed, could lead to the destruction of their own existence. To be sure, this private existence of theirs is holier than the defense of national honor within the country. Yet they gladly risk the nation's future existence for a couple of phrases.

The national border policy becomes downright senseless if we look beyond both the afflictions and tasks of the present to the necessity of shaping a life for our people in the future.

Hence the border policy of our bourgeois-patriotic fatherland circles is especially senseless because it requires the greatest blood stakes and yet contains the smallest prospects for our people's future.

The German nation is less in a position today than in the years of peace to nourish itself on its own territory. All the attempts—either through increasing land yields as such, or by cultivating the last fallow lands—to bring about an increase of the German production of foodstuffs, did not enable our people to nourish itself from its own soil. In fact, the folk-mass now living in Germany can no longer be satisfied with the yield of our soil. Every further increase of these yields, however, would not be applied to the benefit of the increment to our population, but instead would be completely spent in satisfying the increase of the general living requirements of individuals. A model living standard is created here which is primarily determined by a knowledge of conditions and of life in the American Union. Just as the living requirements of rural communities rise as a result of the slow awareness and the influence of life in the big cities, so do the living requirements of entire nations rise under the influence of the life of better-situated and richer nations. Not seldom a people's living standard, which thirty years before would have appeared as a maximum, is regarded as inadequate simply for the reason that in the meanwhile knowledge has been acquired about the living standard of another people. Just as in general, man, even in the lowest circles, takes for granted appointments which eighty years before were unheard-of luxuries even for the upper classes. The more space is bridged through modern technology and especially communication, and nations are brought closer together, the more intensive their mutual relations become, the more also will living conditions reciprocally leave their mark on each other and seek to approximate one another. It is an erroneous opinion that in the long run one can hold a people of a definite cultural capacity and also of a real cultural importance to an otherwise generally valid living standard by an appeal to perceptible facts or even to ideals. The broad masses especially will show no understanding of this. They feel the hardship; either they grumble against those who in their opinion are responsible—something which is dangerous at least in democratic states, since thereby they provide the reservoir for all attempts at revolutionary upheavals —or through their own measures they try to bring about a rectification as they understand it and as it arises from their own insight. The fight against the child begins. They want to lead a life like others and cannot. What is more natural than that the responsibility is put on large families, in which no joy is taken any more, and which are limited as much as possible as a burdensome evil.

Hence it is false to believe that the German people in the future could acquire an increase in number by an increase of its domestic agricultural production. In the most favorable of cases the upshot is only a satisfaction of the increased living requirements as such. But since the increase of these living requirements is dependent on the living standard of other nations which, however, stand in a much more favorable relation of population to land, they, in the future, too will be far ahead in their living equipment. Consequently this stimulus will never die out and one day either a discrepancy will arise between the living standard of these peoples and those poorly provided with land, or the latter will be forced, or believe themselves forced, to reduce their number even further.

The German people's prospects are hopeless. Neither the present living space nor that achieved by a restoration of the borders of 1914 will allow us to lead a life analogous to that of the American people. If we want this, either our people's territory must be considerably enlarged, or the German economy will again have to embark on paths already known to us since the prewar period. Power is necessary in both cases. Specifically, first of all in the sense of a restoration of our people's inner strength, and then in a military mounting of this strength.

Present-day national Germany, which sees the fulfillment of the national task in its limited border policy, cannot deceive herself that the problem of the nation's sustenance will in any way be solved thereby. For even the utmost success of this policy of the restoration of the borders of 1914 would bring only a renewal of the economic situation of the year 1914. In other words, the question of sustenance which then, as now, was completely unsolved, will imperiously force us onto the tracks of world economy and world export. As a matter of fact, the German bourgeoisie, and the so-called national leagues with it, also think only in economic-political terms. Production, export and import are the catchwords with which they juggle and from which they hope for the nation's salvation in the future. It is hoped to raise the export capacity through an increase of production and thereby be able to provide adequately for import needs. Only it is completely forgotten that for Germany this whole problem, as has already been stressed, is not at all a problem of increasing production but rather a question of sales possibility; and that the export difficulties would not at all be obviated by a reduction of German production costs as, again, our bourgeois sly dogs presume. Because inasmuch as this, in itself, is only partly possible in consequence of our limited domestic market, making German export commodities able to compete by lowering production costs—for instance, through the dismantling of our social legislation, and the duties and burdens resulting therefrom—it will only bring us thither, where we had landed on August 4, 1914. It really is part of the whole incredible bourgeois-national naiveté to presume that England would or ever could tolerate a German competition dangerous to her. Yet, these are the very same people who well know, and who always stress, that Germany did not want a war in 1914, but that instead she was literally pushed into it. And that it was England who, out of sheer competitive envy, gathered together former enemies and let loose against Germany. Today, however, these incorrigible economic dreamers imagine that England, after having risked the whole existence of her world empire in the monstrous four-and-one-half-year World War, and in which she remained the victor, will now view German competition differently than at that time. As if for England this whole question were a sporting matter. No. For decades before the war England had tried to break the threatening German economic competition, the growing German maritime trade, etc., with economic counter-measures. Only when they were forced to understand that this would not succeed, and when on the contrary

Germany, by building her navy, showed that she was actually determined to carry out her economic warfare to the extent of the peaceful conquest of the world, did England as a last resort invoke violence. And now, after she has remained the victor, they think they can play the game all over again; whereas, on top of all this, Germany today is not at all in a position to throw any kind of power factor into the scales, thanks indeed to her domestic and foreign policy.

The attempt to restore our people's sustenance and to be able to maintain it by the increase of our production and by reducing the costs of the same, ultimately will fail for the reason that we cannot undertake the final consequence of this struggle because of the lack of military power. Thus the end would be a collapse of the German people's sustenance and of all these hopes along with it. Entirely aside from the fact, too, that now even the American Union is emerging in all fields as the sharpest competitor to all European nations fighting as export nations for the world's markets. The size and the wealth of her domestic market permits production figures and thereby production equipment which so reduce manufacturing costs that, despite enormous wages, it no longer seems possible to undercut her prices. Here the development of the automobile industry may be considered as a warning example. Not only because we Germans, for instance, despite our laughable wages, are not in a position, even only to a degree, to export successfully against American competition, but we must also look on as American cars spread alarmingly even to our own country. This is possible only because the size of her domestic market, her wealth in purchasing power and also in raw materials, guarantees the American automobile industry domestic sales figures which alone make possible manufacturing methods which in Europe would be impossible in consequence of the lack of these domestic sales potentials. The consequence of this is the enormous export possibilities of the American automobile industry. Thus here it is a question of the general motorizing of the world that is a matter of incommensurable importance for the future. For the replacement of human and animal power by motors is only at the beginning of its development, whose end cannot at all be foreseen today. At any rate, for the American Union the modern automobile industry is on the whole at the forefront of all other industries.

Thus in many other areas, our continent will increasingly appear as an economic factor, in an aggressive form, and thereby help to sharpen the struggle for the sales market. From an examination of all factors, especially in view of the limitation of our own raw materials and the ensuing threatening dependence on other countries, Germany's future perforce appears very gloomy and sad.

But even if Germany were to master all her increasing economic difficulties, she would still be in the same spot as she had already been on August 4, 1914. The ultimate decision as to the outcome of the struggle for the world market will lie in power, and not in economics.

It has been our curse, however, that even in peacetime a great part of the national bourgeoisie, precisely, was permeated by the idea that power could be renounced through an economic policy. Today, its chief representatives are also to be sought in those more or less pacifistic circles who, as the adversaries and enemies of all heroic, folkish virtues, would be glad to see a state-preserving, indeed even a state-forming strength in economics. But the more a people accepts the belief that it can maintain its life only through peaceful economic activity, the more will its very economy be surrendered to collapse. For, ultimately, economics, as a purely secondary matter in national life, is linked to the primary existence of a strong state. The sword had to stand before the plough and an army before economics.

If it is believed that we can renounce this in Germany, our people's sustenance will be wrecked.

As soon, however, as a people in general once impregnates its life with the thought that it can find its daily subsistence through peaceful economic activity alone, the less will it think of a violent solution in case this attempt should fail; on the contrary, it will then all the more try to take the easiest path to overcome the miscarriage of the economy without thereby having to risk its blood. As a matter of fact, Germany already finds herself in the middle of this situation. Emigration and birth control are the medicines recommended for our nation's salvation by the representatives of pacifistic economic policy and the Marxist view of the state.

The result of following these counsels, especially for Germany, will be of the most fateful importance. Germany is racially composed of so many unequal constituent elements that a permanent emigration perforce will remove from our nation people who have the greatest capacity for resistance, who are the boldest and most determined. These, above all, like the Vikings of yore, will also today be the bearers of Nordic blood. This slow diminution of the Nordic element leads to a lowering of our general race value and thus to a weakening of our technical, cultural, and also civic-political productive forces. Hence, the consequences of this weakening will be especially grievous for the future because there now appears as a dynamic actor in world history a new state which, as a truly European colony, has for centuries received the best Nordic forces of Europe by way of emigration; aided by the community of their original blood, these have built a new, fresh community of the highest racial value. It is no accident that the American Union is the state in which at the present time most inventions are being made by far, some of which are of an incredible boldness. Americans, as a young, racially select people, confront old Europe which has continually lost much of its best blood through war and emigration. Just as little as one can equate the accomplishment of one thousand degenerate Levantines in Europe, say in Crete, with the accomplishment of one thousand racially still more valuable Germans or Englishmen, so can one just as little equate the accomplishment of one thousand racially questionable Europeans to the capacity of one thousand racially highly valuable Americans. Only a conscious folkish race policy would be able to save European nations from losing the law of action to America, in consequence of the inferior value of European peoples vis-à-vis the American people. If in place of this, however, the German people, along with a bastardization systematically conducted by Jews with inferior human material and a lowering of its racial value as such caused thereby, also lets its best blood-bearers be taken away by a continuation of emigration in hundreds upon hundreds of thousands of individual specimens, it will slowly sink to the level of an equally inferior race and hence to that of an incompetent and valueless people. The danger is especially great since, because of the complete indifference on our side, the American Union itself, inspired by the teachings of its own ethnologists, has established special standards for immigration. By making entry to American soil dependent on definite racial prerequisites on the one hand, as well as on the definite physical health of the individual as such, bleeding Europe of its best people has, indeed, perforce been legally regulated. This is something which our whole so-called national bourgeois world and all its economic politicians either do not see or, at least, will not hear of because it is unpleasant to them and because it is much cheaper to pass over these things with a couple of general national phrases.

To this nature-imposed lowering of the general value of our people by forced emigration in consequence of our economic policy, is added birth control as a second disadvantage. I have already set forth the consequences of the fight against the child. They lie in a reduction of the count of individuals brought to life, so that a further selection cannot take place. On the contrary, the people take pains that all who are once born are kept alive under any circumstances. Since, however, ability, energy, etc., are not necessarily connected with the first born, but instead become visible in each case only in the course of the struggle for existence, the possibility of a weeding-out and a selection according to such criteria is removed. Nations become impoverished in talents and energies. Again, this is especially bad in nations in which the dissimilarity of basic racial elements extends even into families. For then, according to the Mendelian law of division, a separation takes place in every family which can partly be attributed to one racial side, partly to the other. If, however, these racial values vary in their importance for a people, then even the value of the children of one family already will be dissimilar on racial grounds. Since the firstborn in no way must grow according to the racially valuable sides of both parents, it lies in the interest of a nation that later life at least search out the more racially valuable from among the total number of children, through the struggle for existence, and preserve them for the nation and, conversely, put the nation in the possession of the accomplishments of these racially valuable individuals. But if man himself prevents the procreation of a greater number of children and limits himself to the first-born or at least to the second-born, he will nevertheless want to preserve especially these inferior racial elements of the nation, even if these do not possess the most valuable characteristics. Thus he artificially hinders nature's process of selection, he prevents it, and thereby helps to impoverish a nation of powerful personalities. He destroys the peak value of a people.

The German people which, as such, does not have that average value, as for example the English, will be especially dependent on personality values. The extraordinary extremes that we can observe everywhere in our people are only the aftereffects of our blood-determined disruption into superior and inferior racial elements. In general, the Englishman will have a better average. Perhaps he will never arrive at the harmful depths of our people, but also never at its heights of brilliance. Therefore, his life will move along a more average line and be filled with a greater steadiness. In contrast, German life in everything is infinitely unstable and restless and acquires its importance only by its extraordinarily high achievements, through which we make amends for the disquieting aspects of our nation. Once, however, the personal bearers of these high achievements are removed through an artificial system, these very achievements cease. Then our people moves toward a permanent pauperization of personality values and thereby to a lowering of its whole cultural and spiritual importance.

If this condition should continue for just several hundred years, our German people would be, at the least, so weakened in its general importance that it would no longer be able to raise any kind of claim to be called a people of world consequence. In any case, it will no longer be in a position to keep pace with the deeds of the considerably younger, healthier American people. Then, because of a great number of causes, we ourselves will experience what not a few old cultural peoples prove in their historical development. Through their vices, and in consequence of their thoughtlessness, the Nordic blood-bearer was slowly eliminated as the most racially valuable element of the bearers of culture and founders of states, and thereby they left behind a human hodgepodge of such slight intrinsic importance that the law of action was wrested from their hands to pass over to other younger and healthier peoples.

All of southeast Europe, especially the still older cultures of Asia Minor and Persia, as well as those of the Mesopotamian lowlands provide classroom examples of the course of this process.

Thus, just as here history was slowly shaped by the racially more valuable peoples of the Occident, the danger likewise arises that the importance of racially inferior Europe slowly is leading to a new determination of the world's fate by the people of the North American continent.

That this danger threatens all Europe has, after all, already been perceived by some today. Only few of them wish to understand what it means for Germany. Our people, if it lives with the same political thoughtlessness in the future as in the past, will have to renounce its claim to world importance once and for all. Racially, it will increasingly atrophy until it finally sinks to degenerate, animallike feed bags lacking as well the memory of past greatness. As a state in the future order of world states, they will at best be like that which Switzerland and Holland have been in Europe up to now.

This will be the end of the life of a people whose history has been two thousand years of world history.

This fate will no longer be changed with stupid national-bourgeois phrases whose practical senselessness and worthlessness must already have been proved by the success of development up to now. Only a new reformation movement, which sets a conscious knowledge against racial thoughtlessness and draws all the conclusions from this knowledge, can still snatch our people back from this abyss.

It will be the task of the National Socialist movement to carry over into a policy applied in practice the knowledge and scientific insights of race theory, either already existing or in the course of development, as well as the world history clarified through it.

Since today Germany's economic fate vis-à-vis America is in fact also the fate of other nations in Europe, there is again a movement of credulous followers, especially among our people, who want to oppose a European union to the American Union in order thereby to prevent a threatening world hegemony of the North American continent.

For these people, the Pan-European movement, at least at first sight, really seems to have much that is alluring about it. Indeed, if we could judge world history according to economic viewpoints, it could even be pertinent. Two are always more than one for the mechanic of history and thus for the mechanical politician. But values, not numbers, are decisive in the life of nations. That the American Union was able to achieve such a threatening height is not based on the fact that . . . . million people form a state there, but on the fact that . . . . square kilometers of the most fertile and the richest soil is inhabited by . . . . million people of the highest race value. That these people [Thus just the fact that she] form a state has a heightened importance for the other parts of the world, despite the territorial size of their living area, insofar as an all-encompassing organization exists thanks to which, indeed, the racially conditioned individual value of these people, can find a compact deployment of collective forces for fighting through the struggle for existence.

If this were not correct, if the importance of the American Union thus lay in the size of the population alone, or else in the size of the territory, or in the relation in which this territory stands to the size of the population, then Russia would be at least as dangerous for Europe. Present-day Russia encompasses . . . . million people on . . . . million square kilometers. These people are also comprised in a state structure whose value, taken traditionally, would have to be even higher than that of the American Union. Despite this, however, it would never occur to anybody to fear a Russian hegemony over the world for this reason. No such inner value is attached to the number of the Russian people, so that this number could become a danger for the freedom of the world. At least never in the sense of an economic and power-political rule of the other parts of the globe, but at best in the sense of an inundation of disease bacilli which at the moment have their focus in Russia.

If, however, the importance of the threatening American position of hegemony seems to be conditioned primarily by the value of the American people and then only secondarily by the size of this people's given living space and the favorable relation between population and soil resulting therefrom, this hegemony will not be eliminated by a purely formal numerical unification of European nations, so far as their inner value is not higher than that of the American Union. Otherwise, present-day Russia would necessarily appear as the greatest danger to this American Union, as would China, still more, which is inhabited by over 400 million people.

Thus, first and foremost the Pan-European movement rests on the fundamental basic error that human values can be replaced by human numbers. This is a purely mechanical conception of history which avoids an investigation of all shaping forces of life in order, in their stead, to see in numerical majorities the creative sources of human culture as well as the formative factors of history. This conception is in keeping with the senselessness of our western democracy as with the cowardly pacificism of our high economic circles. It is obvious that it is the ideal of all inferior or half-breed bastards. Likewise, that the Jew especially welcomes such a conception. For logically pursued, it leads to racial chaos and confusion, to a bastardization and Negrification of cultural mankind and thereby ultimately to such a lowering of its racial value that the Hebrew who has kept free of this can slowly rise to world domination. At least, he fancies that ultimately he will be able to develop [ascend] into the brain of this mankind which has become worthless.

Aside from this fundamental basic error of the Pan-European movement, even the idea of a unification of European states, forced by a general insight emerging from a threatened distress, is a fantastic, historically impossible childishness. Thereby, I do not mean to say that such a unification under a Jewish protectorate and Jewish impulsion as such would not be possible from the outset, but only that the result could not match the hopes for which the whole monkey business sets the stage. Let no one believe that such a European coalition could mobilize any strength that would manifest itself externally. It is an old experience that a lasting unification of nations can take place only if it is a question of nations which are racially equivalent and related as such, and if, secondly, their unification takes place in the form of a slow process of struggle for hegemony. Thus did Rome once subjugate the Latin states one after the other until finally her strength sufficed to become the crystallization point of a world empire. But this is likewise the history of the birth of the English world empire. Thus, further, did Prussia put an end to the dismemberment of Germany and thus only in this way could a Europe one day rise that could attend to the interests of its population in a compact governmental form. But—this would only be the result of a centuries-long struggle, since an infinite quantity of old customs and traditions must be overcome and an assimilation of peoples who are already extraordinarily divergent racially would have to materialize. The difficulty, then, of giving a unitary state language to such a structure can likewise be solved only in a centuries-long process.

However all this would not be the realization [fulfillment] of the present Pan-European train of thought but rather the success of the struggle for existence of the strongest nations of Europe. And what remained would as little be a Pan-Europe as, for instance, the unification of the Ladin states formerly was a Pan-Ladinization. The power which at that time had fought through this unification process in centuries-long battles gave its name forever to the whole structure. And the power which would create a Pan-Europe along such natural ways would thereby at the same time rob it of the designation Pan-Europe.

But even in such a case, the desired success would not materialize.

For once any European great power today—and naturally it could involve only a power which was valuable according to its folkdom, that is, racially important—brings Europe to unity along these lines, the final completion of this unity would signify the racial submersion of its founders and thereby remove even the last value from the whole structure. It would never be possible thereby to create a structure which could bear up against the American Union.

In the future only the state which has understood how to raise the value of its folkdom and to bring it to the most expedient state form for this, through its inner life as well as through its foreign policy, will be able to face up to North America. By posing such a solution as possible, a whole number of states will be able to participate, which can and will lead to a heightened fitness if for no other reason than the mutual competition.

It is again the task of the National Socialist movement to strengthen and to prepare to the utmost its own fatherland itself for this task.

The attempt, however, to realize the Pan-European idea through a purely formal unification of European nations, without having to be forced in centuries-long struggles by a European ruling power, would lead to a structure whose whole strength and energy would be absorbed by the inner rivalries and disputes exactly as formerly the strength of the German clans in the German Union. Only when the internal German question had been finally solved through Prussia's power superiority could a commitment of the nation's united strength beyond its borders ensue. It is frivolous, however, to believe that the contest between Europe and America will always be only of a peaceful economic nature, if economic motives develop into determining vital factors. In general, it lay in the nature of the rise of the North American state that at first it could exhibit little interest in foreign policy problems. Not only in consequence of the lack of a long governmental tradition, but rather simply in consequence of the fact that within the American continent itself extraordinarily large areas stood at the disposal of man's natural urge for expansion. Hence, the policy of the American Union, from the moment of breaking away from the European mother state to most recent times, was primarily a domestic one. Indeed, the struggles for freedom were themselves at bottom nothing but the shaking off of foreign policy commitments in favor of a life viewed exclusively in terms of domestic policy. In proportion as the American people increasingly fulfill the tasks of internal colonization, the natural, activist urge that is peculiar to young nations will turn outward. But then the surprises which the world may perchance still experience could least of all be seriously opposed by a pacifistic-democratic Pan-European hodgepodge state. According to the conception of that everybody's bastard, Coudenhove, this Pan-Europe would one day play the same role vis-à-vis the American Union or a nationally awakened China that was formerly played by the old Austrian state vis-à-vis Germany or Russia.

Really there is no need to refute the opinion that just because a fusion of peoples of different nationalities has taken place in the American Union, this must also be possible in Europe. The American Union, to be sure, has brought people of different nationalities together into a young nation. But closer scrutiny discloses that the overwhelming majority of these different ethnic groups racially belong to similar or at least related basic elements. For since the emigration process in Europe was a selection of the fittest, this fitness in all European peoples lying primarily in the Nordic admixture, the American Union, in fact, has drawn to itself the scattered Nordic elements from among peoples who were very different as such. If, in addition, we take into account that it involved people who were not the bearers of any kind of theory of government, and consequently were not burdened by any kind of tradition, and, further, the dimensions of

107

the impact of the new world to which all people are more or less subject, it becomes understandable why a new nation, made up of peoples from all European countries, could arise in less than two hundred years. It must be considered, however, that already in the last century this fusion process became more difficult in proportion as, under the pressure of need, Europeans went to North America who as members of European national states not only felt themselves united with them folkishly for the future, but who particularly prized their national tradition more highly than citizenship in their new homeland. Moreover, even the American Union has not been able to fuse people of alien blood who are stamped with their own national feeling or race instinct. The American Union's power of assimilation has failed vis-à-vis the Chinese as well as vis-à-vis the Japanese element. They also sense this well and know it, and therefore they would best prefer to exclude these alien bodies from immigration. But thereby American immigration policy itself confirms that the earlier fusion presupposed peoples of definite equal race foundations and immediately miscarried as soon as it involved people who were fundamentally different. That the American Union itself feels itself to be a Nordic-German state and in no way an international mishmash of peoples further emerges from the manner in which it allots immigration quotas to European nations. Scandinavians, that is, Swedes, Norwegians, further Danes, then Englishmen, and finally Germans, are allotted the greatest contingents. Rumanians and Slavs very little, Japanese and Chinese they would prefer to exclude altogether. Consequently, it is a Utopia to oppose a European coalition or a Pan-Europe, consisting of Mongols, Slavs, Germans, Latins, etc., in which all others than Teutons would dominate, as a factor capable of resistance, to this racially dominant, Nordic state. A very dangerous Utopia, to be sure, if we consider that again countless Germans see a rosy future for which they will not have to make the most grievous sacrifices. That this Utopia of all things came out of Austria is not without a certain comedy. For after all, this state and its fate is the liveliest example of the enormous strength of structures artificially glued together but which are unnatural in themselves. It is the rootless spirit of the old imperial city of Vienna, that hybrid city of the Orient and the Occident, which thereby speaks to us.

X

Summing up, therefore, it can be reiterated that our bourgeois national policy, the foreign policy aim of which is the restoration of the borders of the year 1914, is senseless and indeed catastrophic. It perforce brings us into conflict with all the states which took part in the World War. Thus it guarantees the continuance of the coalition of victors which is slowly choking us. It thereby always assures France a favorable official opinion in other parts of the world for her eternal proceedings against Germany. Even were it successful, it would signify nothing at all for Germany's future in its results, and nevertheless compel us to fight with blood and steel. Further it altogether prevents in particular any stability of German foreign policy.

It was characteristic of our prewar policy that it necessarily gave an outside observer the image of decisions often as wavering as they were incomprehensible. If we disregard the Triple Alliance, the maintenance of which could not be a foreign policy aim but only a means to such an aim, we can discover no stable idea in the leaders of our people's fate in the prewar period. This is naturally incomprehensible. The moment the foreign policy aim no longer signified a struggle for the German people's interests but rather the preservation of world peace, we lost the ground under our feet. I can certainly outline a people's interests, establish them, and regardless of how the possibilities of their advocacy stand, I can nevertheless keep the great aim uninterruptedly in view. Gradually the rest of mankind will also acquire a general knowledge of a nation's special, definite, chief foreign policy ideas. This then offers the possibility of regulating mutual relations in a permanent way, either in the sense of an intended resistance against the known operation of such a power, or a reasonable awareness of it, or also in the sense of an understanding since, perhaps, one's own interests can be achieved along a common path.

This stability in foreign policy can be established with a whole series of European states. For long periods of her existence Russia exhibited definite foreign policy aims which dominated her whole activity. In the course of the centuries France has always represented the same foreign policy aims regardless who embodied political power in Paris at the moment. We may speak of England not only as a state with a traditional diplomacy but above all as a state with a foreign policy idea become a tradition. With Germany such an idea could be discerned only periodically in the Prussian state. We see Prussia fulfill her German mission in the short period of the Bismarckian statecraft, but thereafter any foreign policy aim staked out far in advance came to an end. The new German Reich, especially after Bismarck's retirement, no longer had such an aim since the slogan of preserving peace, that is of maintaining a given situation, does not possess any kind of stable content or character. Just as any passive slogan is doomed in reality to be the plaything of an aggressive will. Only he who himself wants to act can also determine his action according to his will. Hence the Triple Entente, which wanted to act, also had all the advantages which lie in the self-determination of action, whereas the Triple Alliance through its contemplative tendency to preserve world peace was at a disadvantage to the same degree. Thus the timing and opening of a war was established by nations with a definite foreign policy aim, whereas conversely the Triple Alliance powers were surprised by it at an hour that was everything but favorable. If we in Germany ourselves had had even the slightest bellicose intention, it would have been possible through a number of measures, which could have been carried out without effort, to have given another face to the start of the war. But Germany never had a definite foreign policy aim in view, she never thought of any kind of aggressive steps for the realization of this aim, and consequently events caught her by surprise.

From Austria-Hungary we could hope for no other foreign policy aim as such save that of wriggling through the hazards of European politics, so that the rotten state structure as much as possible nowhere bumps into anything, in order thus to conceal from the world the real inner character of this monstrous corpse of a state.

The German national bourgeoisie, which alone is under discussion here—since international Marxism as such has no other aim but Germany's destruction—even today has learned nothing from the past. Even today it does not feel the necessity of setting for the nation a foreign policy aim that may be regarded as satisfactory and thereby give our foreign policy endeavors a certain stability for a more or less long time. For only if such a possible foreign policy goal appears fundamentally staked out can we discuss in detail the possibilities that can lead to success. Only then does politics enter the stage of the art of the possible. As long, however, as this whole political life is not dominated by any leading idea, individual actions will not have the character of utilizing all possibilities for the achievement of a certain success as such. Instead they are but individual stations along the way of an aimless and planless muddling through from today to tomorrow. Above all is lost that certain persistence which the execution of great aims always requires; that is: one will try this today and that tomorrow and the day after one will have this foreign policy possibility in view and suddenly pay homage to a wholly opposite intention—insofar, that is, as this visible confusion as confusion is not actually in keeping with the wish of that power which rules Germany today and in truth does not wish for a resurgence of our people ever. Only international Jewry can possess a lively interest in a German foreign policy which by its continual, seemingly irrational sudden transitions lacks that clear plan, and which as its only justification at best asserts: "Indeed, we too naturally don't know what should be done, but we do something precisely because something must be done." Yes, not seldom can we actually hear that these men are so little convinced of the inner sense of their foreign policy actions that as highest motivation they can only inquire whether somebody else may know a better one. This is the foundation on which the statecraft of a Gustav Stresemann rests.

In contrast, precisely today more than ever is it necessary for the German people to set itself a foreign policy goal which meets its real inner needs and, conversely, guarantees an unconditional stability to its foreign policy activity for the humanly predictable proximate period of time. For only if our people fundamentally determines and persistently fights for its interests in such a way can it hope to induce this or that state whose interests are not opposed to ours, now at last

111

established, and which indeed may even be parallel, to enter into a closer union with Germany. For the idea of wanting to solve our people's distress through the League of Nations is exactly as unjustified as it was to let the German question be decided by the Frankfurt Federal Parliament.

The satisfied nations dominate the League of Nations. Indeed it is their instrument. To a large measure they have no interest in allowing a change in the territorial distribution of the globe, unless it again appeals to their interests. And while they talk about the rights of small nations, in reality it is only the interests of the largest they have in view.

If Germany again wants to achieve a real freedom so that under its blessing she can give the German people its daily bread, she must take the measures thereto outside the parliament of the League of Nations in Geneva. But then for the lack of sufficient strength it will be necessary that she find allies who can believe that they may also serve their own interests by going along with Germany. Such a situation, however, will never arise if Germany's real foreign policy aim has not become fully clear to these nations. And above all Germany by herself will never acquire the strength and inner force for that persistence necessary, alas, to sweep away the obstacles of world history. For then one will never learn how to have patience in particulars, and also to renounce them if necessary, in order finally to be able to achieve the vitally necessary aim on a large scale. For even among allies relations will never be completely frictionless. Disturbances of reciprocal relations can arise over and over again to assume threateningly dangerous forms if the strength to overcome these petty unpleasantnesses and obstacles does not lie in the very dimensions of the foreign policy aim ultimately staked out. Here the French national leadership of the prewar decades may serve as an exemplary model. How it lightly passed over small matters, indeed even remained silent before the most bitter events so as not to lose the possibility of organizing a war of revenge against Germany, in such contrast to our eternally bawling hurrah-patriots and, consequently, their frequent barking at the moon.

The staking out of a clear foreign policy aim appears as important, furthermore, for the reason that otherwise the representatives of other interests among one's own people will always find it possible to confuse public opinion and to make, and in part even provoke, petty incidents into a cause for the radical change of opinion on foreign policy. Thus, out of the petty disputes which result from conditions themselves or which are artificially fabricated, France will again and again try to bring about ill-feeling, indeed estrangement, among nations which, by the whole nature of their real vital interests, would be dependent upon each other, and which perforce would have to take a stand against France in concert. Such attempts, however, will be successful only if in consequence of the lack of an unshakeable political aim, one's own political actions do not possess a true stability, and above all, because persistence in the preparation of measures serviceable to the fulfillment of one's own political aim is also lacking.

The German people, which possesses neither a foreign policy tradition nor a foreign policy aim, will by itself rather be inclined to pay homage to Utopian ideals and thereby neglect its real vital interests. For what has our people not raved over in the last hundred years? Now it was Greeks whom we wanted to save from the Turks, then Turks on whom we bestowed our affection against Russians and Italians, after which our people again found an enchantment in waxing enthusiastic over Polish freedom fighters, and then in indulging their feelings for the Boers, etc. But what have all these most stupid soulful gushings, as incompetent politically as they were garrulous, cost our people?

Thus the relation to Austria, as was emphasized with special pride, was not one of practical understanding but a true inner alliance of the heart. If only reason instead of the heart had spoken at this time, and understanding had decided, Germany would be saved today. But for the very reason that we are the kind of a people which lets its political actions be determined too little according to the grounds of a really reasonable, rational insight—for which reason we cannot look back on any great political tradition—we must, at least for the future, give our people an unshakable foreign policy aim which seems suitable for making the political measures of the state leadership understandable to the broad masses in their particulars. Only thus will it be ultimately possible that millions with a divining faith will stand behind a government leadership which carries out decisions which in their particulars may have something painful about them. This is a prerequisite for bringing about a mutual understanding between the people and the state leadership and, to be sure, also a prerequisite for anchoring the state leadership itself in a certain tradition. It will not do that every German government have its own foreign policy goal. One can quarrel only over the means, one can dispute over them, but the goal itself must be established as unchangeable once and for all. Then politics can become the great art of the possible, that is, it is reserved to the brilliant abilities of the individual government leaders to perceive the possibilities, from instance to instance, of bringing the people and the Reich nearer to its foreign policy aim.

This setting of a foreign policy goal is altogether nonexistent in present-day Germany. Hence the unguided, wavering and unsure manner of attending to our people's interests becomes understandable, as does also the whole confusion of our public opinion. Hence also the incredible capers of our foreign policy which always end unhappily without the people being even at least capable of judging the persons responsible and really calling them to account. No, one does not know what to do.

To be sure there are not a few people today who fully believe we should do nothing. They boil down their opinion to the effect that Germany today must be clever and reserved, that she engage herself nowhere, that we must keep the development of events well in view but ourselves not take part in them, in order one day to assume the role of the laughing third who reaps the benefits while the other two quarrel.

Yes, yes, our present bourgeois statesmen are so clever and wise. A political judgment which is troubled by no knowledge of history. There are not a few proverbs which have become a real curse for our people. For example, "the wiser one yields," or "clothes make the man," or "one can get through the whole land with hat in hand," or "when two fight, the third rejoices."

In the life of nations, at least, the last proverb applies only in a wholly conditional sense. [And this for the following reason] Namely, if two quarrel hopelessly within a nation then a third who is outside

114

a nation can win. In the life of nations with one another, however, the ultimate success will be had by states which deliberately engage in disputes because the possibility of increasing their strength lies only in a quarrel. There is no historical event in the world that cannot be judged from two points of view. The neutrals on one side always confront the interventionist on the other. And, in general, the neutrals will always get the worst of it, whereas the interventionists rather can claim the benefits for themselves, insofar, indeed, as the party on which they wagered does not lose.

In the life of nations this means the following: if two mighty powers quarrel on this globe the more or less small or large surrounding states either can take part in this struggle or keep their distance from it. In one case the possibility of a gain is not excluded, insofar as the participation takes place on the side which carries off the victory. Regardless who wins, however, the neutrals will have no other fate save enmity with the remaining victor state. Up to now none of the globe's great states has arisen on the basis of neutrality as a principle of political action, but only through struggle. If towering power-states as such are on earth, all that remains for small states to do is either to renounce their future altogether or to fight with the more favorable coalition and under its protection and thus increase their own strength. For the role of the laughing third always presupposes that this third already has a power. But whoever is always neutral will never achieve power. For to the extent that a people's power lies in its inner value, the more does it find its ultimate expression in the organizational form of a people's fighting forces on the battlefield, created by the will of this inner value. This form, however, will never rise if it is not put to the test from time to time. Only under the forge-hammer of world history do a people's eternal values become the steel and iron with which history is made. But he who avoids battles will never attain the strength to fight battles. And he who never fights battles will never be the heir of those who struggle with each other in a military conflict. For the previous heirs of world history were not, for instance, peoples with cowardly concepts of neutrality but young peoples with better swords. Neither antiquity nor the Middle Ages nor modern times knows even a single example of any power-states coming into being save in permanent

115

struggle. Up to now, however, the historical heirs have always been power-states. In the life of nations, to be sure, even a third can be the heir when two quarrel. But then from the very outset this third is already the power which deliberately lets two other powers quarrel in order to defeat them once and for all later without a great sacrifice on its part. Thereby neutrality loses the character of passive nonparticipation in events altogether and instead assumes that of a conscious political operation. Obviously no sagacious state leadership will begin a struggle without weighing the size of its possible stakes and comparing it with the size of the adversary's stakes. But if it has perceived the impossibility of being able to fight against a certain power, all the more so will it be forced to try to fight together with this power. For then the strength of the hitherto weaker power can eventually grow out of this common struggle, in order if necessary to fight for its own vital interests also against the latter. Let no one say that then no power would enter into an alliance with a state which some day itself might become a danger. Alliances do not present policy aims, but only means to the aims. We must make use of them today even if we know a hundred times that the later development can possibly lead to the opposite. There is no alliance that lasts forever. Happy the nations which, in consequence of the complete divergence of their interests, can enter into an alliance relationship for a definite time without being forced to a mutual conflict after the cessation of the same. But a weak state especially, which wants to achieve power and greatness, must always try to take an active part in the general political events of world history.

When Prussia entered her Silesian war, this too was a relatively secondary phenomenon alongside the violent dispute between England and France which at that time was already in full swing. Perhaps Frederick the Great can be reproached for having pulled English chestnuts out of the fire. But would the Prussia ever have arisen with which a Bismarck could create a new Reich if at that time a Hohenzollern prince had sat on the throne who, in the knowledge of the future greater events of world history, preserved his Prussia in a state of pious neutrality? The three Silesian wars brought Prussia more than Silesia. On these battlefields grew those regiments which in the future were to carry the German banners from Weissenburg and Wörth up to Sedan, in order finally to greet the new emperor of the new Reich in the Hall of Mirrors in the palace of Versailles. Prussia at that time was certainly a small state, unimportant in population and territorial size. But by leaping into the middle of the great actions of world history this little state had gotten for itself a legitimation for the founding of the later German Reich.

And once, even the neutralists triumphed in the Prussian state. This was in the period of Napoleon I. At that time it was believed at first that Prussia could remain neutral, and for this she was later punished with the most terrible defeat. Both conceptions confronted one another sharply even in the year 1812. The one for neutrality and the other, headed by Baron vom Stein, for intervention. The fact that the neutralists won out in 1812 cost Prussia and Germany infinite blood and brought them infinite suffering. And the fact that at last in 1813 the interventionists broke through saved Prussia.

The World War gave the clearest answer to the opinion that one can achieve political success by preserving a careful neutrality as a third power. What have the neutrals of the World War achieved practically? Were they the laughing third, for instance? Or does one believe that in a similar event Germany would play another role? And let no one think that the reason for this lies only in the magnitude of the World War. No, in the future all wars, insofar as they involve great nations, will be people's wars of the most gigantic dimensions. As a neutral state in any other European conflict, Germany, however, would possess no more importance than Holland or Switzerland or Denmark, etc. in the World War. Does one really think that after the event we would get out of nowhere the strength to play the role against the remaining victor which we did not venture to play in a union with one of the two combatants?

At any rate the World War has proven one thing explicitly: whoever conducts himself as a neutral in great world-historical conflicts may perhaps at first make a little business, but in terms of power politics he will thereby ultimately also be excluded from a co-determination of the world's fate.

Thus, had the American Union preserved her neutrality in the World War, today she would be regarded as a power of the second rank regardless of whether England or Germany had emerged as a victor. By entering the war she raised herself to England's naval strength,

117

but in international-political terms marked herself as a power of decisive importance. Since her entry into the World War the American Union is appraised in a completely different way. It lies in the nature of mankind's forgetfulness no longer to know [to forget], after only a short time, what the general judgment of a situation had been only a few years before. Just as today we detect a complete disregard of Germany's former greatness in the speeches of many foreign statesmen, just as little, conversely, can we appraise the extent of the increase in value that the American Union has experienced in our judgment since her entry into the World War.

This is also the most compelling statesmanlike justification for Italy's entry into the war against her former allies. Had Italy not taken this step she would now share the role of Spain, no matter how the dice had rolled. The fact that she carried out the much criticized step to an active participation in the World War brought a rise in her position and a strengthening of the same which has found its ultimate crowning expression in fascism. Without her entry into the war the latter would have been a completely unthinkable phenomenon.

The German can ponder this with or without bitterness. It is important to learn from history, especially if its teachings speak to us in such a compelling way.

Thus the belief that through a prudent, reserved neutrality vis-à-vis the developing conflicts in Europe and elsewhere one can someday reap the benefits thereof as a laughing third is false and idiotic. In general freedom is preserved neither by begging nor by cheating. And also not by work and industry but exclusively by struggle, and indeed by one's own struggle. Thus it is very easily possible that more weight is attached to the will than to the deed. Not seldom, in the framework of a wise alliance policy, nations have achieved successes unrelated to the success of their arms. But fate does not always measure a nation which boldly stakes its life according to the dimensions of its deeds but rather, very frequently, according to the dimensions of its will. The history of Italian unification in the nineteenth century is noteworthy for this. But the World War also shows how a whole number of states can achieve extraordinary political successes less through their military accomplishments [successes] than through the foolhardy boldness with which they take sides and the doggedness with which they hold out.

If Germany wants to put an end to her period of enslavement by all, she must under all circumstances actively try to enter into a combination of powers in order to participate in the future shaping of European life in terms of power-politics.

The objection that such participation contains a grievous risk is correct. But, after all, does one really believe that we will achieve freedom without taking a risk? Or does one think that there has ever been a deed of world history which was not linked with a risk? Was Frederick the Great's decision, for instance, to participate in the first Silesian war not linked with a risk? Or did Germany's unification by Bismarck entail no dangers? No, a thousand times no! Beginning with man's birth up to his death everything is questionable. Only death seems certain. But for this very reason the ultimate commitment is not the worst for the reason that one day, in one way or another, it will be demanded.

Naturally it is a matter of political sagacity to choose the stake in such a way that it yields the highest possible gain. But not to stake anything at all for fear, perhaps, of picking the wrong horse means to renounce a people's future. The objection that such an action may have the character of a risky gamble can most easily be refuted by simple reference to previous historical experience. By a risky gamble we understand a game in which from the outset the chances of winning are subject to the fate of chance. This will never be the case in politics. For the more the ultimate decision lies in the darkness of the future, the more is the conviction of the possibility or impossibility of a success erected on humanly perceptible factors. The task of a nation's political leadership is to weigh these factors. The result of this examination, then, must also lead to a decision. Thus this decision is consonant with one's own insight and is sustained by faith in possible success on the basis of this insight. Hence I can just as little call a politically decisive deed a risky gamble, just because its outcome is not one hundred per cent certain, as an operation undertaken by a surgeon the outcome of which likewise will not necessarily be successful. From time immemorial it has always been in keeping with the nature of great men to execute deeds whose success is even doubtful and indefinite with the utmost energy if the necessity thereof as such lay before them, and if after a mature examination of all conditions this very action alone could be considered.

The joy of responsibility in the framing of great decisions in the struggles of nations will of course be all the greater the more the actors, by observation of their people, can conclude that even a miscarriage will not be able to destroy the nation's vital strength. For in the long run a people, inwardly healthy at its core, can never be effaced through defeats on the battlefield. Thus insofar as a people possesses this inner health, with the prerequisite of a sufficient racial importance, the courage for difficult undertakings can be the greater since even the failure of the same would not, by far, signify the downfall of such a people. And here Clausewitz is right, when in his principles he asserts that with a healthy people such a defeat may repeatedly lead to a later resurgence and that, conversely, only cowardly subjection, that is, a supine surrender to fate, can lead to ultimate destruction. The neutrality, however, which is today recommended to our people as the only action possible is really nothing but a volitionless surrender to a fate determined by foreign powers. And only therein lies the symptom and the possibility of our decline. If, on the contrary, our people itself had undertaken abortive attempts to achieve freedom, a factor that could be beneficial to our people's strength would lie in the very manifestation of this attitude. For let it not be said that it is political sagacity which holds us back from such steps. No, it is a wretched cowardice and a lack of principle which in this case, as so often in history, one tries to confuse with intelligence. Obviously a people under the duress of foreign powers can be forced by circumstances to endure years of foreign oppression. But the less a people can seriously do outwardly against overpowering forces the more, however, will its internal life press toward freedom and leave nothing untried that could be suitable for changing the momentarily given condition one day by staking such a people's entire strength. One will then endure the yoke of a foreign conqueror but with clenched fists and gritted teeth, waiting for the hour which offers the first opportunity of shaking off the tyrant. Something like this can be possible under the pressure of conditions. But what presents itself today as political sagacity, however, is as a matter of fact a spirit of voluntary subjection, of unprincipled renunciation of any resistance, indeed the shameless persecution of those who dare to think of such a resistance and whose work obviously could serve their people's resurgence. It is the spirit of inner self-disarmament, of the destruction of all moral factors which one day could serve a resurrection of this people and state. This spirit can really not give itself the airs of political sagacity, for actually it is a state-destroying dishonorableness.

And, to be sure, this spirit must hate every attempt at an active participation of our people in future European developments, because the necessity of a struggle against this spirit indeed lies in the mere attempt at such a participation.

If, however, a state leadership seems to be affected by this corrupting spirit, it becomes the task of the opposition which perceives, represents and thus espouses a people's real vital forces to inscribe the struggle [the education] for national resurgence, and through it for national honor, on its banners. And it must not let itself be intimidated by the assertion that foreign policy is the task of responsible state leadership, for there has not been such a responsible leadership for a long time. On the contrary it must adhere to the conception that besides the formal laws of momentary governments there exist eternal [of formal governments also eternal] obligations which compel every member of a nation to do what is perceived as necessary for the existence of the folk-community. Even if this stands a thousand times in opposition to the intentions of bad and incompetent governments.

Hence precisely in Germany today the highest obligation should devolve on the so-called national opposition, in view of the unworthiness of the general leadership of our people to establish a clear foreign policy aim and to prepare and educate our people for the execution of these ideas. Primarily, it must launch the sharpest war against the hope, widely spread today, that our fate can be changed somewhat by active cooperation with the League of Nations. In general it must see to it that our people gradually realizes that we must not expect an amelioration of the German situation from institutions the representatives of which are the interested parties in our present misfortune. Further, it must deepen the conviction that all social aspirations are Utopian promises devoid of any real worth without the regaining of German freedom. It must further bring our people the knowledge that for this freedom, one way or another, only the staking of its own strength can be considered. And that, consequently, our whole domestic and foreign policy must be such that by virtue of it our people's inner strength grows and increases. Finally it must enlighten the people to the effect that this staking of strength must take place for a really worthwhile aim, and that for this purpose we cannot go forward to meet our fate alone, but will need allies.

XI

The size of the possible military commitment as well as the relation of this means of power to those of the surrounding states is of decisive importance for the question of the future shaping of German foreign policy, apart from the inner power of our people, of its strength and assessment of character.

I need not express myself further on the moral inner weakness of our present-day people in this work. Our general weaknesses which are in part grounded in a matter of blood, and in part lie in the nature of our present governmental organization or must be attributed to the effects of our poor leadership, are perhaps less familiar to the German public than, unfortunately, they are to the rest of the world which knows them well. Most of the measures of our oppressors are occasioned by knowledge of this weakness. But with all acknowledgment of the factual conditions it should still never be forgotten that the same people of today hardly ten years ago accomplished deeds unrivaled in history. The German people which at the moment leaves such a depressing impression has, nevertheless, more than once proved its powerful merit in world history. The World War itself is the most glorious evidence of our people's heroism and spirit of sacrifice, of its death-defying discipline and its brilliant capability in thousands upon thousands of areas in the organization of its life. Its purely military leadership has also achieved immortal successes. Only the political leadership has failed. It was already the precursor of that of today, even so much worse.

Today the inner qualities of our people may be a thousandfold unsatisfactory, but in one blow they will yield another image, as soon as another fist takes the reins of events in order to lead our people out of its present decline.

In our own history we see how wonderful is precisely our people's capacity for transformation. Prussia in 1806 and Prussia in 1813. What a difference. In 1806 the state characterized by the most abject capitulation everywhere, an unheard-of wretchedness in the civic attitude, and in 1813 the state characterized by the most glowing hatred against foreign domination and a sense of patriotic sacrifice for one's own people, the most heroic will to fight for freedom. What in truth has changed since then? The people? No, in its inner essence it has remained as before, only its leadership had come into other hands. A new spirit followed the weakness of the Prussian governmental administration and the ossified and aged leadership of the post-Frederick period. Baron vom Stein and Gneisenau, Scharnhorst, Clausewitz and Blücher were the representatives of the new Prussia. And the world in a few months had again forgotten that seven years before this Prussia had undergone the experience of Jena.

And was it, for instance, otherwise before the founding of the Reich? Hardly a decade was required for a new Reich, which in the eyes of many seemed to be the most powerful embodiment of German power and mastery, to arise out of the German decline, the German disunity and the general political dishonorableness. A single head, towering above all, had restored freedom of development to the German genius in a battle against the mediocrity of the majority. Let us dispense with Bismarck in our history and only wretched mediocrity would fill the most glorious period for our people in centuries.

Just as the German people could in a few years be hurled down from its unprecedented greatness by the mediocrity of its leadership, into its present chaos, so can it be pulled up again by an iron fist. Its inner value will then make its appearance so visibly before the entire world that merely the actuality of its existence must compel a regard for and an appraisal of this fact.

If at the start, however, this value is a slumbering one, it is more than ever necessary to provide clarity on Germany's real power-value existing at the moment.

I have already tried to draw a brief picture of the momentary German instrument of military power, the *Reichswehr*. Here I wish to sketch Germany's general military situation in relation to the surrounding world. Germany at the present time is encircled by three power factors or power groups. England, Russia and France are at present militarily the most threatening of Germany's neighbors. At the same time French power appears strengthened by a system of European alliances which reach from Paris to Belgrade via Warsaw and Prague.

Germany lies wedged between these states with completely open borders. What is especially threatening thereby is that the western border of the Reich runs through Germany's greatest industrial region. [That further the coastline is defenseless against the whole overseas trade for few. . . .] This western border, however, in consequence of its length and of the lack of all real natural barriers, offers only a few possibilities for defense by a state whose military means seem most extremely limited. [The attempt to make the Rhine a military line of resistance] Even the Rhine cannot be viewed as a fully effective line of military resistance. Not only because the possibility of finding the necessary technical preparations for this has been taken away from Germany by the peace treaties, but because the river itself offers even fewer obstacles to the passage of armies with modern equipment than the slight means of German defense which must be dispersed over too long a front. Moreover, this river runs through Germany's greatest industrial area and consequently a struggle over it from the outset would mean the destruction of the industrial areas and factories technically most important for national defense. But if in consequence of a Franco-German conflict Czechoslovakia should come under consideration as a further opponent of Germany, a second great industrial region, Saxony, which could be useful industrially for the conduct of the war, would be exposed to the greatest danger of war. Here too the border, without natural defense, runs down to Bavaria, so broadly and openly that the prospect of a resistance promising success can hardly be considered. If Poland also were to take part in such a war, the entire eastern border in addition, apart from a few inadequate fortifications, would be defenseless against attack.

Whereas on the one hand the German borders are militarily indefensible and are surrounded openly in long lines by enemies, our North Sea coast is especially small and confined. The naval power for its defense is laughable and completely worthless as such. The

125

fleet which we claim today, beginning with our so-called battleships, is at best the finest target material for enemy firing practice. The two newly built ships, light cruisers, modern in themselves, have no decisive value, indeed not even an apparent one. The fleet we are allowed is inadequate even for the Baltic Sea. All in all the only value of our fleet is at most that of a floating gunnery school.

Thus in case of a conflict with any naval power, not only would German trade be ended in a moment, but there would also be the danger of landings.

The entire unpropitiousness of our military situation stems from this other consideration:

Berlin, the Reich's capital, is barely 175 kilometers from the Polish border. It lies scarcely 190 kilometers from the nearest Czech border, just as far as the distance between Wismar and the Stettin lagoon as the crow flies. Thus this means that Berlin can be reached by modern aircraft in less than one hour from these borders. If we draw a line stretching 60 kilometers east of the Rhine, within it will lie almost the entire west German industrial region. From Frankfurt to Dortmund there is hardly one major German industrial locality which does not lie within this zone. As long as France occupies a part of the left bank of the Rhine she is in a position to push forward by aircraft into the heart of our west German industrial region in hardly 30 minutes. Munich is just as far from the Czech borders as Berlin is from the Polish and Czech borders. Czech military aircraft would need approximately 60 minutes to reach Munich, 40 minutes to Nuremberg, 30 minutes to reach Regensburg; even Augsburg lies only 200 kilometers from the Czech border and consequently could also be easily reached in scarcely an hour by present-day airplanes. As the crow flies, however, Augsburg is almost as distant from the Czech border as it is from the French border. From Augsburg to Strasbourg the line of flight is 230 kilometers, but it is only 210 kilometers to the nearest French border. Hence Augsburg also lies within a zone which can be reached by hostile aircraft in an hour. Indeed, if we examine the German border from this point of view it turns out that within an hour's flight time the following can be reached: the entire industrial region in west Germany including Osnabrück, Bielefeld, Kassel, Würzburg, Stuttgart, Ulm, Augsburg. In the east: Munich, Augsburg, Würzburg, Magdeburg, Berlin, Stettin. In other words, with the present situation of the German borders, there is only a very small area embracing a few square kilometers which could not be visited by hostile aircraft within the first hour.

Hence France must be considered as the most dangerous enemy because she alone, thanks to her alliances, is in a position to be able to threaten almost the whole of Germany with aircraft, even an hour after the outbreak of a conflict.

At the present time the military counteractions Germany could take against the application of this weapon, all in all, are quite nil.

This single observation already shows the hopeless situation into which a German resistance against France, based only on itself, must land at once. Whoever has himself been often subjected in the field to the effects of an enemy air attack best knows how to appraise especially the moral effects resulting therefrom.

But Hamburg and Bremen too, in general all our coastal cities, would today no longer escape this fate since the large navies have the possibility of bringing floating landing-places very close to the coast by means of aircraft carriers.

But Germany today not only has no technically effective weapons in a sufficient amount to oppose to air attacks. Even otherwise the purely technical equipment of our small *Reichswehr* is hopelessly inferior to that of our enemy. The lack of heavy artillery might be put up with more easily than the lack of a really promising possibility of defense against armored tanks. If Germany today were thrust into a war against France and her allies without beforehand being in a position to be able to find at least the most necessary preparations for defense, the issue would be decided in a few days on the basis of the purely technical superiority of our adversaries. Measures required for defense against such a hostile attack could no longer be taken during the struggle itself.

Likewise false is the opinion that we will be able to put up a resistance at least for a certain time by improvised means, since these very improvisations already require a certain amount of time which is no longer available in case of a conflict. For events would roll more quickly and thereby produce more facts than there would be time left for us to organize counter-measures against these events.

127

Hence from whatever side we consider the possibilities of foreign policy, for Germany one case must in principle be excluded: we will never be able to proceed against the forces now mobilized in Europe by relying only on our military means. Thus any combination which brings Germany into conflict with France, England, Poland and Czechoslovakia, etc., without beforehand giving her the possibility of a thorough preparation, is therefore void.

This fundamental perception is important because there are still among us in Germany, even today, well-meaning national-minded men who in all earnestness believe that we must enter into an association with Russia.

Even if considered only from a purely military point of view such an idea is unviable or catastrophic for Germany.

Just as before the year 1914, today also we can assume as unconditionally established for always that in any conflict involving Germany, regardless on what grounds, regardless for what reasons, France will always be our adversary. Whatever European combinations may emerge in the future, France will always take part in them in a manner hostile to Germany. This lies in the traditionally anchored intention of French foreign policy. It is false to believe that the outcome of the war has changed anything on this score. On the contrary the World War did not bring about for France the complete fulfillment of the war aim she had in mind. For this aim was by no means only the regaining of Alsace-Lorraine, but on the contrary Alsace-Lorraine itself represents only a small step in the direction of the goal of French foreign policy. That the possession of Alsace-Lorraine in no way abolished the tendencies of French policy, aggressively directed against Germany, is most strikingly proved by the fact that at the very time France possessed Alsace-Lorraine, the tendency of French foreign policy directed against Germany was, nevertheless, already in existence. The year 1870 showed more clearly than the year 1914 what France ultimately intended. At that time no need was felt to veil the aggressive character of French foreign policy. In the year 1914, perhaps wisened by experiences, perhaps also influenced by England, the French considered it more correct to profess general ideals of humanity on the one hand and to limit their aim to Alsace-Lorraine on the other. These tactical considerations, however, did not in the least signify an inner deflection from the former goals of French policy, but only a concealment of the same. Afterward, as before, the leading idea of French foreign policy was the conquest of the Rhine borders whereby the mutilation of Germany into individual states, linked as loosely as possible to each other, was viewed as the best defense of this border. That this safeguarding of France in Europe, achieved thereby, was to serve the fulfillment of greater world political aims does not alter the fact that for Germany these French continental-political intentions are a question of life and death.

As a matter of fact, indeed, France also had never taken part in a coalition in which German interests in any way would have been promoted. In the last three hundred years Germany had been attacked by France twenty-nine times all told up to 1870. A fact which on the eve of the battle of Sedan moved Bismarck to oppose the French general Wimpffen most sharply when the latter tried to achieve a mitigation of the terms of surrender. It was Bismarck at that time who, in response to the declaration that France would not forget a German concession but would remember it gratefully forever in the future, immediately stood up and confronted the French negotiator with the hard, naked facts of history. Bismarck stressed, in this sense, that France had attacked Germany so often in the last three hundred years, regardless of the prevailing form of government, that for all the future he was convinced that regardless how the capitulation was formulated, France would immediately attack Germany anew as soon as she felt strong enough for it either through her own strength or through the strength of allies.

Thereby Bismarck had more correctly appraised French mentality than our present political leaders of Germany. He could do this because he, who himself had a policy aim in view, could also have an inner understanding of the policy goals others set themselves. For Bismarck the intention of French foreign policy was clearly established. It is incomprehensible to our present-day leaders, however, because they are lacking in every clear political idea.

If, moreover, France, on the occasion of her entry into the World War, had only the intention of regaining Alsace-Lorraine as a definite aim, the energy of the French war leadership would not have been nearly what it was. The political leadership, especially, would not have come around to a determination which seemed worthy of the greatest admiration during many situations during the World War. It lay, however, in the nature of this greatest coalition war of all times that a complete fulfillment of all wishes was all the less possible since the internal interests of the participant nations themselves had exhibited very great divergences. The French intention [desire] of a complete effacement of Germany in Europe still stood opposed to the English desire to prevent an unconditional French position of hegemony, as much as such a one for Germany.

Thus for the curtailment of French war aims it was important that the German collapse take place in forms that did not yet make public opinion fully aware of the whole dimension of the catastrophe. In France they had come to know the German grenadier in such a way that only with hesitation could they look forward to a possibility that France might be forced to step forth alone for the fulfillment of her ultimate political goal. Later, however, under the impact of Germany's inner defeat, now become generally visible, when they might have been more determined on such an action, the war-psychosis in the other parts of the world had already so widely abated that a unilateral action by France for a final aim of such magnitude could no longer have been carried out without opposition on the part of her former allies.

Thereby we are not saying that France renounced her aim. On the contrary, she will try as persistently as before to achieve in the future what the present prevented. France will also in the future, as soon as she feels capable of this through her own power or the power of her allies, attempt to dissolve Germany, and try to occupy the bank of the Rhine in order in this way to be able to commit French strength elsewhere with no threat to her rear. That thereby France is not in the least irritated in her intention by changes in the forms of German government is all the more comprehensible since the French people itself, indeed, without any regard to its constitutions of the moment, clings equally to its foreign policy ideas. A people which itself always pursues a definite foreign policy goal, paying no regard as to whether as rulers it has a republic or a monarchy, bourgeois democracy or a Jacobin terror, will have no understanding that another people perhaps by a change of its form of government could also undertake a change of its foreign policy aims. Hence nothing will change France's attitude to Germany as such, regardless whether in Germany an empire or a republic represents the nation, or even socialist terror rules the state.

Obviously France is not indifferent vis-à-vis German events, but at the same time her attitude is determined only by the probability of a greater success, that is of a facilitation of its foreign policy action by a definite German form of government. France will wish Germany the constitution which will leave France to expect the least resistance to Germany's destruction. If, therefore, the German republic as a special sign of its value tries to induce French friendship, in reality this is the most devastating certificate of its incapacity. For it is welcomed in Paris only because France regards it as poor in values for Germany. In no way is it thereby said that France will confront this German republic otherwise than as it has in analogous conditions of our governmental weakness in past times. On the Seine they were always fonder of German weakness than German strength because it seemed to guarantee France's foreign policy activity an easier success.

This French tendency will in no way be changed by the fact that the French people suffer from no lack of territory. For in France policy for centuries has least been determined by sheer economic distress, but much more by impulses of feeling. France is a classic example of the fact that the sense of a healthy territorial-gain policy can easily change over into its opposite once folkish principles are no longer determining, and so-called governmental-national principles take their place. French national chauvinism has departed from folkish points of view to such an extent that for the gratification of a mere power-titillation they Negrify their own blood just to maintain the character of a "grand nation" numerically. Hence France will also be an eternal disturber of world peace for as long as a decisive and fundamental lesson is not administered to this people some day. Moreover nobody has better characterized the nature of French vanity than Schopenhauer with his utterance: "Africa has its monkeys, Europe has its French."

French foreign policy has always received its inner impulse from this mixture of vanity and megalomania. Who in Germany wants to wait and hope that the more France is estranged from rational clear thinking, in consequence of her general Negrification, she will yet one day undertake a change in her disposition and intentions toward Germany?

No, regardless of how the next development in Europe proceeds, France, by utilizing momentary German weaknesses and all the diplomatic and military possibilities at her disposal, will always seek to inflict harm on us and to split our people so that she can ultimately bring it to a complete disintegration.

Hence for Germany any coalition which does not signify a binding of France is by itself impermissible.

The belief in a German-Russian understanding is in itself fantastic as long as a regime rules in Russia which is permeated by only one aim: to carry over the Bolshevist poisoning to Germany. It is natural, therefore, for communist elements to agitate for a German-Russian alliance. They thereby hope, rightfully, to be able to lead Germany herself to Bolshevism. It is incomprehensible, however, if national Germans believe that it is possible to achieve an understanding with a state whose greatest interest is the destruction of this very national Germany. Obviously, should such an alliance finally come into being today its result would be the complete rule of Jewry in Germany exactly as in Russia. Likewise incomprehensible is the opinion that one can wage a war against the capitalist West European world with this Russia. For in the first place present-day Russia is anything but an anti-capitalist state. It is, to be sure, a country that has destroyed its own national economy but, nevertheless, only in order to give international finance capital the possibility of an absolute control. If this were not so how could it be, secondly, that the very capitalist world in Germany takes a position in favor of such an alliance? It is after all the Jewish press organs of the most outspoken stock-exchange interests who espouse the cause of a German-Russian alliance in Germany. Does one really believe that the *Berliner Tagblatt* or the *Frankfurter Zeitung* and all their illustrated papers speak more or less overtly for Bolshevik Russia because the latter is an anti-capitalist state? In political matters it is always a curse when the wish becomes father to the thought.

To be sure, it is conceivable that in Russia itself an internal change within the Bolshevik world may ensue to the extent that the Jewish element, perhaps, could be crowded out by a more or less Russian national element. Then the possibility might not be excluded that present-day Bolshevik Russia, in reality Jewish-capitalistic, would be driven toward [to a] national-anti-capitalist tendencies. In this case, to which many things seem to point, it would be conceivable, to be sure, that West European capitalism would seriously take a position against Russia. But then an alliance of Germany with this Russia would also be complete insanity. For the idea that such an alliance could somehow be held secret is as unjustified as the hope to arm ourselves for the conflict through military preparations that are made quietly.

Then there would only be two real possibilities: either this alliance would be viewed by the Western European world, poising itself against Russia, as a danger, or not. If yes, then I don't know who can seriously believe that there will be time for us to arm ourselves in a manner suitable at least to prevent a collapse in the first twenty-four hours. Or do people really believe in earnest that France will wait until we have built our air defense and our tank defense? Or do they believe that this can happen secretly in a country in which treason is no longer considered shameless, but a courageous deed worthy of emulation? No, if Germany really wants to enter into an alliance with Russia against Western Europe then Germany will again become a historic battlefield tomorrow. On top of this it requires an entirely uncommon phantasy to fancy that Russia could somehow come to Germany's help, in what way I know not. The only success of such an action would be that Russia could thereby still escape a catastrophe for a certain time, as it would first break over Germany. But a popular inducement for such a struggle against Germany could hardly exist, especially in the western states. Just imagine Germany allied with a real anti-capitalist Russia and then picture how this democratic world Jewish press would mobilize all the instincts of the other nations against Germany. How especially in France complete harmony would immediately be established between French national chauvinism and the Jewish stock-exchange press. For let one not confuse such a process with the struggle of White Russian generals against the Bolshevism of an earlier time. In the years '19 and '20 national White Russia fought against the Jewish stock-exchange revolution, in truth international-capitalist red revolution in the highest sense. Today, however, anti-capitalist Bolshevism, become national, would stand in a struggle against world Jewry. Whoever understands the importance of press propaganda, and its infinite possibilities for inciting nations and besotting people, can imagine to what orgies of hate and passion against Germany the European western nations would be whipped. For then Germany would no longer be allied with the Russia of a great, noteworthy, ethical, bold idea, but with the despoilers of the culture of mankind.

Above all there could be no better chance for the French government to master its own inner difficulties than to undertake a fully danger-free struggle against Germany in such a case. French national chauvinism could be all the more satisfied since then, under the protection of a new world coalition, it could come much closer to the fulfillment of the ultimate war aim. For regardless of the nature of the alliance between Germany and Russia, militarily, Germany alone would have to sustain the most terrible blows. Wholly apart from the fact that Russia does not border directly on Germany and, consequently, must itself first overrun the Polish state—even in the case of a subjugation of Poland by Russia which as such is quite improbable—in the best of circumstances such Russian help could essentially arrive on German territory only when Germany no longer existed. But the idea of a landing of Russian divisions anywhere in Germany is completely excluded as long as England and France have complete control of the Baltic Sea. Moreover, the landing of Russian troops in Germany would fail because of countless technical deficiencies.

Thus should a German-Russian alliance some day have to undergo the test of reality, and there is no such thing as an alliance without the idea of war, Germany would be exposed to the concentrated attacks of all West Europe without being able to provide for her own defense in a serious way.

But now there remains the question of just what meaning a German-Russian alliance should have in general. Only the one of preserving Russia from destruction and sacrificing Germany for that? Regardless of how this alliance would turn out in the end, Germany could not arrive at setting a decisive foreign policy goal. For thereby nothing would be changed regarding the fundamental vital question, indeed regarding the vital needs, of our people. On the contrary Germany, thereby, would be more than ever cut off from the only rational territorial policy in order to pad out her future with the scuffle over unimportant border adjustments. For the question of space for our people cannot be solved either in the west or in the south of Europe.

The hope in a German-Russian alliance, which haunts the minds of even many German national politicians, however, is more than questionable for still another reason.

In general, it seems self-evident in national circles that we cannot very well ally ourselves with a Jewish-Bolshevist Russia since the result, according to all probability, would be a Bolshevization of Germany. Obviously, we do not want this. But we base ourselves on the hope that one day the Jewish character—and thereby the most fundamentally international capitalistic character of Bolshevism in Russia—might disappear in order to make place for a national communism, anti-capitalist on a world scale. Then this Russia, permeated once more by national tendencies, might very well come up for consideration in terms of an alliance with Germany.

This is a very great error. It rests on an extraordinary ignorance of the psyche of the Slavic folk-soul. This should not amaze anybody if we reflect on how little knowledge even politically minded Germany had of the spiritual conditions of her erstwhile allies. Otherwise we would never have fallen so low. If, therefore, today the national politicians in favor of friendship with Russia try to motivate their policy by reference to Bismarck's analogous attitudes, they disregard a whole multitude of important factors which at that time, but not today, spoke in favor of Russian friendship.

The Russia which Bismarck knew was not a typical Slavic state, at least insofar as it was a question of the political leadership of the same. In general, Slavdom is lacking in state-forming forces. In Russia especially government formations were always attended to by foreign elements. Since the time of Peter the Great there were, above all, very many Germans (Balts!) who formed the skeleton and the brains of the Russian state. In the course of centuries countless thousands of these Germans have been Russified but only in the sense in which our own bourgeoisie, our national bourgeoisie, would like to Germanize or Teutonize Poles or Czechs. Just as in this case the new-fledged "German" is in truth only a German-speaking Pole or Czech, likewise did these artificial Russians remain German, or better, Teutons, according to their blood and hence their capabilities. Russia is indebted to this Teutonic upper stratum for her political state as well as for what little exists of her cultural value. A great Russia would neither have arisen nor would she have been able to preserve herself without this really German upper and intellectual stratum. As long as Russia had been a state with an autocratic form of government this upper stratum, which in truth was not at all Russian, also decisively influenced the political life of the gigantic empire. Even Bismarck knew this Russia at least in part. It was with this Russia that the master of German political statesmanship had political dealings. But even in his lifetime the reliability and stability of Russian policy, both domestic and foreign, fluctuated precariously and became in part incalculable. This lay in the gradual suppression of the German upper stratum. This process of the transformation of the Russian intelligentsia was caused in part by a bleeding of the Russian nation in consequence of many wars, which, as has been already mentioned in this book, primarily decimate the racially more valuable forces. Actually the officer corps especially was for the most part non-Slav by descent, but in every case not of Russian blood. On top of this came the slight increase in the upper stratum of the intelligentsia as such, and finally the artificial training by the schools of a real Russiandom with regard to blood. The slight state-preserving value of the new Russian intelligentsia as such was grounded on blood and revealed itself most sharply perhaps in the nihilism of the Russian universities. Most fundamentally, however, this nihilism was nothing but the blood-determined opposition of real Russiandom to the racially alien upper stratum.

The Pan-Slavic idea was counterposed to the Russian idea of the state in proportion as Russia's Teutonic, state-forming upper stratum was replaced by a racially pure Russian bourgeois class.

From the first hour of its birth it was folkish, Slavish [Russian] and anti-German. The anti-German disposition of the newly emerging Russiandom, especially in the strata of the so-called intelligentsia, however, was not only a pure reflex action against the former autocratic alien upper class in Russia, for instance, on the grounds of politically liberal modes of thought. Rather, in the most intrinsic sense, it was the protest of the Slavic nature against the German. They are two folk souls which have only very little in common, whereby indeed it must first be established whether this littleness they have in common has its cause in the confusedly broken racial individual elements of which the Russian as well as the German people seems to be constituted. Thus what is common to us and to the Russians is as little consonant with the German as with the Russian character but, instead, is to be ascribed only to our mixture of bloods which has brought just as many eastern Slavic elements to Germany as Nordic German ones to Russia. But if as a test of the two spiritual endowments we were to take a purely Nordic German, from Westphalia let us say, and place a purely Slavic Russian opposite to him, an infinite chasm would yawn between these two representatives of the two peoples. Actually the Slavic-Russian people has always felt this and has therefore always had an instinctive antipathy toward the German. Solid thoroughness as well as the cold logic of sober thought, are something which the real Russian inwardly finds unsympathetic and in part even incomprehensible. Our sense of order will not only find no reciprocal love but will always elicit aversion. What with us is felt as something self-evident is for the Russian, however, an affliction, since it represents a restriction of his natural, differently structured spiritual and instinctual life. Hence Slavic Russia will feel itself drawn more and more to France. And indeed to an increasing degree, since the Frankish-Nordic element is also being suppressed in France. The facile, superficial, more or less effeminate French life was more able to fascinate the Slav because inwardly it is closer to him than the severities of our German struggle for existence. Hence it is no accident if Pan-Slavic Russia waxes politically enthusiastic over France, exactly as the Russian intelligentsia of Slavic blood found in Paris the Mecca of its own needs for civilization.

The process of the rise of a Russian national bourgeoisie at the same time caused [signified] an inner alienation of this new Russia vis-à-vis Germany which now could no longer build on a racially related Russian upper stratum.

As a matter of fact already at the turn of the century the anti-German orientation of the representatives of the folkish-Pan-Slav idea was so strong and its influence on Russian policy had grown to such an extent that even Germany's more than decent attitude vis-à-vis Russia, on the occasion of the Russo-Japanese war, could no longer check the further estrangement of the two states. Then came the World War which to no little extent had also been kindled by the Pan-Slavist agitation. The real governmental Russia, insofar as it had been represented by the erstwhile upper stratum, therefore could hardly put in a word anymore.

The World War itself then brought about a further [the last] bleeding of Russia's Nordic German elements, and the last remains were finally extirpated by the revolution and Bolshevism. It was not as if the Slav race instinct had deliberately carried out the struggle for the extermination of the former non-Russian upper stratum by itself. No, it had acquired new leaders meantime in Jewry. Jewry, pressing toward the upper strata and therefore toward supreme leadership, has exterminated the former alien upper class with the help of the Slav race instinct. Thus it is a quite understandable process if Jewry has taken over the leadership of all areas of Russian life with the Bolshevik revolution, since by itself and out of itself Slavdom is altogether lacking in any organizing ability and thereby also in any state-forming and state-preserving power. Take away all the elements which are not purely Slavic from Slavdom and it will immediately succumb to disintegration as a state. To be sure, fundamentally any formation of states may at first have its innermost inducement in the encounter between peoples of a higher and lower order, whereby the bearers of the higher blood value—for reasons of self-preservation—develop a definite community spirit which first allows them the possibility of an organization and a rule over inferior peoples. Only the overcoming of common tasks compels the adoption of organizational forms. But the difference between the state-forming and the non-state-forming elements lies precisely in the fact that the formation of an organization for the preservation of their stock vis-à-vis other types becomes possible for the former, whereas the non-state-forming incompetents are not capable by themselves of finding those organizational forms which would guarantee their existence vis-à-vis others.

Thus present-day Russia or, better said, present-day Slavdom of Russian nationality, has received as master the Jew, who first eliminated the former upper stratum and now must prove his own state-forming power. In view of the endowment of Jewry, which after all is only destructive, it will operate even here only as the historical "ferment of decomposition." It has summoned to its help spirits of which it can no longer rid itself, and the struggle of the inwardly anti-state Pan-Slav idea against the Bolshevist Jewish state idea will end with the destruction of Jewry. What will then remain will be a Russia as insignificant in governmental power as she will be deeply rooted in an anti-German attitude. Since this state will no longer possess a state-preserving upper stratum anchored anywhere, it will become a source of eternal unrest and eternal insecurity. A gigantic land area will thus be surrendered to the most variegated fate and instead of stabilization of relations between states on earth a period of the most restless changes will begin.

Thus the first phase of these developments will be that the most different nations of the world will try to enter into relations with this enormous complex of states in order thereby to bring about a strengthening of their own position and intentions. But such an attempt will always be linked to the effort also to exert their own intellectual and organizational influence on Russia at the same time.

Germany may not hope to come up for consideration in any way during this development. The whole mentality of present-day and future Russia is opposed to this. For the future an alliance of Germany with Russia has no sense for Germany, neither from the standpoint of sober expediency nor from that of human community. On the contrary, it is good fortune for the future that this development has taken place in just this way because thereby a spell has been broken which would have prevented us from seeking the goal of German foreign policy there where it solely and exclusively can lie: territory in the East.

XII

In view of Germany's hopeless military situation the following must be borne in mind in the formulation of future German foreign policy.

1) Germany cannot bring about a change in her present situation by herself, so far as this must ensue by means of military power.

2) Germany cannot hope that a change of her situation will emerge through measures taken by the League of Nations, as long as the determining representatives of this institution are at the same time the parties interested in Germany's destruction.

3) Germany cannot hope to change her present situation through a combination of powers which brings her into conflict with the French system of alliances surrounding Germany, without first acquiring the possibility of eliminating her sheer military powerlessness so that in case the commitments [of an application] of the alliance go into effect she may be able to come forward immediately with the prospect of military success.

4) Germany cannot hope to find such a combination of powers as long as her ultimate foreign policy aim does not seem clearly established, and, at the same time does not contradict the interests of those states which can be considered in terms of an alliance with Germany—indeed even appear serviceable to them.

5) Germany cannot hope that these states can be found outside the League of Nations. On the contrary her only hope must consist in her eventual success in extricating individual states from the coalition of victor states and building a new group of interested parties with new aims which cannot be realized through the League of Nations because of its whole nature.

6) Germany may only hope to achieve success in this way if she

finally renounces her former vacillating see-saw policy and fundamentally decides upon a single direction, and at the same time assumes and bears all the consequences.

7) Germany should never hope to make world history through alliances with nations whose military value seems sufficiently characterized by the fact of their former defeats, or whose general racial importance is inferior. For the struggle for the regaining of German freedom will thereby again raise German history to the level of world history.

8) Germany should never forget for a moment that regardless how, and along what ways, she thinks to change her fate, France will be her enemy, and that France from the outset can count on any combination of powers that turns against Germany.

XIII

We cannot examine Germany's foreign policy possibilities without first possessing clarity on what we want in Germany itself, that is on how Germany itself thinks to shape her future. Further, we must then try to determine clearly the foreign policy goals of those powers in Europe which, as members of the coalition of victors, are important as world powers.

I have already dealt with Germany's various foreign policy possibilities in this book. Nevertheless I shall once more briefly present the possible foreign policy goals so that they may yield a basis for the critical examination of the relations of these individual foreign policy aims to those of other European states.

1) Germany can renounce setting a foreign policy goal altogether. This means that in reality she can decide for anything and need be committed to nothing at all.

Thus in the future she will continue the policy of the last thirty years, but under other conditions. If now the world consisted just of states with a similar political aimlessness, Germany could at least endure this even though it could hardly be justified. But this is not at all the case. Thus just as in ordinary life a man with a fixed life-goal that he tries to achieve at all events will always be superior to others who live aimlessly, exactly likewise is it in the life of nations. But, above all, this is far from saying that a state without a political goal is in the position to avoid dangers which such a goal may bring in its train. For just as it seems exempt from an active function, in consequence of its own political aimlessness, in its very passiveness it can also just as easily become the victim of the political aims of others. For the action of a state is not only determined by its own will, but also by that of others, with the sole difference that in one case it itself can determine the law of action, whereas in the other case the latter is forced upon it. Not to want a war because of a peaceful sentiment, is far from saying that it can also be avoided. And to avoid a war at any price is far from signifying saving life in the face of death.

Germany's situation in Europe today is such that she is far from allowing herself to hope that she may go forward to a condition of contemplative peace with her own political aimlessness. No such possibility exists for a nation located in the heart of Europe. Either Germany itself tries actively to take part in the shaping of life, or she will be a passive object of the life-shaping activity of other nations. All the sagacity hitherto supposedly able to extricate nations from historical dangers through declarations of a general disinterest has, up to now, always shown itself to be an error as cowardly as it is stupid. Whoever will not be a hammer in history, will be an anvil. In all its development up to now our German people has had a choice only between these two possibilities. When it itself wanted to make history, and accordingly joyfully and boldly staked all, then it was still the hammer. When it believed that it could renounce the obligations of the struggle for existence it remained, up to now, the anvil on which others fought out their struggle for existence, or it itself served the alien world as nutriment.

Hence, if Germany wants to live she must take the defense of this life upon herself, and even here the best parry is a thrust. Indeed Germany may not hope at all that she can still do something for shaping her own life, if she does not make a strong effort to set a clear foreign policy aim which seems suitable for bringing the German struggle for existence into an intelligent relation to the interests of other nations.

If we do not do this, however, aimlessness on a large scale will cause planlessness in particulars. This planlessness will gradually turn us into a second Poland in Europe. In the very proportion that we let our own forces become weaker, thanks to our general political defeatism, and the only activity of our life is spent in a mere domestic policy, we will sink to being a puppet of historical events whose motive forces spring from the struggle for existence and for their interests waged by other nations.

Moreover, nations which are not able to take clear decisions over their own future and accordingly would like best of all not to participate in the game of world development, will be viewed by all the other players as a spoil-sport and equally hated. Indeed, it can even happen that, on the contrary, the planlessness of individual political actions, grounded in the general foreign policy aimlessness, is regarded as a very shrewd impenetrable game and responded to accordingly. It was this which befell us as a misfortune in the pre-war period. The more impenetrable, because they were incomprehensible, were the political decisions of the German governments of that time, the more suspicious they seemed. And all the more, therefore, were especially dangerous ideas suspected behind the most stupid step.

Thus if today Germany no longer makes an effort to arrive at a clear political goal, in practice she renounces all possibilities of a revision of her present fate, without in the least being able to avoid future dangers.

2) Germany desires to effect the sustenance of the German people by peaceful economic means, as up to now. Accordingly even in the future she will participate most decisively in world industry, export and trade. Thus she will again want a great merchant fleet, she will want coaling stations and bases in other parts of the world and finally she wants not only international sales markets, but also her own sources of raw material if possible in the form of colonies. In the future such a development will necessarily have to be protected especially by maritime means of power.

This whole political goal for the future is a utopia, unless England is seen as defeated beforehand. It establishes anew all the causes which in 1914 resulted in the World War. Any attempt by Germany to renew her past along this way must end with England's mortal enmity, alongside which France may be reckoned as a most certain partner from the outset.

From a folkish standpoint setting this foreign policy aim is calamitous, and it is madness from the point of view of power politics.

3) Germany establishes the restoration of the borders of the year 1914 as her foreign policy aim.

This goal is insufficient from a national standpoint, unsatis-

144

factory from a military point of view, impossible from a folkish standpoint with its eye on the future, and mad from the viewpoint of its consequences. Thereby even in the future Germany would have the whole coalition of former victors against her in a compact front. In view of our present military position, which with a continuation of the present situation will worsen from year to year, just how we are to restore the old borders is the impenetrable secret of our national-bourgeois and patriotic government politicians.

4) Germany decides to go over to [her future aim] a clear, far-seeing territorial policy. Thereby she abandons all attempts at world-industry and world-trade and instead concentrates all her strength in order, through the allotment of sufficient living space for the next hundred years to our people, also to prescribe a path of life. Since this territory can be only in the East, the obligation to be a naval power also recedes into the background. Germany tries anew to champion her interests through the formation of a decisive power on land.

This aim is equally in keeping with the highest national as well as folkish requirements. It likewise presupposes great military power means for its execution, but does not necessarily bring Germany into conflict with all European great powers. As surely as France here will remain Germany's enemy, just as little does the nature of such a political aim contain a reason for England, and especially for Italy, to maintain the enmity of the World War.

XIV

It is fitting to review the great foreign aims of the other European powers for a closer understanding of the possibilities just adduced. In part these aims are recognizable in the previous activity and efficacy of these states, in part they are virtually laid down programmatically, and otherwise lie in vital needs th: t are so clearly recognizable that even if the states momentarily embark on other paths, the compulsion of a harsher reality necessarily leads them back to these aims.

That England has a clear foreign policy goal is proved by the fact of the existence and therewith of the rise of this giant empire. Let no one fancy, after all, that a world empire can ever be forged without a clear will thereto. Obviously not every single member of such a nation goes to work every day with the idea of setting a great foreign policy goal, but in a completely natural way even an entire people will be gripped by such a goal so that even the unconscious acts of individuals nevertheless lie in the general line of the aim that has been set and actually benefit it. Indeed the general political goal will slowly stamp itself on the very character of such a people, and the pride of the present-day Englishman is no different from the pride of the former Romans. The opinion that a world empire owes its rise to chance or that, at least, the events which conditioned its establishment were accidental historical processes which always turned out luckily for a nation is false. Ancient Rome owed its greatness, exactly as does present-day England, to the soundness of Moltke's assertion that in the long run luck is always with the fit. This fitness of a people in no way lies only in racial value, but also in the ability and skill with which these values are applied. A world empire of the size of ancient Rome, or of present-day Great Britain, is always the result of a marriage between the highest race value and the clearest political aim. As soon as one of these two factors begins to be lacking, first a weakening sets in and ultimately perhaps even a decline.

Present-day England's aim is conditioned by the race value of Anglo-Saxonism as such and by her insular position. t lay in the I race value of Anglo-Saxonism to strive for territorial space. Of necessity this drive could find fulfillment only outside present-day Europe. Not that the English had not, from time to time, also attempted to take soil in Europe for their expansionist lusts. But all these enterprises failed because of the fact that they were opposed by states which at that time were of a no less great racial fitness. Later English expansion in the so-called colonies led at the outset to an extraordinary increase of English maritime life. It is interesting to see how England, which at first exported men, ultimately went over to the export of commodities and thereby weakened her own agriculture. Although now a great part of the English people, indeed the average in general, is inferior to the German peak value, nevertheless the centuries-old tradition of this people has become so much part of its own flesh and blood that vis-à-vis our own German people it possesses considerable political advantages. If today the globe has an English world empire, then for the time being there is also no people which, on the grounds of its general civic-political characteristics as well as its average political sagacity, would be more fitted for it.

The fundamental idea which dominated English colonial policy, on the one hand, was to find a territorial market for English human material and to keep the latter in a governmental relation with the motherland; and on the other to secure the English economy's markets and sources of raw material. It is understandable that the Englishman is convinced that the German cannot colonize just as it is understandable, conversely, that the German believes the same about the Englishman. Both peoples take different standpoints in judging colonizing capacities. Thus the English standpoint was infinitely more practical, more sober, and the German standpoint more romantic. When Germany strove for her first colonies, she was already a military state in Europe and thereby a power state of the first

147

rank. She had wrested the title of a world power through imperishable accomplishments in all fields of human culture as well as in that of military skill. It was now noteworthy that especially in the nineteenth century a general impulse toward colonies permeated all nations, whereas the original leading idea had already fully declined. For example, Germany motivated her claim to colonies with her ability and her desire to spread German culture. As such it was nonsense. For culture, which is the general life-expression of a definite people, cannot be transmitted to another people with wholly other psychic prerequisites. This may, at best, go with a so-called international civilization which stands in the same relation to culture as jazz music to a Beethoven symphony. But wholly apart from this, it would never have occurred to an Englishman at the time England's colonies were founded to motivate his actions otherwise than with the very real and sober advantages which they might bring with them. If later England espoused the freedom of the seas or of oppressed nations, it was never for the purpose of justifying her colonial activity but to destroy ugly competitors. Hence English colonial activity was perforce successful in part because of the most natural reasons. For the less the Englishman ever gave a thought to such a notion as wanting to impose English culture or English breeding on savages, the more sympathetic did such a government necessarily seem to savages who were absolutely not hungry for culture. On top of this, to be sure, there was also the whip which one likewise could all the sooner use since thereby one did not run the danger of departing from a cultural mission. England needed markets and sources of raw material for her commodities and she secured these markets for herself through power politics. This is the sense of English colonial policy. If later even England nevertheless mouthed the word culture, it was only from a purely propagandistic viewpoint, so that she also could morally embroider her own exceedingly sober actions somewhat. In reality the living conditions of the savages were a matter of complete indifference to the English as long, and to the extent, that they did not affect the living conditions of the English themselves. That later still other ideas, of a political prestige character, were linked with colonies of the size of India is conceivable and understandable. But no one can dispute

148

that, for instance, Indian interests never determined English living conditions, but instead English living conditions determined India's. Likewise it cannot be disputed that even in India the Englishman does not set up any cultural institution of any kind so that, for instance, the natives may share in English culture but rather so that, at best, the Englishman can draw more benefits from his colonies. Or does one believe that England brought railroads to India just to put Indians in possession of European transport possibilities and not in order to make possible a better utilization of the colony as well as to guarantee an easier domination? If today in Egypt England again follows in the footsteps of the Pharaohs and stores the water of the Nile by means of gigantic dams, it is certainly not done in order to make the earthly life of the poor *fellah* easier, but only in order to make English cotton independent of the American monopoly. But these are all viewpoints which Germany never dared to think about openly in her colonial policy. The English were the educators of the natives for England's interests, the German was the teacher. That in the end the natives might have felt better with us than they did under the English would, for a normal Englishman, be far from speaking for our kind of colonization policy but surely for that of the English instead.

This policy of a gradual conquest of the world, in which economic power and political strength always went hand in hand, conditioned England's position vis-à-vis other states. The more England grew into her colonial policy, the more she required dominion over the seas, and the more she achieved dominion over the seas the more, in consequence of this, she became again a colonial power. But then also, the more jealously did she finally begin to watch that nobody competed with her for dominion of the seas or of colonial possessions.

There is a very erroneous and widespread notion, especially in Germany, according to which England would immediately fight against any European hegemony. As a matter of fact this is not correct. England actually concerned herself very little with European conditions as long as no threatening world competitor arose from them, so that she always viewed the threat as lying in a development which must one day cut across her dominion over the seas and colonies.

149

There is no conflict of England in Europe in which the former did not have to protect her trade and overseas interests. The struggles against Spain, Holland and later France had their ground not in the threatening military might of these states as such, but only in the way this power was founded as well as in the effects of the same. If Spain had not been an overseas power and thereby a power in competition with England, the latter would presumably have taken little notice of Spain. The same applies to Holland. And even England's later gigantic struggle against France was never waged against Napoleon's continental France but rather against Napoleonic France which viewed her continental policy only as a springboard and as a basis for greater, altogether non-continental aims. In general, France, given her geographical position, will be the power most threatening to England. It was perhaps the only state in which even a limited continental development could contain dangers for England's future. It is all the more noteworthy and instructive for us Germans that despite this, England decided to enter the World War together with France. It is instructive because it proves that despite all the steadfast adherence to the great fundamental ideas of English foreign policy, momentary existing possibilities are always taken into account there and never renounced merely because a threat to England could likewise rise from one of them in the near or distant future. Our German "God punish England" politicians are always of the opinion, to wit, that a good relationship with England in the future must always founder on the fact that England would never seriously give a thought to promoting Germany's interests by an alliance with her in order to see Germany counterposed to her again one day as a dangerous and threatening power. Obviously England will not conclude an alliance to promote Germany's interests, but only in order to foster British interests. But up to now England has provided many examples that she could, very often, couple the representation of her interests with the representation of the interests of other nations. And that then she had recourse to alliances, although according to human prediction, even these were bound to change into later enmity. For divorces sooner or later underly political marriages since, indeed, they do not serve the representation of the common interests of both sides, but instead aim only with common means at promoting or defending the interests of two states which as such are different but which for the time being are not opposed.

England's relations vis-à-vis Prussia prove that she does not fundamentally oppose resistance to a European great power of superior military importance, as long as the foreign policy aims of this power are manifestly of a purely continental character. Or will one dispute that under Frederick the Great, Prussian military power was beyond all doubt by far the strongest in Europe? Let no one believe that England did not fight against the Prussia of that time only for the reason that, despite its military hegemony, she had to be numbered among the smaller states in terms of territorial size in Europe. Not at all. For when England herself had previously fought out her wars against the Dutch, Dutch territory in Europe was still considerably smaller than the Prussia of late Frederickian time. And one could really not talk of a threatening hegemony or dominant power position on the part of Holland. If nevertheless England pressed Holland hard in decades-long struggles the reason lay exclusively only in the thwarting of England's dominion of the sea and trade by Holland, as well as in the general colonial activity of the Dutch. Thus one should not deceive oneself: if the Prussian state had not so exclusively dedicated itself to purely continental aims, it would at all times have had England as its sharpest enemy regardless of the size of Prussia's purely military means in Europe or the danger of a hegemonization of Europe by Prussia. Our national-patriotic politicians, who do little thinking, have not seldom bitterly reproached the successors of the great Elector for neglecting the overseas possessions brought into being by the Elector, indeed for surrendering them and thereby having no interest in the maintenance and further construction of a Brandenburg-Prussian fleet. It was Prussia's good fortune, and later Germany's, that this was the case.

Nothing speaks so well for the outstanding statesmanship, especially of Frederick William I, than the fact that, with all the scanty and surely infinitely limited means of the small Prussian state, he concentrated exclusively on the promotion of the land army. Not only for the reason that through it this small state could maintain a superior position in one weapon, but was thereby also spared England's enmity. A Prussia following in Holland's footsteps would not have been able to fight the three Silesian wars with England as an added enemy at her back. Aside from the fact that any achievement of a real naval standing by the small Prussian state would necessarily miscarry in the long run in consequence of the territorial base of the motherland which was exceedingly limited and unfavorably situated in a military sense. Even at that time it would have been child's play for the English to rid themselves of a dangerous competitor in Europe through a general coalition war. In general the fact that the later Prussia could develop out of little Brandenburg and in turn a new German Reich out of the later Prussia was due only to that sagacious insight into the real power relations as well as into the possibilities of the Prussia of that time, so that the Hohenzollerns, up to the time of Bismarck, limited themselves almost exclusively to a strengthening of land power. It was the only clear, consequential policy. If German-Prussia and then later Germany in general wanted to go toward a future it could only be guaranteed by a supremacy on land which matched the English supremacy on the seas. It was Germany's misfortune that we slowly moved away from this insight and built up our land power insufficiently and instead went over to a naval policy whose end result had been inadequate anyway. Even the Germany of the post-Bismarckian period could not afford the luxury of creating and maintaining a superior armament on land and sea simultaneously. It has been one of the most important principles of all times that a nation recognize which weapon is most necessary and indispensable for the preservation of its existence, and then promote it to the extreme by staking all its means on it. England recognized and followed this principle. For England dominion of the seas was really the substance of her existence. Even the most brilliant military periods on the mainland, the most glorious wars, the most matchless military decisions could not move the English to see in land power for England anything but something ultimately subordinate, and to concentrate the whole strength of the nation on the maintenance of a superior dominion of the seas. In Germany, to be sure, we let ourselves be swept along by the great colonial waves of the nineteenth century, strengthened perhaps by romantic memories of the old Hansa as well as driven by the peaceful economic policy, to shelve the exclusive promotion of the land army and to take up the construction of a fleet. This policy acquired its final expression in the proposition, as preposterous as it was calamitous, "Our future lies on the water." No, exactly to the contrary, it lay and lies for us in Europe on land, just as exactly as the causes of our decline will always be of a purely continental character: our unfortunate territorial and terrible military-geographical position.

As long as Prussia limited herself to purely European aims in her foreign policy aspirations, she had no serious danger to fear from England. The objection that nevertheless a pro-French mood already prevailed in England in the year 1870-71 is not relevant and in any case signifies nothing at all. For at that time a pro-German attitude prevailed just as much in England; indeed France's action was branded as a sacrilege from the pulpit in English churches. Moreover, it was the official attitude adopted which is decisive. For it is entirely obvious that France will indeed have continual sympathies in a state of England's importance, all the more so as the influence of a country's press is not seldom exerted through foreign capital. France has always known how to mobilize sympathy for herself adroitly. Thus she has always played Paris as her most remarkable auxiliary weapon. But this did not take place only in England, for instance, but even in Germany. In the very middle of the war in *anno* 70/71 a not small clique was to be found in Berlin society, indeed at the Berlin court, who made no bones about their pro-French sympathies. At any rate they knew how to postpone the bombardment of Paris for a long time. And it is humanly understandable that English circles should have viewed German military success with mixed joy. But in any case they could not move the official attitude of the British government toward an intervention. Even the opinion that this is to be ascribed only to the fact that the rear was covered by Russia, which Bismarck had assured, changes nothing. For this covering of the rear was thought of primarily against Austria. If, however, England had given up her neutral attitude at that time, even Russia's covering of the rear would not have been able to avert an immense conflagration. For then Austria would naturally have been involved and, one way or the other, the success of the year 1871 would hardly have come to pass. As a matter of fact Bismarck had a continual quiet fear of meddling by other states not only in the war, but even in the peace negotiations. For what took place several years later vis-à-vis Russia, the intervention of other powers,* could have been staged against Germany by England just as well.

The course of the anti-German attitude of the English can be exactly followed. It parallels our development on the seas, rises with our colonial activity to an overt antipathy and finally ends up with our naval policy in a frank hatred. One cannot take it amiss that in England a really solicitous state leadership scented a threatening danger for the future in this development of a people as efficient as the Germans. We must never apply our German sins of omission as a measure for judging the actions of others. The frivolousness with which post-Bismarckian Germany allowed her position in terms of power politics to be threatened in Europe by France and Russia without undertaking any serious counter-measures, far from allows us to impute similar neglect to other powers or to denounce them in moral indignation if indeed they attend to the vital needs of their peoples better.

If prewar Germany had decided upon a continuance of the former Prussian continental policy instead of her peaceful world and economic policy with its fateful repercussions, then first of all she could have raised her land power to that superior height formerly enjoyed by the Prussian state, and secondly she need not have feared an unconditional enmity with England. For this much is sure: if Germany had used all the enormous means which she squandered on the fleet for the strengthening of her land army then her interests might have been fought for in a different way, at least on the decisive European battlefields. And the nation would have been spared seeing a land army, worse than inadequately armed, slowly bleed to death against an overwhelming world coalition while the navy, at least in its decisive combat units, rusted away in the harbors in order finally to terminate its existence in a more than ignominious surrender. Let us not find excuses for the leaders, but have the courage rather to admit that this lay in the very nature of such a weapon for us. For at the same time the field army was pulled out of one battle and hurled into another without regard to losses and any other

* Hitler refers here to the Congress of Berlin in 1878.—*T.T.*

154

hardships. The land army was really the German weapon, grown out of a hundred-year tradition, but in the end our fleet was only a romantic plaything, a parade piece that was built for its own sake and which again for its own sake could not be risked. The whole benefit which it brought us is disproportionate to the terrible enmity with which it saddled us.

If Germany had not taken this development, at the turn of the century we still could have reached an understanding with England, which at that time was ready for one. To be sure such an understanding would have lasted only if had been accompanied by a fundamental shift in our foreign policy goal. Even at the turn of the century Germany could have decided upon a resumption of the former Prussian continental policy and together with England prescribed the further development of world history. The objection of our eternal temporizers and doubters that this would nevertheless have been uncertain is based on nothing but personal opinions. English history up to now speaks against it in any case. By what right can such doubters presume that Germany could not have played the same role as Japan? The stupid phrase that Germany thereby would have hauled England's chestnuts out of the fire could just as much be applied to Frederick the Great who, ultimately, on European battlefields, helped to facilitate England's conflicts with France outside Europe. It is almost stupid to cite the further objection that nevertheless England one day would have gone against Germany. For then even in such a case Germany's position, following a successful defeat of Russia in Europe, would be better than it was at the start of the World War. On the contrary if the Russo-Japanese war had been fought in Europe between Germany and Russia, Germany would have received such a purely moral increase in power that for the next thirty years every other European power would have carefully weighed whether to break the peace and let itself be incited into a coalition against Germany. But all these objections always spring from the mentality of prewar Germany which itself as an opposition knew everything but did nothing.

The fact is, at that time England made an approach to Germany, and there is the further fact that Germany for her part could not make up her mind to emerge from the mentality of this eternal

155

temporizing and hesitation and come to a clear stand. What Germany refused at that time was solicitously tended to by Japan and thereby she achieved the fame of a world power in a relatively cheap way.

If nobody in Germany wanted to do this under any circumstances, then we necessarily should have joined the other side. Then we could have utilized the year 1904 or '05 in a conflict with France and had Russia at our rear. But these temporizers and delayers wanted that just as little. Out of sheer caution, sheer hesitation and sheer knowledge they were never able to establish what they really wanted at any hour. And only therein lies the superiority of English statesmanship, for that country is not ruled by such smart-alecks who can never brace themselves for an action, but by men who think naturally and for whom politics most surely is an art of the possible but who also take all possibilities by the forelock and really strike with them.

Once Germany, however, had shunned such a fundamental understanding with England, which, as already noted, would have made durable sense only if in Berlin a clear continental territorial-political aim had been arrived at, England began to organize the world resistance against the country threatening British interests as regards her dominion of the seas.

The World War did not proceed as had been thought at the beginning in view of our people's military efficiency, which was not presumed to be what it was even in England. To be sure Germany was finally overcome but only after the American Union had made its appearance on the battlefield and Germany had lost the support of her rear in consequence of the internal collapse of the homeland. But the actual English war aim had not been achieved thereby. Indeed the German threat to English supremacy on the seas was eliminated but the American threat, with a considerably stronger base, took its place. In the future the greatest danger to England would not be in Europe any more at all but in North America. In Europe itself at this time France is the state that is most dangerous to England. Her military hegemony has an especially threatening significance for England in consequence of the geographical position which France occupies vis-à-vis England. Not only for the reason that a great number of vitally important English centers seems to be almost defenselessly exposed to French aerial attacks, but even by means of artillery fire a number of English cities can be reached from the French coast. Indeed, if modern technology succeeds in producing a considerable increase in the firing power of the heaviest artillery then a bombardment of London from the French mainland does not lie beyond the limits of the possible. But it is even more important that a French submarine war against England would possess a wholly different basis than the earlier German one during the World War. France's broad encampment on two seas would make it very difficult to carry out sealing-off measures which could be easily successful vis-à-vis the confined triangle of water.

Whoever in present-day Europe tries to find natural enemies against England will always chance upon France and Russia. France as a power with continental political aims which in truth, however, are only a cover for very widely demarcated intentions of a general international political character. Russia as a threatening enemy of India and the possessor of oil sources which today have the same importance once possessed by iron and coal mines in past centuries.

If England herself remains true to her great world-political aims, her potential opponents will be France and Russia in Europe, and in the other parts of the world especially the American Union in the future.

In contrast no inducement exists to make eternal England's enmity against Germany. Otherwise English foreign policy would be determined by motives that lie far beyond all real logic and therefore could have a decisive influence on the determination of the political relations among nations perhaps only in the head of a German professor. No, in the future in England positions in accordance with purely expedient points of view will be taken up just as soberly as has happened for three hundred years. And just as for three hundred years allies could become England's enemies and enemies again become allies, so will this also be the case in the future as long as general and particular necessities call for it. If, however, Germany comes to a fundamentally new political orientation which no longer contradicts England's sea and trade interests but spends itself in continental aims, then a logical ground for England's enmity, which would then be just hostility for hostility's sake, would no longer exist. For even the European balance of power interests England only as long as it hinders the development of a world trade and sea power that may threaten England. There is no foreign policy leadership at all which is less determined by doctrines that bear no relation to life's realities than the English. A world empire does not come into being by means of a sentimental or purely theoretical policy.

Hence the sober perception of British interests will be determining for English foreign policy in the future too. Whoever cuts across these interests will thereby also be England's enemy in the future. Whoever does not touch them, his existence will also not be touched by England. And whoever can be useful to her from time to time will be invited on England's side regardless of whether he had been an enemy in the past or perhaps can again become one in the future.

Only a bourgeois-national German politician can manage to refuse a useful alliance for the reason that later, perhaps, it can end in enmity. To impute such an idea to an Englishman is an insult to the political instinct of this people.

Naturally if Germany does not set herself any political goal and we muddle through planlessly from one day to the other as up to now without any guiding thought; or if this goal lies in the restoration of the borders and territorial conditions of the year 1914 and thereby in the end lands into a policy of world trade, colonization and naval power, England's future enmity with us will indeed be certain. Then Germany will suffocate economically under her Dawes burdens, politically decay under her Locarno treaties, and increasingly weaken racially in order finally to terminate her life as a second Holland or a second Switzerland in Europe. This can certainly be achieved by our bourgeois-national and patriotic armchair politicians; for this all they need do is continue further along their present path of phrasemongering, shooting off their mouths in protests, making war on all Europe and then crawling cravenly into a hole before every act. This then is what the national-bourgeois-patriotic policy of Germany's resurgence means. Thus, just as our bourgeoisie in the course of barely sixty years has known how to degrade and to compromise the national concept, so in its decline does it destroy the beautiful concept of the fatherland by degrading it also to a mere phrase in its patriotic leagues.

To be sure, yet another important factor emerges in regard to

England's attitude toward Germany: the decisive influence world Jewry also possesses in England. Just as surely as Anglo-Saxonism itself can overcome its war-psychosis vis-à-vis Germany, world Jewry just as surely will neglect nothing to keep the old enmities alive so as to prevent a pacification of Europe from materializing and thereby enable it to set its Bolshevist destructive tendencies into motion amid the confusion of a general unrest.

We cannot discuss world policy without taking this most terrible power into account. Therefore I will deal especially with this problem further in this book.

XV

Certainly if England is under no compulsion to maintain her war-time enmity toward Germany forever on grounds of principle, Italy has even less grounds to do so. Italy is the second state in Europe that must not be fundamentally hostile to Germany. Indeed, her foreign policy aims need not cross with Germany's at all. On the contrary, with no other state does Germany have perhaps more interests in common than precisely with Italy, and conversely.

At the same time that Germany tried to achieve a new national unification, the same process also took place in Italy. To be sure the Italians lacked a central power of gradually growing, and ultimately towering, importance such as Germany in the making possessed in Prussia. But as German unification was primarily opposed by France and Austria as true enemies, so likewise did the Italian unification movement also have to suffer most under these two powers. The chief cause, of course, lay with the Hapsburg state which must have and did have a vital interest in the maintenance of Italy's internal dismemberment. Since a state of the size of Austria-Hungary is unthinkable without direct access to the sea, and the only territory which could be considered for this—at least in regard to its cities—was inhabited by Italians, Austria necessarily disapprovingly opposed the rise of a united Italian state for fear of the possible loss of this territory in case of the founding of an Italian national state. At that time even the boldest political aim of the Italian people could lie only in its national unification. This then perforce also conditioned the foreign policy attitude. Hence as Italian unification [that through Savoys] slowly took shape, Cavour, its brilliant great statesman, utilized all possibilities which could serve this particular aim. Italy owes the possibility of her unification to an extraordinarily cleverly chosen alliance policy. Its aim was primarily to bring about the paralysis of the chief enemy of unification, Austria-Hungary, indeed finally to induce this state to leave the north Italian provinces. Withal, even after the conclusion of the provisional unification of Italy there were more than 800,000 Italians in Austria-Hungary alone. The national aim of the further unification of people of Italian nationality was at first bound to undergo a postponement when for the first time there began to arise the dangers of an Italian-French estrangement. Italy decided to enter the Triple Alliance, chiefly in order to gain time for her inner consolidation.

The World War at last brought Italy into the camp of the Entente for reasons that I have already discussed. Thereby Italian unity had been carried a powerful step forward. Even today, however, it is not yet completed. For the Italian state, though, the great event was the elimination of the hated Hapsburg empire. To be sure, its place was taken by a south-Slav structure which already presented a danger hardly less great for Italy on the basis of general national viewpoints.

For just as little as the bourgeois-national and purely border-policy conception in Germany could in the long run satisfy our people's vital needs, equally little could the purely bourgeois-national unification policy of the Italian state satisfy the Italian people.

Like the German people the Italian people lives on a small soil surface which in part is scantily fertile. For centuries, indeed many centuries, this over-population has forced Italy to a permanent export of people. Even though a great part of these emigrants, as seasonal laborers, return to Italy in order to live there on their savings, this leads more than ever to a further aggravation of the situation. Not only is the population problem not solved thereby, but it is sharpened rather. Just as Germany through her export of goods fell into a state of dependence on the ability, potentiality and willingness of other powers and countries to receive these goods, likewise and exactly did Italy with her export of people. In both cases a closing of the receiving market, resulting from events of any kind whatsoever, perforce led to catastrophic consequences within these countries.

Hence Italy's attempt to master the problem of sustenance through an increase of her industrial activity cannot lead to any ultimate success because, at the outset, the lack of natural raw materials in the Italian motherland robs her in great measure of the required ability to compete.

Just as in Italy the conceptions of a formal bourgeois national policy are being overcome and a folkish feeling of responsibility is taking its place, likewise will this state also be forced to deviate from its former political conceptions in order to turn to a territorial policy on a grand scale.

The shore-basins of the Mediterranean Sea constitute, and hence remain, the natural area of Italian expansion. The more present-day Italy departs from her former unification policy and goes over to an imperialist policy the more will she fall into the ways of ancient Rome, not out of any presumption to power but out of deep, internal necessities. If today Germany seeks soil in east Europe this is not the sign of an extravagant hunger for power, but only the consequence of her need for territory. And if today Italy seeks to enlarge her influence on the shores of the Mediterranean basin and ultimately aims to establish colonies, it is also only the release ensuing from sheer necessity, out of a natural defense of interests. If the German prewar policy had not been struck with total blindness it would necessarily have supported and fostered this development with every means. Not only because it would have meant a natural strengthening of an ally, but because it might perhaps have offered the only possibility of drawing Italian interests away from the Adriatic Sea and thereby lessened the sources of irritation with Austria-Hungary. Such a policy, in addition, would have stiffened the most natural enmity which can ever exist, namely that between Italy and France, the repercussions of which would have strengthened the Triple Alliance in a favorable sense.

It was Germany's misfortune that at that time not only did the Reich leadership flatly fail in this respect but that, above all, public opinion—led on by insane German-national patriots and foreign policy dreamers—took a stand against Italy. Especially, moreover, for the reason that Austria discovered something unfriendly about the Italian operation in Tripoli. At that time, however, it appertained to the political wisdom of our national bourgeoisie to back every stupidity or baseness of Viennese diplomacy, indeed if possible to undertake stupid and base acts itself in order thereby to demonstrate the inner harmony and solidarity of this cordial alliance before the world in the best possible way.

Now Austria-Hungary is wiped out. But Germany has even less cause than before to regret a development of Italy which one day must necessarily proceed at the expense of France. For the more present-day Italy discovers her highest folkish tasks and the more, accordingly, she goes over to a territorial policy conceived along Roman lines the more must she run into the opposition of her greatest competitor in the Mediterranean Sea, France. France will never tolerate Italy's becoming the leading power in the Mediterranean. She will try to prevent this either through her own strength or through a system of alliances. France will lay obstacles in the path of Italy's development wherever possible, and finally she will not shrink from recourse to violence. Even the so-called kinship of these two Latin nations will change nothing on this score, for it is no closer than the kinship between England and Germany.

On top of that, in proportion as France declines in her own people's power, this state proceeds to the opening up of her reservoir of black people. Thus a danger of unimaginable proportions draws near for Europe. The idea of French Negroes, who can contaminate white blood, on the Rhine as cultural guards against Germany is so monstrous that it would have been regarded as completely impossible only a few decades ago. Surely France itself would suffer the greatest harm through this blood-pollution, but only if the other European nations remain conscious of the value of their white race. Viewed in purely military terms France can very well supplement her European formations, and as the World War has shown, also commit them effectively. Finally, this completely un-French black army indeed vouchsafes a certain defense against communist demonstrations, since utter subordination in all situations will be easier to preserve in an army which is not at all linked by blood to the French people. This development entails its greatest

163

danger for Italy first of all. If the Italian people wants to shape its future according to its own interests it will ultimately have black armies, mobilized by France, as its enemy. Thus it cannot in the least lie in Italy's interest to be in a state of enmity with Germany, something which even in the best of cases cannot make a profitable contribution to the shaping of Italian life in the future. On the contrary, if any state can finally bury war enmity, this state is Italy. Italy has no inherent interest in a further oppression of Germany if, for the future, both states want to attend to their most natural tasks.

Bismarck had already perceived this fortunate circumstance. More than once did he confirm the complete parallel between German and Italian interests. It was he who even then pointed out that the Italy of the future must seek her development on the shores of the Mediterranean Sea, and it was he who further ascertained the harmony of German and Italian interests by stressing that only France could think of disturbing this shaping of Italian life, whereas Germany was bound to welcome it from her viewpoint. Actually in the whole future he sees no necessary cause for an estrangement, let alone enmity, between Italy and Germany. If Bismarck rather than Bethmann-Hollweg had guided Germany's destiny before the World War, indeed, even this terrible enmity, incurred only on account of Austria, would never have come to pass.

Moreover, with Italy as with England, it is a positive fact that a continental expansion of Germany in north Europe is no threat and thereby can give no cause for an estrangement by Italy against Germany. Conversely, for Italy the most natural interests speak against any further increase of French hegemony in Europe.

Hence Italy, above all, would warrant consideration in terms of an alliance relation with Germany.

The enmity with France has already become obvious ever since fascism in Italy brought a new idea of the state and with it a new will to the life of the Italian people. Therefore France, through a whole system of alliances, is not only trying to strengthen herself for a possible conflict with Italy but also to hamper and separate Italy's possible friends. The French aim is clear. A French system of states is to be built that reaches from Paris via Warsaw, Prague, Vienna up to Belgrade. The attempt to draw Austria into this system is in no way as hopeless as it may seem at first sight. In view of the dominating character of the influence which Vienna with its two million inhabitants exerts over the rest of Austria, which encompasses only six million people, this country's policy will always be determined primarily by Vienna. The fact that an alliance with Paris is far more likely as such than one with Italy lies in the cosmopolitan nature [character] of Vienna which has been revealed even more pointedly in the last decade. This was already taken care of by the manipulation of public opinion guaranteed by the Vienna press. But this activity threatens to become especially effective since this press, with the help of the clamor over the South Tyrol, has also succeeded in stirring up the completely instinctless bourgeois-national province against Italy. Thus a danger of an incommensurable extent draws near. For the Germans, more than any other people, can be brought to the most incredible, in reality truly suicidal, decisions by an agitational press campaign conducted consistently over many years.

If, however, France succeeds in fitting Austria into the chain of her "friendship," Italy one day will be forced into a two-front war or she must again renounce a real representation of the interests of the Italian people. In both cases for Germany there is the danger that a possible German ally is finally excluded for an unpredictable period of time, and that France thus increasingly becomes the master of Europe's fate.

Let no one indulge in any illusions as to what this entails for Germany. Our bourgeois-national border politicians and protesters from the patriotic leagues will then have their hands full in order again, in the name of national honor, to eliminate the traces of the mistreatments which they would have to endure from France thanks to their farsighted policy.

Since the National Socialist movement concerns itself with ideas of foreign policy I have tried to educate it to become a bearer of a clear foreign policy aim by a consideration of all the arguments discussed. It is unjust to raise the reproach that this is primarily the task of the government, in a state, first of all, the official governments of which come from the bosom of parties who neither have any cognizance of Germany nor want a happy future for this

Germany. Since those who were responsible for arranging the November crime have become qualified to govern, it is no longer the interests of the German nation which are represented but instead those of the wrongly acting parties. In general we cannot very well expect the promotion of Germany's vital needs by people to whom the fatherland and the nation are but means to an end and which, if necessary, they shamelessly sacrifice for their own interests. Indeed the instinct of self-preservation of these people and parties, so often visible, in truth by itself speaks against any resurgence of the German nation, since the freedom-struggle for German honor perforce would mobilize forces which must lead to the fall and destruction of the former defilers of German honor. There is no such thing as a struggle for freedom without a general national resurgence. But a resurgence of the national conscience and the national honor is unthinkable without first bringing those responsible for the previous degradation to justice. The naked instinct of self-preservation will force these degenerate elements and their parties to thwart all steps that could lead to a real resurrection of our people. And the seeming insanity of many acts of these Herostrats of our people, once we properly gauge the inner motives, becomes a planned, adroit, albeit infamous and contemptible, action.

In a time such as this when public life acquires its shape from parties of this kind and is represented solely by people of inferior character, it is the duty of a national reform movement to go its own way even in foreign policy which some day, according to all human prediction and reason, must lead to the success and happiness of the fatherland. Hence so far as the reproach of conducting a policy that does not correspond to official foreign policy comes from the Marxist-democratic-Center camp, it can be set aside with the contempt it deserves. But if bourgeois-national and so-called fatherland circles raise it, this is really only the expression and the symbol of the state of mind of professional joiners which exerts itself only in protests and simply cannot seriously grasp that another movement possesses the indestructible will ultimately to become a power, and that in a prevision of this fact it already undertakes the necessary education of this power.

Since the year 1920 I have tried with all means and most persistently to accustom the National Socialist movement to the idea of an alliance among Germany, Italy and England. This was very difficult, especially in the first years after the war, since the "God punish England" standpoint, first and foremost, still robbed our people of any capacity for clear and sober thinking in the sphere of foreign policy and continued to hold it prisoner.

The situation of the young movement was infinitely difficult even vis-à-vis Italy, especially since an unprecedented reorganization of the Italian people set in under the leadership of the brilliant statesman Benito Mussolini, which drew the protest of all the states directed by Freemasonry. For whereas up to the year 1922 the fabricators of official German opinion took altogether no notice of the sufferings of those parts of our people severed from Germany through their crimes, they now suddenly began to honor the South Tyrol with their attention. With all the means of a cunning journalism and a mendacious dialectic the South Tyrol problem was blown up into a question of extraordinary importance so that in the end Italy incurred a proscription in Germany and Austria conferred on none other of the victor states. If the National Socialist movement honestly wanted to represent its foreign policy mission, sustained by the conviction of the unconditional necessity of the same, it could not draw back from the struggle against this system of lies and confusion. Thus at the same time it could not count on any allies but instead had to be guided by the idea that one should sooner renounce a cheap popularity rather than act against a perceived truth, a necessity that lay before one, and the voice of one's conscience. And even if one would thereby be defeated, this would still be more honorable than to participate in a crime that had been seen through.

When in the year 1920 I pointed to the possibility of a later association with Italy, all the prerequisites thereto, at least at first, actually seemed to be lacking. Italy was in the circle of the victor states and shared in the actual or merely presumed advantages of this situation. In the years 1919 and 1920 there seemed no prospect at all that the inner structure of the Entente would loosen in any predictable time. The powerful world coalition still placed a great value on showing that it was a self-sufficient guarantor of the victory and thus also of the peace. The difficulties which had already come to light in connection with the drawing up of the peace treaties came all the less to the consciousness of a broad public opinion since the directors of an adroitly staged production knew how to preserve the impression of complete unity, at least outwardly. This common action was based just as much on the public opinion which had been created by a generally homogeneous war propaganda as it was on the still insecure fear of the German giant. Only slowly did the outside world get a glimpse of the dimensions of Germany's inner decay. A further reason contributed to the seemingly almost indissoluble solidarity of the victor states: the hope of the individual states that they would thus not be overlooked when the time came to share the spoils. Finally there was the further fear that if at that time a state should actually withdraw, Germany's fate, nevertheless, would have taken no other course, and then perhaps France alone would be the sole beneficiary of our collapse. For in Paris they naturally never gave a thought to bringing about a change in the attitude toward Germany which had been set in motion during the war. "For me the peace is the continuation of the war." With this statement white-haired old Clemenceau expressed the French people's real intentions.

The complete planlessness of German intentions confronted this at least seeming inner solidity of the coalition of victors, the immovable aim of which, inspired by France, was the complete annihilation of Germany even after the event. Next to the contemptible villainy of those who in their country, against all truth and against their own conscience, put the blame for the war on Germany and insolently deduced a justification for the enemy's extortions therefrom, stood a partly intimidated, partly uncertain national side which believed that now after the ensuing collapse it could help matters by means of the most painful possible reconstruction of the nation's past. We lost the war in consequence of a lack of national passion against our enemies. The opinion in national circles was that we must replace this harmful deficiency and anchor this hatred against the former enemies in the peace. At the same time it was noteworthy that from the start this hatred was concentrated more against England, and later Italy, than against France. Against England because, thanks to the Bethmann-Hollwegian soporific policy nobody had believed in a war with England up to the last hour. Therefore her entry into the war was viewed as an extraordinarily shameful crime against loyalty and faith. In the case of Italy the hatred was even more understandable in view of the political thoughtlessness of our German people. They had been so imprisoned in the mist and fog of the Triple Alliance by official government circles that even Italy's non-intervention for the benefit of Austria-Hungary and Germany was viewed as a breach of loyalty. And they saw a boundless perfidy in the later joining up of the Italian people with our enemies. This accumulated hatred was discharged in the typically bourgeois-national fulmination and battle cry: "God punish England." Since God is just as much on the side of the stronger and the more determined, as well as preferably on the side of those who are cleverer, He manifestly refused to inflict this punishment. Nevertheless, at least during the war, whipping up of our national passion by every means was not only allowed but obviously called for. It was only a hindrance in that we were blinded by it to the real actualities, although the passion was never fanned too high among us. In politics there is no standpoint of contrariness, and therefore even during the war it was wrong to draw no other consequences, especially from Italy's entry into the world coalition, except those of a flaming anger and indignation. For, on the contrary, we should have had the duty then especially to keep on reexamining the possibilities of the situation in order to come to those decisions that might have warranted consideration for saving the threatened German nation. For with Italy's entry into the front of the Entente an extraordinary aggravation of the war situation was unavoidable, not only in consequence of the increase in terms of arms which the Entente acquired but much more rather in consequence of the moral strengthening which necessarily lay in the emergence of such a power on the side of the world coalition being formed, especially for France. In terms of duty the nation's political leaders at that time perforce should have decided, cost what it may, to put an end to the two- and three-front war. Germany was not responsible for the further maintenance of the corrupt, slovenly Austrian state. Nor did the German soldier fight for the family power policy of

169

the hereditary house of Hapsburg. This at best lay in the mind of our noncombatant hurrah-shouters but not in that of those at the front shedding their blood. The sufferings and hardships of the German musketeers were already immeasurable in the year 1915. These sufferings could be demanded for the future and the preservation of our German people but not for the salvation of the Hapsburg big-power megalomania. It was a monstrous idea to let millions of German soldiers bleed in a hopeless war only so that a dynasty could preserve a state, the most private dynastic interests of which for centuries had been anti-German. This insanity will become completely understandable to us in its entirety only if we keep in view that the best German blood had to be shed so that, in the most favorable case, the Hapsburgs might again have another chance to denationalize the German people in peacetime. We not only had to undertake the most monstrous bloodshed on two fronts for this madness, which screamed to heaven, no, we were even duty bound again and again to fill the holes which treason and corruption had torn in our worthy ally's front with German flesh and blood. And thereby we made this sacrifice for a dynasty which itself was ready to leave its all-sacrificing ally in the lurch at the first opportunity which offered itself. And who indeed later did just this. To be sure our bourgeois-national fatherland patriots speak as little of the betrayal as they do of the continuous betrayal of the Austrian troops of Slavic nationality allied with us who went over to the enemy's side in whole regiments and brigades, in order finally in their own legions to join the fight against those who had been dragged into this dreadful misfortune by the operations of their state. Moreover, by itself Austria-Hungary would never have participated in a war which might have involved Germany. That here or there some perhaps really believed to gain protection from the Triple Alliance, grounded in reciprocity, can be ascribed only to the boundless ignorance of Austrian conditions which generally prevailed in Germany. The worst disappointment for Germany would have materialized had the World War broken out on account of Germany. The Austrian state, with its Slav majority and with its Hapsburg ruling house, fundamentally anti-German and anti-Reich oriented, would never have taken up arms to defend and assist Germany against all the rest of the world, as Germany stupidly did. As a matter of fact vis-à-vis Austria-Hungary Germany had but one duty to fulfill, namely: to save the German element of this state by all means and to eliminate the most degenerate, most guilt-laden dynasty that the German people ever had to endure.

For Germany, Italy's entry into the World War perforce should have been the occasion for a fundamental revision of her attitude vis-à-vis Austria-Hungary. It is not a political act, let alone an expression of the sagacity and competence of political leaders, in such a case to find no other answer than sullen indignation and impotent rage. Such a thing is usually harmful even in private life, but in political life it is worse than a crime. It is an act of stupidity.

And even if this attempt at a change of the former German attitude had led to no success, it at least would have absolved the nation's political leadership from the guilt of not having tried it. In any case, after Italy's entry into the World War, Germany should have tried to put an end to the two-front war. She should then have striven for a separate peace with Russia, not only on the basis of a renunciation of any utilization of the successes in the East already achieved by German arms but even, if necessary, of a sacrifice of Austria-Hungary. Only the complete dissociation of German policy from the task of saving the Austrian state and its exclusive concentration on the task of helping the German people could still afford a possibility of victory, according to human appraisals.

Moreover with the demolition of Austria-Hungary, the incorporation of nine million German-Austrians into the Reich as such would have been a more worthwhile success before history and for our people's future than the gain, doubtful in its consequences, of a few French coal and iron mines. But it must be stressed again and again that the task—even of a German foreign policy that is only bourgeois-national—should not have been the preservation of the Hapsburg state but exclusively the salvation of the German nation, including the nine million Germans in Austria. Otherwise nothing else at all, indeed absolutely nothing else.

As is known, the reaction of the Reich's leaders to the situation created by Italy's entry into the World War was quite different. They tried more than ever to save the Austrian state with its deserting

Slavic brothers of the alliance by staking German blood in a still greater measure and in the homeland by calling down heaven's revenge on the faithless erstwhile ally. In order to cut themselves off from any possibility of ending the two-front war they let the artful and cunning Vienna diplomacy induce them to found the Polish state. Thereby any hope of arriving at an understanding with Russia, which naturally could have been obtained at the expense of Austria-Hungary, was shrewdly prevented by the Hapsburgs. Thus the German soldier from Bavaria, Pomerania, Westphalia, Thuringia and East Prussia, from Brandenburg, Saxony and from the Rhine was given the high honor, in the most terrible, bloody battles of world history, to sacrifice his life by the hundreds of thousands, not for the salvation [formation] of the German nation, but for the formation of a Polish state to which, in case of a favorable outcome of the World War, the Hapsburgs would have given a representative and which then would have been an eternal enemy for Germany.

Bourgeois-national state policy. But if this reaction to the Italian step had already been an unforgivable absurdity during the war, the preservation of this emotional reaction to the Italian step after the war was a still greater, capital stupidity.

To be sure Italy was in the coalition of victor states even after the war and hence also on the side of France. But this was natural, for Italy had certainly not entered the war out of pro-French feelings. The determining force which drove the Italian people to it was exclusively the hatred against Austria and the visible possibility of being able to benefit their own Italian interests. This was the reason for the Italian step and not any kind of fantastic emotional feeling for France. As a German one can be deeply pained that Italy took far-reaching steps now that the collapse of her hated centuries-old enemy has taken place, but one must not let it deprive his mind of sound reason. Fate had changed. Once Austria had more than 800,000 Italians under her rule and now 200,000 Austrians fell under Italy's rule. The cause of our pain is that these 200,000 who interest us are of German nationality.

Neither the future aims of a national nor of a folkishly conceived

Italian policy are fulfilled by the elimination of the eternally latent Austrian-Italian conflict. On the contrary the enormous increase of the self- and power-consciousness of the Italian people by the war and especially by fascism will only increase its strength to pursue greater aims. Thus the natural conflicts of interest between Italy and France will increasingly appear. We could have counted on that and hoped for it as early as the year 1920. As a matter of fact, the first signs of an internal disharmony between the two states were already visible at that time. Whereas the south-Slav instincts for a further curtailment of the Austrian-German element were sure of France's undivided sympathy, the Italian attitude already at the time of the liberation of Carinthia from the Slavs was at least very well disposed toward the German element. This inner shift vis-à-vis Germany was also displayed in the attitude of the Italian commissions in Germany itself, most pointedly on the occasion of tl.e struggles in Upper Silesia. At any rate at that time one could already discern the beginning of an inner estrangement, albeit only faint at first, between the two Latin nations. According to all human logic and reason and on the basis of all the experiences of history hitherto, this estrangement must increasingly deepen and one day end in an overt struggle. Whether she likes it or not, Italy will have to fight for her state's existence and future against France, just as Germany itself. It is not necessary for this that France always be in the foreground of operations. But she will pull the wires of those whom she has cleverly brought into a state of financial and military dependence on her, or with whom she seems to be linked by parallel interests. The Italian-French conflict can just as well begin in the Balkans, as it may find its end on the lowlands of Lombardy.

In view of this compelling probability of a later enmity of Italy with France, already in the year 1920 this very state came under consideration primarily as a future ally for Germany. The probability increased to certainty when with the victory of fascism the weak Italian government, which ultimately was subject to international influences, was eliminated and a regime took its place which had nailed the exclusive representation of Italian interests as a slogan on its banners. A weak Italian-democratic-bourgeois government, by disregarding Italy's real future tasks, could perhaps have maintained an artificial relation with France. But a nationally conscious and responsible Italian regime, never. The struggle of the Third Rome for the future of the Italian people acquired its historic declaration on the day when the fasces became the symbol of the Italian state. Thus one of the two Latin nations will have to leave its place in the Mediterranean Sea, whereas the other will acquire supremacy as the prize of this struggle.

As a nationally conscious and rationally thinking German, I firmly hope and strongly wish that this state may be Italy and not France.

Thereby my attitude toward Italy will be induced by motives of future expectations and not by sterile reminiscences of the war.

The standpoint "Declarations of war are accepted here" as an inscription on troop transports was a good sign of the victorious confidence of the peerless old army. As a political proclamation, however, it is a mad stupidity. Today it is even more mad if one takes the position that for Germany no ally can warrant consideration which stood on the enemy's side in the World War and shared in the spoils of the World War at our expense. If Marxists, Democrats and Centrists raise such a thought to a leitmotif of their political activity this is clearly for the reason that this most degenerate coalition does not desire a resurgence of the German nation ever. But if national-bourgeois and fatherland circles take over such ideas, then that's the limit. For let one name any power at all which could possibly be an ally in Europe and which has not enriched itself territorially at our expense or that of our allies of that time. On the basis of this standpoint France is excluded from the outset because she stole Alsace-Lorraine and wants to steal the Rhineland, Belgium because it possesses Eupen and Malmedy, England because even if she does not possess our colonies, at least she administers them in large part. And any child knows what this means in the life of nations. Denmark is excluded because she took North Schleswig, Poland because she is in possession of West Prussia and Upper Silesia and parts of East Prussia, Czechoslovakia, because she oppresses almost four million Germans, Rumania because she likewise

174

has annexed more than a million Germans, Yugoslavia because she has nearly 600,000 Germans, and Italy because today she calls the South Tyrol her own.

Thus for our national-bourgeois and patriotic circles the alliance possibilities are altogether impossible. But then they do not need them at all. For through the flood of their protests and the rumble of their hurrahs they will in part stifle the resistance of the other parts of the world, and in part overthrow it. And then without any allies, indeed without any weapons, supported only by the clamorousness of their glib tongue, they will retrieve the stolen territories, let England subsequently still be punished by God, but chastise Italy and deliver her to the deserved contempt of the whole world—so far as up to this point they have not been hanged on lampposts by their own momentary foreign-policy allies, the Bolshevist and Marxist Jews.

At the same time it is noteworthy that our national circles of bourgeois and patriotic origin never at all realize that the strongest proof of the fallacy of their attitude toward foreign policy lies in the concurrence of Marxists, Democrats and Centrists, above all especially in the concurrence of Jewry. But one must know our German bourgeoisie well in order immediately to know why this is so. They are all infinitely happy at least to have found an issue in which the presumed unity of the German people seems to be effected. No matter if this concerns a stupidity. Despite this it is infinitely comforting for a courageous bourgeois and fatherland politician to be able to talk in tones of national struggle without receiving a punch on the jaw for it from the nearest Communist. That they are spared this only for the reason that their political conception is just as sterile in national terms as it is valuable in Jewish-Marxist terms either does not occur to these people or it is concealed in the deepest recesses of their being. The extent which the corruption of lies and cowardice has assumed among us is something unheard of.

When in the year 1920 I undertook to orient the foreign policy position of the movement toward Italy, I at first ran into complete incomprehension on the part of national circles, as well as in so-called fatherland circles. It was simply incomprehensible to these people how, contrary to the general duty of continual protests, one could formulate a political idea which—taken practically—signified the intrinsic liquidation of one of the enmities of the World War. In general, national circles found it beyond comprehension that I did not want to place the main weight of national activity on protests which were trumpeted to the skies in front of the Feldherrenhalle in Munich, or somewhere else, now against Paris, then again against London or also against Rome, but wanted to place it instead on the elimination first within Germany of those responsible for the collapse. A flaming protest demonstration against Paris also took place in Munich on the occasion of the Paris *diktat* which, to be sure, must have caused M. Clemenceau little worry. But it induced me to elaborate with all vigor the National Socialist attitude in opposition to this protest mania. France had only done what every German could know and perforce should have known. Were I myself a Frenchman I would have supported Clemenceau as a matter of course. To bark permanently at an overpowering adversary from a distance is as undignified as it is idiotic. On the contrary, the national opposition of the fatherland circles should have bared its teeth at those in Berlin who were responsible for, and guilty of, the terrible catastrophe of our collapse. To be sure, it was more comfortable to scream against Paris curses which could not be actualized in view of the factual conditions, than to stand up against Berlin with deeds.

This also applied especially to the representatives of that Bavarian government policy, who, to be sure, sufficiently exhibit the nature of their brilliance by the facts of their success up to now. For the very men who continually asserted the desire to preserve Bavaria's sovereignty, and who at the same time also had in view maintenance of the right to conduct foreign policy, should primarily have been obliged to put forth a possible foreign policy of such sort that Bavaria, thereby, could of necessity have obtained leadership of a real national opposition in Germany conceived in its grand aspects. In view of the complete inconsistency of Reich policy or of the deliberate intention to ignore all real avenues of success, it is precisely the Bavarian state that should have risen to the role of spokesman for a foreign policy which, according to human prediction, might one day have brought an end to Germany's dreadful isolation.

But even in these circles they confronted the foreign policy conception of an association with Italy, as espoused by me, with a complete and stupid thoughtlessness. Instead of thus rising in a bold way to the role of spokesmen and guardians of the highest national German interests for the future, they preferred from time to time, with one eye blinking toward Paris while the other was raised up to heaven, to asseverate their loyalty to the Reich on the one hand, and on the other their determination nevertheless to save Bavaria by letting the fires of Bolshevism burn out in the north. Yes, indeed, the Bavarian state has entrusted the representation of its sovereign rights to intellectual characters of a wholly special greatness.

In view of such a general mentality it should surprise nobody that from the very first day my foreign policy conception encountered, if not direct rejection, at least a total lack of understanding. Frankly speaking, I expected nothing else at that time. I still took account of the general war psychosis and strove only to instill a sober philosophy of foreign policy into my own movement.

At that time I did not yet have to endure any kind of overt attacks on account of my Italian policy. The reason for this probably lay on the one hand in the fact that for the moment it was held to be completely devoid of danger, and on the other that Italy herself likewise had a government subject to international influences. Indeed, in the background it was perhaps even hoped that this Italy could succumb to the Bolshevist plague, and then she would be highly welcome as an ally, at least for our Left circles.

Besides, on the Left at that time one could not very well take a position against the elimination of war enmity, since in this very camp they were anyhow making constant efforts to extirpate the hateful, demeaning and—for Germany—so unjustified feeling of hatred born of the war. It would not have been easy to launch a criticism against me from these circles over a foreign policy conception, which as a prerequisite for its realization would after all have caused at least the removal of the war hatred between Germany and Italy.

177

I must, however, stress once more that perhaps the main reason why I found so little positive resistance lay for my enemies in the presumed harmlessness, unviability and thereby also the non-dangerous character of my action.

This situation changed almost in one stroke when Mussolini had begun the March on Rome. As if by a magic word the running fire of poisoning and slander against Italy by the entire Jewish press began from this hour on. And only after the year 1922 was the South Tyrol question raised and made into a pivotal point of German-Italian relations, whether the South Tyroleans themselves wanted it so or not. It did not take long before even Marxists became the representatives of a national opposition. And now one could experience the unique spectacle of Jews and folkish-Germans, Social Democrats and members of the patriotic leagues, Communists and national bourgeois, arm in arm, spiritually marching across the Brenner in order to carry out the reconquest of this territory in mighty battles but, to be sure, without the shedding of blood. A charm of a wholly special character was further added to this bold national front by the fact that even those *urbajuwarischen** representatives of Bavarian sovereign rights, whose spiritual forefathers over a hundred years before had surrendered the good Andreas Hofer to the French and let him be shot, also vigorously interested themselves in the freedom struggle for the country of Andreas Hofer.

Since the influence of the Jewish-press gang, and the national-bourgeois and patriotic dunderheads who run after them, has really succeeded in blowing up the South Tyrol problem to the dimensions of a vital question of the German nation, I see myself induced to take a detailed position toward it.

As has already been emphasized, the old Austrian state had over 850,000 Italians within its borders. Incidentally, the data on nationalities as established by the Austrian census was not wholly accurate. Namely, the count was not made according to the nationality of the individual but rather according to the language he specified as spoken. Obviously this could not give a completely clear picture, but it is in the nature of the weakness of the national bourgeoisie

---

* Out-and-out Bavarian particularist.—*Trans.*

gladly to deceive itself over the real situation. If one does not learn of a matter or at least if it is not talked about openly, then it also does not exist. Ascertained on the basis of such a procedure, the Italians, or better, the people who spoke Italian, in large measure lived in the Tyrol. According to the census figures of the year 1910 the Tyrol had . . . . inhabitants, of whom . . . . per cent were counted as speaking the Italian language, while the rest were counted as German or in part also Ladin. Consequently around . . . . Italians were in the archduchy of Tyrol. Since this whole number is allotted to the territory occupied today by Italians, the ratio of Germans to Italians in the whole part of the territory of the Tyrol occupied by Italians consequently is one of . . . . Germans to . . . . Italians.

It is necessary to establish this because not a few people in Germany, thanks to the mendacity of our press, have no idea at all that in the area understood by the concept South Tyrol actually two thirds of the inhabitants living there are Italians, and one third German. Thus whoever seriously advocates the reconquest of the South Tyrol would bring about a change of things only to the extent that instead of having 200,000 Germans under Italian rule, he would bring 400,000 Italians under German rule.

To be sure the German element in the South Tyrol is now concentrated primarily in the northern part, whereas the Italian element inhabits the south. Thus if someone would find a solution that is just in a national sense, he must first of all completely exclude the concept South Tyrol from the general discussion. For one cannot war on the Italians on moral grounds because they have taken an area in which 200,000 Germans live next to 400,000 Italians if we ourselves, conversely, want to win this territory again for Germany as a redress of this injustice, that is if we want to commit a still greater injustice than is the case with Italy.

Thus the call for a reconquest of the South Tyrol will have the same moral faults in it which we now discover in the Italian rule in the South Tyrol. Hence this call also loses its moral justification. With this still other viewpoints can be asserted, which then must speak for a regaining of the whole South Tyrol. Thus on the basis of morally justified feelings we can, at most, advocate the regaining of that part which is actually inhabited by an overwhelming majority of Germans. This is a spatially limited area of . . . . square kilometers. Even in this, however, there are around 190,000 Germans, 64,000 Italians and Ladins and 24,000 other aliens so that the completely German territory encompasses hardly 160,000 Germans.

At the present time there is hardly a border which does not cut Germans off from the motherland just as in the South Tyrol. Indeed, in Europe alone not less than . . . . million Germans all told are separated from the Reich. Of these . . . . million live under out-and-out alien rule and only . . . . million in German Austria and Switzerland, though under conditions that at least for the moment pose no threat to the nationality. At the same time, here are a whole series of cases involving aggregates of a quite different numerical character as compared to our folkdom in the South Tyrol.

As terrible as this fact is for our people, just so guilty of it are those who today raise their hue and cry over the South Tyrol. Just as little, at any rate, can we make the fate of all the rest of the Reich dependent simply on the interests of these lost territories, let alone on the wishes of one of them, even by taking over a purely bourgeois border policy.

For one thing must first of all be rejected most sharply: there is no holy German people in the South Tyrol as the patriotic leaguers foolishly prattle. Rather, all who must be reckoned as belonging to German folkdom must be equally holy to it. It won't do to appraise a South Tyrolean higher than a Silesian, East Prussian or West Prussian who is enslaved under Polish rule. It also won't do to regard a German in Czechoslovakia as more worthwhile than a German in the Saar territory or also in Alsace-Lorraine. The right to grade the German element of the severed territories according to special values could, at best, grow out of an analytical examination of their specific decisive and dominant fundamental racial values. But this is the very measure which the protest groups against Italy apply least of all. For the Tyroleans in the territories now separated too, it could yield no higher credit factor than, let's say, for an East or a West Prussian.

Now the foreign policy task of the German Reich as such cannot be determined by the interests of the parts split off from the Reich.

For in reality these interests will not be served thereby since practical help indeed presupposes the regained power of the motherland. Hence the sole viewpoint that warrants consideration in regard to the foreign policy position can be only that of the fastest and earliest restoration of the independence and freedom of the remaining part of the nation united under a government.

In other words this means that even if a German foreign policy were cognizant of no aim other than the salvation of the "holy people in South Tyrol," that is the 190,000 Germans who can really come under consideration, first the prerequisite thereto would be the achievement of Germany's political independence as well as means of military power. For it should be rather clear after all that the Austrian protest state will not wrest the South Tyrol from the Italians. But it must be equally clear that even if German foreign policy knew no aim other than the actual liberation of the South Tyrol, its actions must especially then be determined by such viewpoints and factors which guarantee the regaining of the means of political and military power. Thus we should surely not place the South Tyrol in the focal point of foreign policy considerations but, on the contrary, especially then must we be dominated and guided by those ideas which in fact allow us to smash the existing world coalition directed against Germany. For ultimately, even through Germany, the South Tyrol will not be restored to the German element by the droning of a Tibetan prayer-wheel of protests and indignation but by the commitment of the sword.

Thus if Germany herself were to have this aim she must nevertheless ever and again look first of all for an ally who would furnish help for the gaining of German power. Now one can say that France could be considered in this case. As a National Socialist, I however oppose this most sharply.

It may well be that France would declare herself ready to allow Germany to march with her as an ally against Italy. Indeed it can even be that in gracious recognition of our blood-sacrifice and as meager bandages for our wounds they would award the South Tyrol to us. But what would such a victory mean for Germany? Could our nation, for instance, live then because it possesses 200,000 more South Tyroleans? Or does one not believe that France, once she has defeated her Latin competitor in the Mediterranean with

181

German military help, would surely turn once more against Germany? Or in any case that she would surely pursue her old political aim of the liquidation of Germany?

No, if for Germany there remains any choice between France and Italy, then, according to all human reason Italy alone warrants consideration for Germany. For a victory with France over Italy will bring us the South Tyrol and a stronger France to boot as a subsequent enemy. A victory over France with Italy's help will bring us Alsace-Lorraine at the least, and at most, the freedom to carry out a genuine large-scale territorial policy. And in the long run it is through this alone that Germany can live in the future, and not through South Tyrol. Nor will it do to choose one among all the severed territories, and indeed the one most unimportant to us in a vital sense, and to stake the total interests of a nation of 70,000,000 people, actually to renounce its future, just so that wretched fantastic German hurrah-patriots can obtain a momentary gratification. And all this on account of a sheer phantom, for in reality the South Tyrol would be as little helped thereby as it is now.

The National Socialist movement as such must educate the German people to the effect that it must not shrink from staking its blood for the sake of shaping its life. But, likewise, must our people be educated to the effect that such a staking of their blood, at least in future history, must never again take place for the sake of phantoms.

Let our protest patriots and fatherland leaguers for once please say how they envisage the reconquest of the South Tyrol other than by military violence. Let them, for once, summon up the honesty to avow, if they seriously believe it, that one day Italy—made mellow simply by their verbiage and heated protests—will hand over the South Tyrol, or whether they are not also convinced that a state with some existing national consciousness will give up a territory for which it had fought for four long years only under the compulsion of a military decision. Let them not always prattle that we, or I, had renounced the South Tyrol. These infamous liars know very well that, at least as far as regards my own person, I fought at the front at the time when the fate of the South Tyrol was being decided, something which not a few of the present-day meeting-protesters neglected to do at that time. And that at the same time, however, the forces with which our patriotic leaguers and national bourgeoisie make a common foreign policy and agitate against Italy, sabotaged the victory with every means, that international Marxism, democracy and the Center even in peacetime neglected nothing in order to weaken and paralyze the military power of our people, and that finally they organized a revolution during the war which necessarily led to the collapse of the German homeland and with it of the German army.

The South Tyrol was also lost to the German people through the activity of these people and the accursed weakness and impotence of our present-day bourgeois manic protesters. It is a contemptible falsification on the part of these so-called national patriots if today they talk about a renunciation of the South Tyrol. No, dear gentlemen, don't twist and squirm in such a cowardly way over the right word. Don't be too cowardly to come right out and say that today it could only be a question of the conquest of the South Tyrol. For the renunciation, gentlemen of the national leagues, was effected by your worthy present-day allies, the one-time Marxist betrayers of their country, with all legal governmental forms. And the only ones who had the courage to take an open position against this crime at that time were not you, esteemed national leaguers and bourgeois diplomatists, but rather the small National Socialist movement and primarily myself. Indeed, sirs, when you were so quiet that nobody in Germany had an idea of your existence, so deeply had you crawled off into your mouse holes, it was then in the years 1919 and 1920 that I came forth against the shame of signing the peace treaties—and not secretly, behind four walls, but publicly. At that time, however, you were still so cowardly that never once did you dare to come to one of our meetings for fear of being cudgeled by your present foreign policy allies, the Marxist streettramps.

The men who signed the peace treaty of St. Germain were as little National Socialists as the signers of the peace treaty of Versailles. They were the members of the parties who by this signing merely capped their decades-long betrayal of their country. Whoever today wants to change the fate of the South Tyrol in any way cannot renounce anything that was already renounced in all forms by the present-day protesters. At most he can only reconquer it.

I am most fanatically opposed to this, to be sure, and I announce the most extreme resistance to this endeavor, and I shall fight with the utmost fanaticism against the men who are trying to drive our people into this adventure, as bloody as it is insane. I did not learn about the war at a restaurant table reserved for regular customers. Nor was I in this war one of those who had to give orders or to command. I was an ordinary soldier who was given orders for four and a half years, and who nevertheless honorably and truly fulfilled his duty. But I thereby had the good fortune to know war as it is and not as one would like to see it. As a simple soldier, who had known only its dark sides, I was for this war up to the last hour because I was convinced that the salvation of our people could lie only in victory. Since however, there is now a peace which others have perpetrated, I fight to the utmost against a war which would not benefit the German people but instead only those who once before sacrilegiously traded the blood-sacrifice of our people for their interests. I am of the conviction that one day I will not be lacking in the determination, to bear the responsibility even, if necessary, of staking the blood of the German people. But I fight against even a single German being dragged off to a battlefield, for fools or criminals to nourish their plans on his blood. Whoever reflects on the unprecedented horror and the frightful misery of a modern war, or considers the boundless demands on the nervous stamina of a people, must take fright at the idea that such a sacrifice could be demanded for a success which in the most favorable case could never be consonant with this enormous effort. And I also know that if today the people of the South Tyrol, so far as it thinks along exclusively German lines, were gathered in one front and the hundreds and hundreds of thousands of dead which our nation would have to lay down in a struggle for their sake were to appear before these spectators, 300,000 hands would rise protectingly toward heaven and the foreign policy of the National Socialists would be justified.

What is most terrible about all this is that they play with this dreadful possibility without ever giving a thought to really wanting to help the South Tyroleans.

Since the struggle over the South Tyrol is being waged today by those who once surrendered all Germany to ruin, even the South Tyrol is to them only a means to an end which they use with ice-cold unscrupulousness in order to be able to gratify their infamous anti-German—in the most extreme sense of the word—instincts. It is the hate against the present-day nationally conscious Italy, and it is above all a hatred of the new political idea of this country and most of all hatred against the towering Italian statesman which induces them to stir up German public opinion with the help of the South Tyrol. For, in reality, how indifferent after all are these elements to the German people. While they lament the South Tyrol's fate with crocodile tears in their eyes, they are driving all Germany toward a fate which is worse than that of the partitioned territory. While they protest against Italy in the name of national culture, they pollute the culture of the German nation within, destroy our whole cultural sensibility, poison the instinct of our people and annihilate even the accomplishments of earlier times. Does an age which inside the country has depressed our whole theater, our literature, our plastic arts to the level of swine have the right to step forth against present-day Italy, or to protect German culture from her in the name of culture? The gentlemen of the Bavarian People's Party, the German nationalists and even the Marxist defilers of culture are concerned about the German culture of the South Tyrol, but, undisturbed, they let the culture of the homeland be insulted by the most wretched bungling works and surrender the German stage to the race-shame of a *Jonny Spielt Auf*.* And hypocritically they lament the oppression of German cultural life in the South Tyrol while they themselves most cruelly persecute those in the homeland who want to protect German culture from a deliberate and intentional destruction. Here the Bavarian People's Party incites the state power against those who raise a protest against the infamous defilement of our people's culture. What do these solicitous protectors of German

---

* An opera—the title of which might be rendered in English as *Jonny Takes Off*—by the Czech composer Ernst Křenek, first performed in Leipzig in 1927. The protagonist is a Negro band leader and the music is jazzy; these features, together with Křenek's national origin, caused the Nazis to find the work odious. It was, however, widely performed in Europe, and was sung at the Metropolitan Opera House in New York.—*T.T.*

culture in the South Tyrol do in Germany itself for the defense of German culture? They have let the theater sink to the level of a brothel, into sites of demonstrated race-defilement, and destroyed all the foundations of our folk-life with movies holding honesty and morality up to ridicule, they connive at the cubistic and Dadaistic infatuation of our plastic art, they themselves protect the fabricators of this base deception or madness, they let German literature sink into mud and filth and surrender the whole intellectual life of our people to international Jewry. And the same contemptible pack is so brazen-faced as to stand up for German culture in the South Tyrol, whereby the only aim they have in mind, naturally, is to incite two cultured peoples against each other so that in the end they can all the more easily reduce them to the level of their own cultural wretchedness.

Thus is it in everything, however.

They complain about the persecution of the Germans in the South Tyrol and they are the same people who in Germany most cruelly wage war on anyone who understands being national as something other than defenselessly surrendering his people to syphilization by Jews and Negroes. The same people who call for the freedom of conscience of Germans in the South Tyrol oppress it in Germany itself in the meanest way. Never before has the freedom of expression of one's national outlook in Germany been so muzzled as under the rule of these mendacious party riffraff who presume to break a lance for the rights of conscience and national freedoms, of all things, in the South Tyrol. They wail over every injustice that is inflicted on a German in the South Tyrol but they are silent about the murders that these Marxist street-tramps commit from month to month in Germany against national elements. And their silence is shared by the whole fine national bourgeoisie including the fatherland protesters. In a single year—that is to say only five months of this year have gone by—nine men from the ranks of the National Socialist movement alone were murdered under circumstances that in part were bestial, and over six hundred wounded. This entire mendacious brood is silent about this, but how they would roar if only one such deed were committed by fascism against the German element in the South Tyrol. How they would summon the whole world to revolt if only one German in the South Tyrol were slaughtered by fascists under conditions similar to those which the Marxist murder riffraff employs in Germany, without this calling forth the indignation of this fine phalanx for the salvation of the German people. And how indeed these same people, who solemnly protest against the government persecution of the German element in the South Tyrol, persecute the Germans who inconvenience them in Germany itself. Beginning with the U-boat heroes up to the saviors of Upper Silesia, the men who first staked their blood for Germany—how they dragged them in chains before the courts and finally sentenced them to the penitentiary all because they had sacrificed their lives hundreds upon hundreds of times out of a fervent love for the fatherland, whereas this contemptible riffraff of protesters had crawled off somewhere where they could not be found. Let them total the sentences which have been imposed in Germany for acts which in a national-conscious state would be rewarded with the highest decorations. If Italy today puts a German in the South Tyrol in jail the whole German national and Marxist newspaper pack straightaway screams bloody murder. But they completely overlook that in Germany one can go to jail for months merely on the basis of a denunciation, that house searches, violation of the mails, telephone tapping, that is, sheer anti-constitutional deprivation of the personal freedoms guaranteed by the civil rights of this state are the order of the day. And let not our so-called national parties say that this is possible only in Marxist Prussia. First of all they fraternize arm in arm with these same Marxists in regard to foreign policy and second they have taken the same part in the oppression of a real, self-conscious nationalism. In "national Bavaria" they placed the mortally ill Dietrich Eckart* in so-called protective custody, despite the

---

* Dietrich Eckart was a Bavarian writer and *bon vivant* who was closely associated with Hitler in the early years of the Nazi movement, and became editor of the Nazi party newspaper, the *Voelkischer Beobachter*. Eckart died in 1923; the second volume of *Mein Kampf* ends with a tribute to his memory. Alfred Rosenberg's book *Dietrich Eckart—A Testament* was published in 1928.—*T.T.*

available medical testimony, without even the trace of any wrong-doing on his part save, at most, that of his incorruptible national outlook. And he was kept in such custody for so long that he finally collapsed, and died two days after his release. Moreover he was Bavaria's greatest poet. Of course he was a national German and had not perpetrated any *Jonny Spielt Auf* and in consequence he did not exist for these fighters for the national culture. Just as these national patriots first murdered him likewise did they kill his work with silence, for after all he was a German and a good Bavarian in addition and no international Jew polluter of Germany. In that case he would have been holy to this league of patriots, but here they acted in accordance with their national-bourgeois outlook and the open statement in the Munich police administration, "Croak, national pig!" But these are the same German-conscious elements who mobilize the indignation of the world when someone in Italy stupidly does no more than throw a German in jail.

When a few Germans were expelled from the South Tyrol these people again summoned the German people to blazing indignation. They forgot only to add, however, that the greatest incitement was being directed against Germans in Germany itself. Under a bour-geois-national government "national Bavaria" has expelled dozens and dozens of Germans and all only because they did not politically suit the corrupt ruling bourgeois stratum in consequence of their uncompromising nationalism. Suddenly one no longer took cogni-zance of the clan-brotherhood with German Austria but only of the foreigner. But it was not at all limited to the expulsion of so-called alien Germans. No, these same bourgeois-national hypocrites who hurl flaming protests against Italy because a German is expelled from the South Tyrol and packed off to another province, have ex-pelled from Bavaria dozens and dozens of Germans with German citizenship who fought for Germany in the German army for four and a half years and who had been severely wounded and won the highest decorations. Indeed, this is how these bourgeoise-national hypocrites look who now bluster indignantly against Italy, whereas they themselves have burdened themselves with shame upon shame among their own people.

They moan over the denationalization in Italy and at the same time they denationalize the German people in their own homeland. They fight against anyone who opposes poisoning of our people with regard to blood, indeed they persecute every German who does battle against the de-Germanization, Negrification, and Judaization of our people in the big cities which they themselves instigate and sponsor, and in the most shameless and ruthless way. And by means of the mendacious allegation of a danger to religious establishments they try to send them to jail.

When an over-excited Italian in Merano damaged the Empress Elizabeth monument there, they raised a wild clamor and could not be pacified even though an Italian court punished the culprit with two months in prison. That the monuments and mementos of the past greatness of our people are uninterruptedly defiled in Germany itself, interests them not at all. That France has almost entirely destroyed all monuments recalling Germany in Alsace-Lorraine is a matter of indifference to them. It does not excite them that the Poles systematically lay waste to everything that even reminds one of the name of Germany. Indeed they do not get excited over the fact that this very month in Bromberg* the Bismarck tower was officially demolished by the government—all this leaves these champions of the national honor of our people cold. Woe, however, if something like this were the case in the South Tyrol. For this has suddenly become a Holy Land for them. But the fatherland itself, the homeland, it can go to hell.

Certainly, on the Italian side more than one unwise action has taken place in the South Tyrol, and the attempt to denationalize the German element systematically is just as impolitic as its result is questionable. But those who are in part guilty of all this and who, as a matter of fact, know nothing of a national honor of their people, have no right to protest against this. Instead, this right belongs

---

* A city in Poland, known in Polish as Bydgoszcz. It is the capital of Pomorze province, and was part of Prussia from 1772 to 1919, and of the Polish area annexed by Germany in 1939. The episode to which Hitler refers occurred early in May, 1928. If, as is probable, Hitler dictated this book in the order indicated by the typescript, this reference indicates that he had nearly finished it in May, 1928.—*T.T.*

only to those who up to now really fought for German interests and German honor. In Germany this was exclusively the National Socialist movement.

The whole inner mendacity of the agitation against Italy becomes apparent if the actions of the Italians are compared with the actions that the French, Poles, Belgians, Czechs, Rumanians and South Slavs have perpetrated against the German element. That France has expelled more than a quarter-million Germans altogether from Alsace-Lorraine, that is more people than the South Tyrol numbers as inhabitants, means not a rap to them. And that the French today are trying to extirpate every trace of German nationality in Alsace-Lorraine does not prevent them from fraternizing with France, even when continuous blows on the jaw are the answer from Paris. That the Belgians persecute the German element with a matchless fanaticism; that the Poles have massacred over 17,000 Germans in part under downright bestial attendant circumstances gives them no cause for excitement; that they, finally, expelled tens of thousands from house and home, with hardly a shirt on their backs, and drove them across the border, are things that cannot make our bourgeois and fatherland protest-swindlers fly into a passion. Indeed, whoever wants to know the real disposition of this pack must only recall the way and manner in which the refugees were welcomed even then. Their hearts, at that time, bled as little as they do now when those tens of thousands of unfortunate expellees again found themselves on the soil of their dear homeland, in part in veritable concentration camps, and were being shunted from place to place like gypsies. In my mind's eye I still see before me the time when the first Ruhr refugees came to Germany and then were shunted from police administration to police administration as if they were hardened criminals. No, then the hearts of these representatives and defenders of the national element in the South Tyrol did not bleed. But if a single German in the South Tyrol itself is expelled by the Italians or some other injustice is inflicted on him, they tremble with righteous resentment and indignation over this unexampled crime against culture and over this greatest barbarism that the world has ever seen. How they say then: "Never before and nowhere else before has the German element been so oppressed

190

with such terrible and tyrannical methods as in this country." Indeed, but only with one exception, that is namely Germany itself, through your own tyranny.

The South Tyrol, or better, the German element in the South Tyrol, must remain preserved for the German people, but in Germany itself, through their insane policy of un-national dishonorableness, of general corruption and of obsequiousness to the international financial lords, they murder more than double the people that the South Tyrol numbers as German inhabitants. They are silent about the 17,000-22,000 people driven to suicide on an average in recent years by their catastrophic policies, although this number with children included, likewise amounts in ten years alone, to more than the South Tyrol numbers in German inhabitants. They foster emigration and Herr Stresemann's national bourgeoisie characterizes the increase of the emigration quota as an enormous foreign policy success. And yet this means that every four years Germany loses more people than the South Tyrol numbers as inhabitants of German nationality. But in abortions and birth control, year for year, they murder almost double the number of people of German nationality in the South Tyrol all together. And this pack arrogates to itself the moral right to speak on behalf of the interests of the German element abroad.

Or this national official Germany wails over the denationalization of our language in the South Tyrol, but in Germany itself they de-Germanize the German names in Czechoslovakia, in Alsace-Lorraine, etc. in all official ways and manners. Indeed official travel guides are published in which even the German names of cities in Germany are Czechized for the sake of the Czechs. This is all in order. Only when the Italians changed the holy name Brenner into Brennero was this an occasion to demand the most fervent resistance. And it is a spectacle not to be missed when such a bourgeois patriot begins to blaze with indignation when one knows well that it is all a comedy. To simulate national passion suits our passionless, putrified bourgeoisie as exactly as when an old whore mimics love. It is all only an artificial sham and at its worst this is proved most correctly if such an excitement has its homeland in Austria. The black-gold legitimistic element, to whom formerly the German element in the Tyrol was completely a matter of indifference, now joins in a holy national indignation. Something of this kind electrifies all petty-bourgeois associations, especially if they then hear that the Jews are also cooperating. This means that they themselves protest because they know that this time, exceptionally for once, they are permitted to shout their national feelings out loud without being done in by the press-Jews. On the contrary: it is after all fine for an upright national-bourgeois man to appeal for a national struggle and at the same time even be praised by Itzig Veitel Abrahamson. Indeed, even more. The Jewish gazettes scream along with them and with this for the first time the real bourgeois national-German unity front is established from Krotoschin via Vienna up to Innsbruck and our German people, so politically stupid, lets itself be taken in by this show exactly as once before German diplomacy and our German people let themselves be duped and misused by the Hapsburgs.

Germany once before had let her foreign policy be determined exclusively by Austrian interests. The punishment for this was something terrible. Woe, if the young German nationalism lets its future policy be determined by the theatrical babblers of the putrid bourgeois elements or indeed by the Marxist enemies of Germany. And woe if, at the same time, in complete misunderstanding of the real driving forces of the Austrian state in Vienna, it again receives its directives from there. It will be the task of the National Socialist movement to prepare an end to this theatrical hue and cry, and to choose sober reason as the ruler of future German foreign policy.

To be sure, Italy also bears guilt for this whole development. I would view it as stupid and politically childish to rebuke the Italian state for the fact that it pushed its borders up to the Brenner on the occasion of the Austrian collapse. The motives that dominated it at that time were no more base than the motives which once determined bourgeois annexationist politicians, including Herr Stresemann and Herr Erzberger, to prop the German borders against the Belgian Meuse fortresses. At all times a responsible, thinking and acting government will make an effort to find strategically natural and secure frontiers. Surely, Italy did not annex the South Tyrol in order thus to come into possession of a couple of hundred thousand Germans, and surely the Italians would have preferred '+

if only Italians lived in this territory in place of these Germans. For as a matter of fact it was never strategic considerations primarily which induced them to place the borders over the Brenner. But no state would have acted differently in a similar situation. Hence it is aimless to criticize this shaping of the borders as such since ultimately every state must determine its natural borders according to its own interests and not others. To the extent that the possession of the Brenner may serve military interests and strategic purposes, it is irrelevant whether or not 200,000 Germans live within this strategically established and secured border as such, if the population of the country encompasses 42 million people, and a militarily effective adversary on this very border does not come in for consideration. It would have been wiser to have spared these 200,000 Germans any compulsion rather than to have forcibly tried to instill an outlook the result of which, according to experience, is generally without value. Also a folkdom cannot be extirpated in twenty or thirty years regardless of the methods employed and whether one wants or does not want this. On the Italian side one can answer with a certain appearance of right that this was not intended at first and that it developed necessarily by itself as a consequence of the provocative attempts at a continuous interference in domestic Italian affairs on the part of Austrian and German external forces and of the repercussions evoked therefrom on the South Tyroleans themselves. This is correct, for as a matter of fact the Italians at first welcomed the German element in the South Tyrol very honestly and loyally. But as soon as fascism arose in Italy the agitation against Italy in Germany and Austria began on grounds of principle and now led to an increasing heightening of mutual irritability which in the South Tyrol finally had to lead to consequences we see today. Most unfortunate in this was the influence of the Andreas Hofer Bund which, instead of strongly recommending sagacity to the Germans in the South Tyrol and making it clear to them that their mission was to build a bridge between Germany and Italy, aroused hopes in the South Tyroleans beyond any possibility of realization but which, however, were bound to lead to incitements and thereby to rash steps. It is primarily the fault of this Bund if conditions were carried to an extreme. Whoever like myself had many

opportunities to krow important members of this association personally as well must be amazed over the irresponsibility with which an
association with so little real active strength could do so much damage. For when I see the different leading figures in my mind's eye
and think of one of them in particular who had his office in the
Munich police administration then I grow angry at the thought that
men who would never bring their own blood and skins to the market
occasioned a development which in its ultimate consequence must
end with a bloody conflict.

It is also correct that no understanding at all over the South
Tyrol can exist with the real wirepullers of this agitation against
Italy, since to these elements the South Tyrol as such is a matter of
indifference as much as is the German nation in general. Indeed
it is only a question of a suitable means for sowing confusion and
stirring up public opinion, especially in Germany, against Italy.
For this is what concerns these gentlemen. Hence there is a certain
ground for justification in the Italian objection that regardless of
what the treatment of Germans in the South Tyrol may be, these
people will always find something suitable for their agitation, because they want precisely this. But for the very reason that in Germany today, exactly as in Italy, certain elements have an interest
in thwarting an understanding between both nations with all means,
it would be the duty of wisdom to remove these means from them
as far as possible, even despite the danger that they will try further.
The opposite would make sense only if there were altogether nobody in Germany who had the courage to speak for an understanding in opposition to this agitation. This, however, is not the case.
On the contrary, the more present-day Italy by itself seeks to avoid
impolitic incidents, the easier will it become for Italy's friends in
Germany to expose the hate-inciters, to unmask the sanctimoni-
ousness of their reasons and to put a stop to their folk-poisoning activity. But if in Italy they really believe that they cannot compromise in some way, in view of all the clamor and the demands of
foreign organizations, without this looking like a capitulation
rather, and possibly further increasing the arrogance of these elements, then ways could be found. Indeed such an obligingness
could be fundamentally ascribed to those who not only are not in-

volved in this agitation but, on the contrary, are the friends of an understanding with Italy and Germany and themselves lead the sharpest struggle against the poisoners of public opinion in Germany.

The foreign policy aim of the National Socialist movement has nothing to do either with an economic or bourgeois border policy. Our folkish territorial aim, in the future as well, will assign the German people a development which need never bring it into conflict with Italy. We will also never sacrifice the blood of our people in order to bring about small border rectifications, but only for territory in order to win a further expansion and sustenance for our people. This aim drives us eastward. The east coasts of the Baltic Sea are for Germany what the Mediterranean Sea is to Italy. Germany's mortal enemy for any further development, indeed even for the mere maintenance of the unity of our Reich, is France, exactly as she is for Italy. The National Socialist movement will never fall into a superficial insipid hurrah-cry. It will not rattle the sword. Its leaders, almost without exception, have learned about war as it is in reality and truth. Therefore, it will never shed blood for any other aims save those which are serviceable to the whole future development of our people. Hence it also refuses to provoke a war with Italy for the sake of a border rectification which is laughable in view of the German fragmentation in Europe. On the contrary it wants to put an end for all the future to these unfortunate Teutonic marches to the south and wants the advocacy of our interests to take place in a direction which makes the elimination of its need for territory appear possible to our people. By thus delivering Germany from the period of her present enslavement and servitude, we also fight above all for her restoration and thus in the interest of German honor.

If present-day Italy believes that a change in various measures in the South Tyrol would be viewed as a capitulation before foreign interference without in the end leading to the desired understanding, then let her undertake this shift exclusively for the sake of those in Germany who themselves are for an understanding with Italians—thereby openly justifying them—and who not only reject being identified with the agitators against it but who, indeed, have fought the sharpest struggle against these elements for years and who recognize the sovereign rights of the Italian state as existing, as a matter of course.

It is just as little a matter of indifference to Germany whether she keeps Italy as a friend, as it also is to Italy. Just as fascism has given the Italian people a new value, likewise the value of the German people must not be estimated for the future on the basis of its momentary life-expression, but according to the forces which it has so often shown in its former history and which, perhaps, it can again show tomorrow.

Thus, just as Italy's friendship is worth a sacrifice on Germany's part, German friendship is worth just as much to Italy. It would be a good fortune for both peoples if those forces in both countries who are the bearers of this knowledge could come to an understanding.

Thus as much as the agitation against Italy in Germany is responsible for the unfortunate enmity, just as much guilt lies on Italy's side if, in view of the fact that there is a struggle in Germany itself against this agitation, she herself as far as possible does not wrest the means from their hands.

If the sagacity of the fascist regime one day succeeds in making 65 million Germans into friends of Italy this will be worth more than if it educates 200,000 into becoming bad Italians.

Likewise unsound was the Italian stand prohibiting the union of Austria with Germany. The very fact that France primarily espoused this prohibition perforce should have led Rome to take an opposite position. For France itself did not take this step in order to benefit Italy, but much more rather in the hope of being able to inflict harm on her thereby. There are primarily two reasons which induced France to push through the prohibition of the union: first, because thereby she wanted to prevent a strengthening of Germany, and second, because she is convinced that some day she can, in the Austrian state, acquire a member for the French-European alliance. So Rome should not deceive itself that French influence in Vienna is considerably more decisive even than the German, not to speak of the Italian. The French attempt to transfer the League of Nations to Vienna, if possible, stems only from the intention to strengthen the cosmopolitan character of this city as such and to bring it into contact with a country whose character and culture

196

finds a stronger response in the present-day Viennese atmosphere than does that of the German Reich.

As seriously intended as are the tendencies toward a union in the Austrian provinces as such, just as little are they taken seriously in Vienna. On the contrary if in Vienna they really operate with the idea of a union it is always only in order to extricate themselves from some financial difficulty, since France then is always sooner ready to lend a hand to the creditor state. Gradually, however, this very idea of a union will dry up in proportion as an inner consolidation of the Austrian federation occurs and Vienna regains its full dominating position. On top of this the political development in Vienna assumes an increasingly anti-Italian and especially anti-fascist character, whereas Austro-Marxism has at all times made no bones about its strong sympathy for France.

Thus the fact that at that time the union fortunately was prevented, and in part with Italian help, will some day lead to the insertion of the missing link between Prague and Yugoslavia into the French alliance system.

For Italy, however, the prevention of the Austrian union with Germany had been wrong even on psychological grounds. The smaller the fragmented Austrian state remained, the more limited naturally also were its foreign policy aims. A foreign policy goal, conceived on a grand scale, could not be expected from a state structure which has scarcely . . . . square kilometers of territory and hardly . . . . million inhabitants. If German Austria had been annexed to Germany in the year 1919-1920 the tendency of her political thought would gradually have been determined by the great political aims of Germany, which were at least possible, that is for a nation of almost 70,000,000. Preventing this at that time removed foreign policy thinking from greater aims and limited it to small old-Austrian reconstruction ideas. Only thus was it possible that the South Tyrol question could have at all grown to such an importance. For as small as the Austrian state was as such, it was at least large enough to be the bearer of a foreign policy idea which was in keeping with its smallness, just as, conversely, it could slowly poison the political thinking of all Germany. The more limited the political ideas of the Austrian state become in consequence of its territorial limitation the more will they

197

sprout into problems which can certainly have an importance for this state but which cannot be viewed as decisive for the shaping of a German foreign policy for the German nation.

Italy should espouse a union of Austria with Germany if for no other reason than to cut across the French alliance system in Europe. She should further also do this, however, in order to present other tasks to the German border policy germinated in consequence of her incorporation in a great Reich.

Moreover, the reasons which once induced Italy to take a stand against the union are not quite clear. Neither present-day Austria nor present-day Germany can be considered a military adversary of Italy for the time being. But if France succeeds in bringing a general alliance in Europe into being against Italy, in which Austria and Germany take part, the military situation as such will not at all change whether Austria is independent or whether she is with Germany. Moreover one cannot actually speak of a real independence with so small a structure anyhow. Austria will always [They will always] hang on to the strings of a large power of some kind. Switzerland cannot in the least prove the opposite since as a state she possesses her own possibilities of existence, even if on the basis of tourist traffic. For Austria this is already impossible in consequence of the disproportion of the capital of this country to the size of the whole population. Regardless, however, what attitude Austria itself assumes toward Italy, in the very fact of her existence there already lies an easing of the military strategic position of Czechoslovakia which one day, one way or another, can make itself noticeable vis-à-vis Italy's natural ally as such, Hungary.

For the Italians, military and political reasons would speak in favor of regarding prohibition of the union as at least without importance, if not as something which answers the purpose.

I cannot conclude this chapter without establishing in detail who in fact bears the guilt that a South Tyrol question exists altogether. For us National Socialists, politically, the decision has been reached. And at least I—who am most violently opposed to millions of Germans being dragged to a battlefield on which to bleed to death for the interests of France without a gain thereby accruing to Germany which would in some way be consonant with the blood-sacrifice—I also refuse to recognize the standpoint of national honor as being decisive here. For on the basis of this viewpoint I would sooner have to march against France, which by her whole conduct has offended German honor in quite a different way than Italy. I have already enlarged in the introduction to this book on the possibility of formulating a foreign policy on the basis of national honor, so there is no further need to take a position toward it. If now the attempt is made in our protest groups to present this attitude of ours as a betrayal or a renunciation of the South Tyrol this can only be correct if without our attitude South Tyrol would either have not been lost altogether, or were about to return to the other Tyrol in the predictable future.

Therefore I see myself forced once more to establish in this exposition precisely who it was that betrayed the South Tyrol and through whose measures it was lost to Germany [Austria].

1. The South Tyrol was betrayed and lost by the activity of those parties who in long work for peace weakened, or completely refused, the armament to the German people which it needed to assert itself in Europe, and by so doing robbed the German people of the necessary power for victory and thereby of the preservation of the South Tyrol at the critical hour.

2. Those parties who in long work for peace undermined the moral and ethical foundation of our people and, above all, destroyed faith in the right to self-defense.

3. Thus the South Tyrol was also betrayed by those parties, which as so-called state-preserving and national parties, looked on this activity with indifference or, at least, without opposing a serious resistance. Albeit indirectly, they too are accessories to the weakening of our people's armament.

4. The South Tyrol was betrayed and lost by the activity of those political parties who reduced the German people to being the stooge of the Hapsburg big-power idea. And who, instead of setting

199

before German foreign policy the aim of the national unification of our people, viewed the preservation of the Austrian state as the mission of the German nation. Who, therefore, also in peacetime for decades merely looked on as the Hapsburgs systematically carried out their work of de-Germanization, indeed furnishing them assistance. Thereby they are co-responsible for neglecting the solution of the Austrian question by Germany itself, or at least by the decisive cooperation of Germany. In such a case the South Tyrol could have certainly been preserved for the German people.

5. The South Tyrol was lost in consequence of the general aimlessness and planlessness of German foreign policy which in the year 1914 extended also to the establishment of reasonable war aims, or prevented this.

6. The South Tyrol was betrayed by all those who during the course of the war did not cooperate to the utmost in strengthening German resistance and aggressive power. As well as by the parties which deliberately paralyzed the German power of resistance, as well as those who tolerated this paralysis.

7. The South Tyrol was lost in consequence of the inability, even during the war, to undertake a new orientation of German foreign policy and to save the German element of the Austrian state by renouncing the maintenance of the Hapsburg great-power state.

8. The South Tyrol was lost and betrayed by the activity of those who, during the war, by raising the sham hope of a peace without victory broke the German people's moral power of resistance, and who instead of a manifestation of the will to wage the war brought about a peace resolution that was catastrophic for Germany.

9. The South Tyrol was lost by the betrayal of those parties and men who even during the war lied to the German people about the non-existence of Entente imperialistic aims and thereby duped our people, estranged it from the unconditional necessity of resistance and ultimately induced it to believe the Entente more than those who raised their voices in warning at home.

10. The South Tyrol was further lost by the grinding down of the front, attended to by the homeland, and by the infection of

German thinking by the fraudulent declarations of Woodrow Wilson.

11. The South Tyrol was betrayed and was lost by the activity of parties and men who, beginning with conscientious objection to military service up to the organization of munitions strikes, robbed the army of the feeling of the incontestable necessity of its struggle and victory.

12. The South Tyrol was betrayed and lost by the organization and the execution of the November crime, as well as by the contemptible and cowardly tolerance of this ignominy by the so-called state-preserving national forces.

13. The South Tyrol was lost and betrayed by the shameless acts of the men and parties who after the collapse defiled Germany's honor, destroyed the esteem of our people before the world and only thereby encouraged our adversaries to the enormity of their demands. It was further lost by the contemptible cowardice of the national-bourgeois parties and patriotic leagues who dishonorably capitulated everywhere before the terror of baseness and villainy.

14. The South Tyrol was finally lost and betrayed by the signing of the peace treaties and with this by the legal recognition of the loss also of this area.

All the German parties together are guilty of all this. Some have knowingly and intentionally destroyed Germany, and others in their proverbial incapacity and in their cowardice, which cries out to heaven, not only did nothing to stop the destroyers of Germany's future but, on the contrary, they actually played into the hands of these enemies of our people by the incapacity of their direction of domestic and foreign policy. Never before has a people been driven like the German people to ruin by such a marriage of baseness, villainy, cowardice and stupidity.

In these days we have been afforded a glimpse into the activities and effectiveness of this old Germany in the field of foreign policy by the publication of the war memoirs of the head of the American intelligence service, Mr. Flynn.*

---

* Hitler here is referring to an article by William J. Flynn, former head of the United States Secret Service, entitled "Tapped Wires," which appeared in the now defunct *Liberty* magazine, June 2, 1928.—*Trans.*

I let a bourgeois-democratic organ speak on this matter only for the purpose of a broader understanding.

How America Entered the War*

Flynn Writes About the Diplomatic Secret Service
by F. W. Elven, correspondent of the *Münchener Neuesten Nachrichten*

Cincinnati, mid-June

William J. Flynn has published a part of his war memoirs in the weekly *Liberty* which is much read here. During the war Flynn was the head of the United States Secret Service. The Service encompasses the whole country and is brilliantly organized. In peacetime it primarily provides for the personal security of the President. Its attention is enjoyed by whatever else in the national capital is in need of protection, or thinks it needs so. It keeps under surveillance all doubtful elements somehow suspected of connections with political tendencies hostile to the government and its spokesmen. During the war its principal task was to keep an eye on those who more or less loudly had made themselves noticeable in opposition to the war, or who merely were suspected of not being in agreement with the Wilsonian war policy. Germans also enjoyed its special care and at that time many fell into the traps which had been laid everywhere by the Federal Secret Service.

From Flynn's memoirs, however, we learn that the Secret Service had been assigned an important mission even before our entry into the war. In the year 1915, a full two years before the declaration of war, the most efficient telephone expert was summoned to Washington and assigned the task of arranging the leading telephone wires to the German and Austrian embassies in such a way that Secret Service officials could tap every conversation from any source that was held between the ambassadors and their personnel as well as every conversation emanating from the embassy offices. A room was set up with which all the wires were linked in such an ingenious way that not even a single conversation could be

---

* Omitted from Hitler's manuscript, this article is inserted here.—*Trans.*

missed. Secret Service men sat in this room day and night, dictating the overheard conversations to the stenographers seated beside them. Every night the head of the Secret Service Bureau, that is the author of the article in *Liberty,* received a stenographic report of all the conversations held in the preceding twenty-four hours so that on the very same evening he was able to communicate everything important to the State Department and to President Wilson.

Let us bear in mind the time this installation was created, at the beginning of the year 1915, that is, at the time when the United States still lived in peace with Germany and Austria-Hungary, and Wilson never tired of giving assurances that he harbored no hostile intentions against Germany. It was also the time when the German ambassador in Washington, Count Bernstorff, neglected no opportunity to show due appreciation of Wilson's friendly disposition and feelings for Germany and the German people. It was also the time when Wilson gave his confidant Baruch instructions to begin the gradual mobilization of industry for war; also the time in which it became increasingly obvious, as the American historian Harry Elmer Barnes also sets forth in his book on the origins of the great war, that Wilson was firmly decided to enter the war and postponed the execution of his bellicose plans only because public opinion first had to be won over for these plans.

Flynn's memoirs must finally remove the ground from the foolish chatter that Wilson was pushed into the war against his will by German submarine warfare. The tapping of the telephone wires leading to the German embassy took place with his knowledge. We also learn this from Flynn's memoirs. The author adds that the material thus gathered against Germany contributed considerably to the eventual break. This can prove only that this put means in Wilson's hands to win public opinion for the war long planned by him. And in fact this material was wholly and ideally suited for it. The memoirs confirm to the fullest extent what unfortunately must still be said, that Germany at that time was represented in Washington in a downright incredibly incompetent and incredibly unworthy way. If we hear that in one passage Flynn writes that the stenographic reports prepared for him daily contained enough material to keep a divorce lawyer busy for months on end, then we get a general idea of what went on.

The Secret Service maintained women agents in Washington and New York whose job it was to sound out the members of the German embassy, Bernstorff included, whenever anything important happened. One of these woman agents kept a better-class apartment in Washington in which the gentlemen met their ladies, and where occasionally even Secretary of State Lansing dropped in to hear what was new. On New Year's Day, 1916, when the news of the sinking of the liner "Persia" became known in the national capital, Bernstorff telephoned five women one after the other in order to make sweet compliments to them and to receive similar compliments in return, although in view of the mood which news of the sinking of the "Persia" had left behind in the State Department and the White House he really could not have been lacking in more serious pursuits.

One of the ladies complimented Bernstorff on the fact that he was a great lover and always would be, even were he a hundred years old. The rest of the gentlemen of the embassy were not differently built. One, whom Flynn designates as the best diplomatic aide in the embassy, had a lady friend in New York, a married woman, with whom he had a daily telephone conversation which each time cost the German Reich twenty dollars, and whom he visited frequently. He told her about everything that happened and she then took care to bring this information to the right places. Even quite vulgar remarks about Wilson and his consort were made during the telephone conversations and thus we can without difficulty imagine that thereby the mood of the White House vis-à-vis Germany did not get any friendlier.

From the conversation held at the beginning of March, 1916, we learn how little the embassy knew about the country and the people and with what childish plans it concerned itself. At that time a bill introduced by Senator Gore lay before Congress to the effect that a proclamation be issued warning the American people not to use armed commercial vessels. President Wilson most bitterly fought against the proposal. He needed the loss of American lives in order to incite feelings against Germany. People in the German embassy knew that the prospects of the bill were not favorable, so they earnestly concerned themselves with plans to buy Congress. Only at first they did not know where to get the money. On March 3 the Senate decided to postpone the Gore bill provisionally. The vote in the House was supposed to follow a few days later. So the plan first to buy the House was further eagerly pursued, but in this case at least Bernstorff was reasonable enough to advise against the plan decisively.

The reading of the Flynn article must leave a feeling of deep indignation in the veins of every man of healthy German blood, not only over Wilson's treacherous policy but rather, and especially, over the incredible stupidity with which the German embassy played into the hands of this policy. Wilson duped Bernstorff more and more from day to day. When Colonel House, his adviser, returned from his European journey in May, 1916, Bernstorff traveled to New York to meet him there. Wilson, however, who vis-à-vis Bernstorff had acted as though he had no objections to this meeting, secretly instructed House not to have anything to do with the Count and to avoid him at all events. Thus it happened. Bernstorff waited in New York in vain. Then he went to a nearby beach and let himself be photographed in a bathing suit with two lady friends in a very intimate position. The photo accompanies Flynn's article. At that time it fell into the hands of the Russian ambassador Bakhmateff who had it enlarged and sent it to London where it was published in the newspapers under the caption, "The Dignified Ambassador," and it rendered a capital service to Allied propaganda.

This is what the *Münchener Neuesten Nachrichten* writes now. The man thus characterized, however, was a typical representative of German foreign policy before the war, just as he is also the typical representative of the German foreign policy of the Republic. This fellow, who would have been sentenced to hanging by a political tribunal in any other state, is the German representative at the League of Nations in Geneva.

These men bear the guilt and the responsibility for Germany's collapse and, therefore, also for the loss of the South Tyrol. And with them the guilt falls on all parties and men who either caused such conditions, or covered them up, or also tacitly countenanced them or did not fight against them in the sharpest manner.

The men, however, who today brazenly try to deceive public opinion anew and would like to aver that others are guilty of the loss of the South Tyrol must first give a detailed accounting of what they have done for its preservation.

As for my person, at any rate, I can proudly declare that since the time that I became a man I have always been for the strengthening of my people. And when the war came I fought on the German front in the West for four and a half years, and since its end I have been fighting against the corrupt creatures whom Germany can thank for this disaster. Since that time I have entered into no compromise with the betrayers of the German fatherland, either in domestic or foreign policy matters, but immovably proclaim their destruction one day as the aim of my life's work and the mission of the National Socialist movement.

I can all the more calmly endure the yelping of the cowardly bourgeois curs as well as that of the patriotic leaguers, as I know the average poltroon of these creatures, for me unspeakably contemptible, all too well. That they also know me is the reason for their hue and cry.

XVI

As a National Socialist I see in Italy to begin with the first possible ally of Germany who can step out of the camp of the old coalition of enemies without this alliance signifying an immediate war for Germany for which we are not equipped militarily.

According to my conviction this alliance will be of great benefit to Germany and Italy alike. Even if its direct benefit should ultimately no longer exist, it will never become detrimental, as long as both nations represent their interests in the highest sense of the word. As long as Germany views the maintenance of the freedom and independence of our people as the supreme aim of her foreign policy and wants to secure this people the prerequisite for its daily life, for so long will its foreign policy thinking be determined by our people's territorial need. And for so long will we not be able to have any internal or external inducement to fall into enmity with a state which does not in the least stand obstructively in our way.

And as long as Italy wants to serve her real vital needs as a truly national state, for just so long will she, likewise attending to her territorial needs, have to base her political thought and action on the enlargement of Italian soil. The more proud and independent, the more national the Italian people becomes, the less will it in its development ever come into conflict with Germany.

The areas of interest of these two countries, in a most fortunate way, lie so widely apart from each other that there are no natural areas of irritation.

A national-conscious Germany and an equally proud Italy will also ultimately be able to close the wounds left behind by the World War in the understanding of their friendship based on their frank and mutual community of interests.

South Tyrol will thus someday have to fulfill a lofty mission in the service of both peoples. If the Italians and the Germans of this territory, once filled with a responsibility for their own folkdom, perceive and understand the great tasks that Italy and Germany have to solve, the petty disputes of the day will recede vis-à-vis the higher mission of building a bridge of frank, reciprocal understanding on the former borders of Germany and Italy.

I know that under the current regimes in Germany this is as exactly as impossible as it would be under a non-fascist regime in Italy. For the forces which determine German policy today do not desire any German resurgence but our destruction. They likewise want the destruction of the present-day Italian fascist state and therefore will leave nothing untried in order to sink both nations into hate and hostility. France will seize upon any such manifestation, be it only an act of thoughtlessness, and use it to her own advantage with a thousand joys.

Only a National Socialist Germany will find the way to a final understanding with a fascist Italy and finally eliminate the danger of war between the two peoples. For this old Europe was always a territory that was dominated by political systems, and this will not be otherwise at least for the humanly predictable future. General European democracy will either be replaced by a system of Jewish-Marxist Bolshevism, to which all states will succumb one after the other, or by a system of free and unlinked national states who in the free play of forces will set their stamp on Europe in accordance with the number and importance of their specific folkdom.

It is also not good for fascism to exist isolated in Europe as an idea. Either the world of ideas from which it stems is generalized, or Italy will one day again succumb to the general ideas of another Europe.

———

Thus if we submit Germany's foreign policy possibilities to a closer examination only two states remain in Europe as possible valuable allies for the future: Italy and England. Italy's relation to England itself is already a good one today and, for reasons which I have discussed in another passage, will hardly be clouded in the immediate future. This, too, has nothing to do with mutual sympathies but rests, on the Italian side above all, on a rational appraisal of the actual power relations. Thus an aversion to a boundless and unlimited French hegemony in Europe is common to both states. For Italy because her most vital European interests are threatened, for England because an over-powerful France in Europe can inflict a new threat on England's present-day naval and world supremacy which in itself is no longer completely unquestionable.

That already today probably Spain and Hungary are also to be reckoned as belonging to this community of interests, even if only tacitly, lies grounded in Spain's aversion to French colonial activity in North Africa as well as in Hungary's hostility to Yugoslavia, which is at the same time supported by France.

If Germany would succeed in taking part in a new state coalition in Europe, which either must lead to a shift of emphasis in the League of Nations itself or allow decisive power factors altogether outside the League of Nations to develop, then the first domestic political prerequisite for a later active foreign policy would be realizable. The weaponlessness imposed on us by the Versailles treaty and thus our practical defenselessness could come to an end, albeit slowly. This is possible only if the coalition of victors itself quarrels over this question but never, however, in an alliance with Russia, let alone in a union with other so-called oppressed nations, against the front of the coalition of the former victor states that encircle us.

Then in the far future it may be possible to think of a new association of nations, consisting of individual states with a high national value, which could then stand up to the threatening overwhelming of the world by the American Union. For it seems to me that the existence of English world rule inflicts less hardships on present-day nations than the emergence of an American world rule.

Pan-Europe cannot be summoned to the solution of this problem, but only a Europe with free and independent national states whose areas of interest are divergent and precisely delimited.

Only then can the time ripen for Germany, secured by a France pushed back within her own boundaries and supported by her army born anew, to lead the way toward the elimination of her territorial need. Once our people, however, will have grasped this great geopolitical aim in the East the consequence will not only be clarity regarding German foreign policy but also stability, at least for a humanly predictable time, will make it possible to avoid political insanities like those which ultimately entangled our people in the World War. And then we will also have ultimately overcome the period of this petty daily clamor and of the completely sterile economic and border policy.

Germany then, also domestically, will have to take steps toward the strongest concentration of her means of power. She will have to realize that armies and navies are set up and organized not along romantic lines but according to practical requirements. Then she will automatically select as our greatest task the formation of a superior strong land army since our future as a matter of fact does not lie on the water, but in Europe rather.

Only if we will have completely perceived the meaning of this proposition and put an end to our people's territorial need, in the East and on the largest scale, along the lines of this perception will German economy also cease to be a factor of world unrest which brings a thousand dangers down upon us. It will then at least serve the satisfaction of our domestic needs in their major aspects. A people which no longer needs to shunt off its rising rural generations into the big cities as factory workers, but which instead can settle them as free peasants on their own soil, will open up a domestic sales market to German industry which can gradually remove and exempt it from the frenzied struggle and scramble for the so-called place in the sun in the rest of the world.

It is the foreign policy task of the National Socialist movement to prepare and ultimately to carry out this development. It must also place foreign policy in the service of the reorganization of our folkdom on the basis of its philosophical range of ideas. Even here it must anchor the principle that we do not fight for systems but for a living people, that is for flesh and blood, which must be preserved and whose daily bread must not be lacking so that in consequence of its physical health it can also be healthy spiritually.

Just as it must step over a thousand obstacles, misunderstandings and malignities in its struggle for reform in its domestic policy, likewise in foreign policy must it also clear away not only the conscious betrayal of the country by Marxism but also the rubbish heap of worthless, indeed harmful phrases and ideas of our national, bourgeois world. Thus the less understanding there will be for the significance of our struggle at the moment, all the more powerful will be its success some day.

Why Italy today can primarily be considered as an ally for Germany is connected with the fact that this country is the only one whose domestic and foreign policy is determined by purely Italian national interests. These Italian national interests are the only ones which do not contradict German interests and, conversely, German interests do not run counter to them.

And this is important not only for factual reasons, but also on the basis of the following:

The war against Germany was fought by an overpowering world coalition in which only a part of the states could have a direct interest in Germany's destruction. In not a few countries the shift to war was brought by influences which in no way sprang from the real domestic interests of these nations or even which could also be to their benefit. A monstrous war propaganda began to befog public opinion of these peoples and to stir it into enthusiasm for a war which for these very peoples in part could not bring any gain at all and indeed sometimes ran downright counter to their real interests.

International world Jewry was the power which instigated this enormous war propaganda. For as senseless as the participation in the war by many of these nations may have been, seen from the viewpoint of their own interests, it was just as meaningful and logically correct seen from the viewpoint of the interests of world Jewry.

It is not my task here to enter into a discussion of the Jewish question as such. This cannot take place in the framework of a necessarily brief and compressed presentation. The following is said here only [so much] in the interests of a better understanding:

Jewry is a people with a racial core that is not wholly unitary. Nevertheless as a people it has special intrinsic characteristics which separate it from all other peoples living on the globe. Jewry is not a religious community but the religious bond between Jews rather is in reality the momentary governmental system of the Jewish people. The Jew has never had a territorially bounded state of his own in the manner of Aryan states. Nevertheless his religious community is a real state since it guarantees the preservation, the increase and the future of the Jewish people. But this is solely the task of the state. That the Jewish state is subject to no territorial limitation, as is the case with Aryan states, is connected with the character of the Jewish people which is lacking in the productive forces for the construction and preservation of its own territorial state.

Just as every people as a basic tendency of all its earthly actions possesses a mania for self-preservation as its driving force, likewise is it exactly so with Jewry too. Only here, in accord with their basically different dispositions, the struggle for existence of Aryan peoples and Jewry is also different in its forms. The foundation of the Aryan struggle for life is the soil, which he cultivates and which provides the general basis for an economy satisfying primarily its own needs within its own orbit through the productive forces of its own people.

Because of the lack of productive capacities of its own the Jewish people cannot carry out the construction of a state, viewed in a territorial sense, but as a support of its own existence it needs the work and creative activities of other nations. Thus the existence of the Jew himself becomes a parasitical one within the lives of other peoples. Hence the ultimate goal of the Jewish struggle for existence is the enslavement of productively active peoples. In order to achieve this goal, which in reality has represented Jewry's struggle for existence at all times, the Jew makes use of all weapons that are in keeping with the whole complex of his character.

Therefore in domestic politics within the individual nations he fights first for equal rights and later for super-rights. The characteristics of cunning, intelligence, astuteness, knavery, dissimulation, etc., rooted in the character of his folkdom, serve him as weapons thereto.

They are as much strategems in his war of survival as those of other peoples in combat.

In foreign policy he tries to bring nations into a state of unrest, to divert them from their true interests, and to plunge them into reciprocal wars and in this way gradually rise to mastery over them with the help of the power of money and propaganda.

His ultimate goal is the denationalization, the promiscuous bastardization of other peoples, the lowering of the racial level of the highest peoples as well as the domination of this racial mish-mash through the extirpation of the folkish intelligentsia and its replacement by the members of his own people.

The end of the Jewish world struggle therefore will always be a bloody Bolshevization. In truth this means the destruction of all the intellectual upper classes linked to their peoples so that he can rise to become the master of a mankind become leaderless.

Stupidity, cowardice and baseness, therefore, play into his hands. In bastards he secures for himself the first openings for the penetration of an alien nation.

Hence the result of Jewish domination is always the ruin of all culture and finally the madness of the Jew himself. For he is a parasite of nations and his victory signifies his own end as much as the death of his victim.

With the collapse of the ancient world the Jews encountered young, in part still completely unspoiled, peoples sure in racial instinct who protected themselves against being infiltrated by them. He was a foreigner and all his lies and dissimulation helped him little for nearly one and a half thousand years.

It was the feudal domination and the government of the princes which first created a general situation which allowed him to attach himself to the struggle of an oppressed social class, indeed to make this struggle his own in a short time. He received civil equality with the French Revolution. With that the bridge was constructed over which he could stride to the conquest of political power within nations.

The nineteenth century gave him a dominating position within the economy of nations through the building up of loan-capital based on ideas regarding interest. Finally, through the subterfuge of stockholdings he placed himself in possession of a great part of the production sites and with the help of the stock exchange he gradually became not only the ruler of public economic life but ultimately also of political life. He supported this rule by means of the intellectual contamination of nations with the help of Freemasonry as well as by the work of the press become dependent upon him. He found the potential strength for the destruction of the bourgeois intellectual regime in the newly rising fourth estate of the handicraftsmen, just as once before the bourgeoisie had been the means for the demolition of feudal domination. At the same time bourgeois stupidity and dishonest lack of principle, avarice and cowardice worked into his hands. He formed the vocational estate of the handicraftsmen into a special class which he now allowed to take up the struggle against the national intelligentsia. Marxism became the spiritual father of the Bolshevik revolution. It is the weapon of terror which the Jew now applies ruthlessly and brutally.

The economic conquest of Europe by the Jews was pretty much completed around the turn of the century, and now he began to safeguard it politically. That means, the first attempts to extirpate the national intelligentsia were undertaken in the form of revolutions.

He utilized the tensions between European nations, which are in great part to be ascribed to their general need for territory with the consequences which arise therefrom, for his own advantage by systematically inciting them to the World War.

The aim is the destruction of inherently anti-Semitic Russia as well as the destruction of the German Reich which in the administration and the army still offers resistance to the Jew. The further aim is the overthrow of those dynasties which had not yet been made subject to a democracy dependent upon and led by Jews.

This Jewish war aim has at least in part been completely achieved. Czarism and Kaiserism in Germany were eliminated. With the help of the Bolshevik revolution the Russian upper classes and also the Russian national intelligentsia were murdered and completely extirpated amid inhuman agonies and atrocities. For the Russian people the total number of victims of this Jewish struggle for hegemony in Russia amounted to 28-30 million people in number of dead. This is fifteen times more than the World War cost Germany. After the successful revolution he completely tore down [further] the bonds of order, of morality, of custom, etc., abolished marriage as a lofty institution and instead proclaimed a general copulation with the aim of breeding a general inferior human mish-mash, by way of a chaotic bastardization, which by itself would be incapable of leadership and which ultimately would no longer be able to do without the Jews as its only intellectual element.

The future will show to what extent this has succeeded and to what extent now forces of a natural reaction can still bring about a change of this most terrible crime of all times against mankind.

At the moment, he exerts himself to lead the remaining states toward the same condition. Thereby he is supported and covered in his strivings and his actions by the bourgeois national parties of the so-called national fatherland leagues, whereas Marxism, democracy and the so-called Christian Center emerge as aggressive shock troops.

The bitterest struggle for the victory of Jewry at the present time is being waged in Germany. Here it is the National Socialist movement which alone has taken upon itself the struggle against this execrable crime against mankind.

In all European states at the moment a struggle, in part quiet and violent albeit often under wraps, is being waged for political power.

Outside Russia this struggle has first been decided in France. There the Jew, favored by a number of circumstances, has entered into a community of interests with French national chauvinism. Since then Jewish stock exchanges and French bayonets have been allies.

This struggle is undecided in England. There the Jewish invasion still meets with an old British tradition. The instincts of Anglo-Saxondom are still so sharp and alive that one cannot speak of a complete victory of Jewry but rather, in part, the latter is still forced to adjust its interests to those of the English.

If the Jew were to triumph in England, English interests would recede into the background, just as in Germany today German in-terests no longer are decisive but rather Jewish interests. On the other hand if the Briton triumphs then a shift of England's attitude vis-à-vis Germany can still take place.

The struggle of Jewry for its hegemony is also decided in Italy. With the victory of fascism in Italy the Italian people has triumphed. Even if the Jew is compelled to try to adjust himself to fascism in Italy today, his attitude toward fascism outside Italy nevertheless reveals his inner view of it. Only her own national interest is decisive and determining for Italy's fate since the memorable day when the fascist legions marched on Rome.

For this reason also no state is better suited than Italy as an ally for Germany. It is consonant only with the bottomless stupidity and dissembling baseness of our so-called folkish representatives that they reject the only state that today is ruled along national lines, and as authentic German-folkish elements they prefer to enter a world coalition with Jews. It is fortunate that the time of these fools is played out in Germany. Thus the German-folkish concept is released from the embrace of these creatures, as petty as they are pitiful. It will infinitely gain thereby.

INDEX

219

221

Egypt, 83, 149
Eher Verlag, xiv, xix
Elector, the Great, 151
Emigration, 10, 11, 12, 51, 70, 99, 100, 101, 107, 191
Empress Elizabeth (monument), 189
England, xviii, 49, 68, 72, 73, 74, 80, 81, 83, 93, 97, 98, 102, 108, 110, 116, 117, 125, 128, 134, 144, 145, 146, 147, 148, 149, 150, 151, 152, 153, 154, 155, 156, 157, 158, 159, 160, 163, 164, 167, 168, 169, 174, 175, 209, 215
English, 26, 71, 94, 102, 148, 149, 154
  anti-English attitude, 68
  breeding, 148
  centers, 157
  chestnuts, 116
  circles, 153
  cities, 157
  citizen, 93
  colonial activity, 148
  cotton, 149
  culture, 149
  declaration of war, 73
  economy, 147
  expansion, 147
  fleet, 83
  foreign policy, xxv, 150
  human material, 147
  history, 155
  in Australia, 71
  independence, 83
  interests, 81, 215
  living conditions, 149
  maritime life, 147
  mercenary army, 80, 83
  people, 147
  power of resistance, 81
  settlement, 71
  standpoint, 147
  statesmanship, 156
  supremacy on seas, 152, 156
  war aim, 156
  world empire, 105, 147
  world rule, 209
Entente, 76, 161, 167, 169, 200
Epp, Franz Ritter von, xvii
Erzberger, Matthias, 76, 192
Eupen, 174

Fascism, 118, 164, 173, 193, 196, 215
Flynn, William J., xviii, 201, 202, 203, 204, 205
"Folkish," 18, 45, 47, 56, 63, 73, 79, 80, 99, 131, 137, 138, 162, 163, 172, 216
France, 47, 49, 59, 66, 67, 73, 74, 81, 82, 109, 110, 113, 116, 125, 127, 128, 129, 130, 131, 132, 133, 134, 137, 140, 144, 145, 150, 153, 154, 156, 157, 160, 162, 163, 164, 165, 168, 169, 172, 173, 174, 176, 181, 182, 189, 190, 196, 197, 198, 199, 208, 209
Franco-German conflict, xviii, xxii, 125

222

Francophile, 3, 57, 59
Frankfurt, 126
Frankfurt Federal Parliament, 112
Frankfurter Zeitung, 132
Frederick the Great, 9, 42, 82, 116, 119, 151, 155
Frederick William I, 151
Freemasonry, 167, 214
French
  action vs. German element, 190
  aim, 164
  alliance system, 140, 197, 198
  aerial attacks, 157
  army, 82
  attempts to transfer League of Nations, 196
  black army, 163
  border, 126
  chauvinism, 82, 131, 133, 134, 215
  civilization, 67
  coal and iron mines, 171
  coast, 157
  colonial activity, 209
  continental-political intentions, 129
  European alliance, 196
  foreign policy, 128, 129, 132
  governments, 67, 134
  hegemony in Europe, 164, 209
  hegemony in North Africa, 67
  influence in Vienna, 196
  life, 137
  mentality, 129
  nation, 67
  national leadership, 112
  Negroes, 163
  opening up of Dark Continent, 67
  people, 131, 163
  policy, 82, 129
  strength, 130
  system, 164
  vanity, 131
  war aims, 130
  war leadership, 129
Frenchmen, 47, 93, 176
French Revolution, 8, 213

Geneva, 205
German Empire, 38
  (*see also* Reich)
German-Austrian, 60
German Federal State, 50
German element, 91, 92, 171, 173, 179, 180, 181, 190, 191, 193
Germanism (*see also* German element), 60, 61, 62
German-Russian
  alliance, xxi, 132, 134, 135
  understanding, 132
German Union, 49, 64, 106
Gessler, Otto, xxi
Gneisenau, Neithardt von, General, 124
Gore, Thomas Pryor, Senator, 204, 205
Gravelotte, 60
Great Britain, 147
Greeks, 113

223

Selected Grove Press Paperbacks

E773   CLURMAN, HAROLD, ed., / Nine Plays of the Modern Theater (Waiting for Godot by Samuel Beckett, The Visit by Friedrich Durrenmatt, Tango by Slawomir Mrozek, The Caucasian Chalk Circle by Bertolt Brecht, The Balcony by Jean Genet, Rhinoceros by Eugene Ionesco, American Buffalo by David Mamet, The Birthday Party by Harold Pinter, and Rosencrantz and Guildenstern are Dead by Tom Stoppard) / $11.95

E771   COCTEAU, JEAN / Opium: The Diary of a Cure / $6.95

E793   COHN, RUBY / New American Dramatists: 1960-1980 / $7.95

E742   COWARD, NOEL / Three Plays (Private Lives, Hay Fever, Blithe Spirit) / $4.50

E739   CROCKETT, JIM, ed. / The Guitar Player Book (Revised and Updated Edition) / $9.95

E190   CUMMINGS, E. E. / 100 Selected Poems / $2.45

E159   DELANEY, SHELAGH / A Taste of Honey / $3.95

E639   DOSS, MARGOT PATTERSON / San Francisco at Your Feet (Second Revised Edition) / $4.95

E808   DURAS, MARGUERITE / Four Novels: The Square; 10:30 on a Summer Night; The Afternoon of Mr. Andesmas; Moderato Cantabile / $9.95

E380   DURRENMATT, FRIEDRICH / The Physicists / $2.95

E344   DURRENMATT, FRIEDRICH / The Visit / $2.95

E817   FANON, FRANTZ / Black Skin, White Masks / $6.95

B342   FANON, FRANTZ / The Wretched of the Earth / $3.95

E772   FAWCETT, ANTHONY / John Lennon: One Day At A Time. A Personal Biography (Revised Edition) / $8.95

E47   FROMM, ERICH / The Forgotten Language / $4.95

E223   GELBER, JACK / The Connection / $3.95

E577   GENET, JEAN / The Maids and Deathwatch: Two Plays / $5.95

B322   GENET, JEAN / The Miracle of the Rose / $3.95

B389   GENET, JEAN / Our Lady of the Flowers / $2.45

E760   GERVASI, TOM / Arsenal of Democracy II / $9.95

E792   GETTLEMAN, MARVIN et. al. eds., / El Salvador: Central America in the New Cold War / $7.95

E704   GINSBERG, ALLEN / Journals: Early Fifties Early Sixties / $6.95

B437   GIRODIAS, MAURICE, ed. / The Olympia Reader / $3.95

E720   GOMBROWICZ, WITOLD / Three Novels: Ferdydurke, Pornografia and Cosmos / $9.95

B448	GOVER, ROBERT / One Hundred Dollar Misunderstanding / $2.95
B376	GREENE, GERALD and CAROLINE / SM: The Last Taboo / $2.95
E71	H. D. / Selected Poems of H. D. / $8.95
B152	HARRIS, FRANK / My Life and Loves / $4.95
E769	HARWOOD, RONALD / The Dresser / $5.95
E446	HAVEL, VACLAV / The Memorandum / $5.95
E695	HAYMAN, RONALD / How To Read A Play / $2.95
B205	HEDAYAT, SADEGH / The Blind Owl / $1.95
B306	HERNTON, CALVIN / Sex and Racism in America / $2.95
B154	HOCHHUTH, ROLF / The Deputy / $3.95
B436	HODEIR, ANDRE / Jazz: Its Evolution and Essence / $3.95
E351	HUMPHREY, DORIS / The Art of Making Dances / $3.95
B417	INGE, WILLIAM / Four Plays (Come Back, Little Sheba; Picnic; Bus Stop; The Dark at the Top of the Stairs) / $5.95
E456	IONESCO, EUGENE / Exit the King / $2.95
E101	IONESCO, EUGENE / Four Plays (The Bald Soprano, The Lesson, The Chairs, Jack or The Submission) / $4.95
E259	IONESCO, EUGENE / Rhinoceros & Other Plays / $4.95
B421	JAMES, HENRY / The Sacred Fount / $2.95
B418	JAMES, HENRY / Italian Hours / $2.95
E216	KEENE, DONALD, ed. / Anthology of Japanese Literature: Earliest Era to Mid-19th Century / $7.95
E573	KEENE, DONALD, ed. / Modern Japanese Literature: An Anthology / $7.95
B394	KEROUAC, JACK / Dr. Sax / $3.95
B253	KEROUAC, JACK / Lonesome Traveler / $3.95
E552	KEROUAC, JACK / Mexico City Blues / $4.95
B135	KEROUAC, JACK / Satori in Paris / $2.25
B454	KEROUAC, JACK / The Subterraneans / $3.50
B479	LAWRENCE, D. H. / Lady Chatterley's Lover / $3.50
B262	LESTER, JULIUS / Black Folktales / $2.95
E163	LEWIS, MATTHEW / The Monk / $5.95
E578	LINSSEN, ROBERT / Living Zen / $3.95
B351	MALCOLM X (Breitman, ed.) / Malcom X Speaks / $3.95
E741	MALRAUX, ANDRE / Man's Hope / $6.95

E697	MAMET, DAVID / American Buffalo / $3.95
E778	MAMET, DAVID / Lakeboat / $4.95
E709	MAMET, DAVID / A Life in the Theatre / $3.95
B61	MILLER, HENRY / Black Spring / $3.95
B325	MILLER, HENRY / Sexus / $4.95
B10	MILLER, HENRY / Tropic of Cancer / $3.95
B59	MILLER, HENRY / Tropic of Capricorn / $3.50
E789	MROZEK, SLAWOMIR / Striptease, Tango, Vatzlav: Three Plays / $12.50
E636	NERUDA, PABLO / Five Decades: Poems 1925–1970. Bilingual ed. / $5.95
E364	NERUDA, PABLO / Selected Poems. Bilingual ed. / $6.95
B429	ODETS, CLIFFORD / Six Plays (Waiting for Lefty; Awake and Sing; Golden Boy; Rocket to the Moon; Till the Day I Die; Paradise Lost) / $7.95
E807	OE, KENZABURO / A Personal Matter / $6.95
E413	O'HARA, FRANK / Meditations in an Emergency / $4.95
E359	PAZ, OCTAVIO / The Labyrinth of Solitude: Life and Thought in Mexico / $5.95
B359	PAZ, OCTAVIO / The Other Mexico: Critique of the Pyramid / $2.45
E315	PINTER, HAROLD / The Birthday Party & The Room / $3.95
E299	PINTER, HAROLD / The Caretaker & The Dumb Waiter / $2.95
E411	PINTER, HAROLD / The Homecoming / $4.95
E764	PINTER, HAROLD / The Hothouse / $4.95
E690	PINTER, HAROLD / The Proust Screenplay / $3.95
E641	RAHULA, WALPOLA / What the Buddha Taught / $6.95
B438	REAGE, PAULINE / Story of O, Part II: Return to the Chateau / $2.95
B213	RECHY, JOHN / City of Night / $2.95
B171	RECHY, JOHN / Numbers / $2.95
E710	REED, ISHMAEL & YOUNG, AL, eds. / Yardbird Lives! / $5.95
E828	ROBBE-GRILLET, ALAIN / For A New Novel: Essays on Fiction / $9.95
E698	ROBBE-GRILLET, ALAIN / Topology of a Phantom City / $3.95
B133	ROBBE-GRILLET, ALAIN / The Voyeur / $2.95
B313	SELBY, HUBERT / Last Exit to Brooklyn / $2.95

GROVE PRESS, INC., 196 West Houston St., New York, N.Y. 10014